The changing geography of advanced producer services

The changing geography of advanced producer services

Theoretical and empirical perspectives

Edited by

Peter W. Daniels
and
Frank Moulaert

Belhaven Press
London and New York

First published in Great Britain in 1991 by
Belhaven Press (a division of Pinter Publishers),
25 Floral Street, London WC2E 9DS

British Library Cataloguing in Publication Data
A CIP catalogue record for this book is available from the
British Library

ISBN 1 85293 171 X

For enquiries in North America please contact PO Box 197,
Irvington, NY 10533

Library of Congress Cataloging in Publication Data

The Changing geography of advanced producer services : theoretical and
  empirical perspectives / edited by Peter W. Daniels and Frank
  Moulaert.
    p.   cm.
  Includes bibliographical references and index.
  ISBN 1-85293-171-X
  1. Service industries—Location.   I. Daniels, P. W.
II. Moulaert, Frank.
HD9980.5.C45   1991
338.6'042—dc20
                                            91-19252
                                                 CIP

Typeset by Florencetype Limited, Kewstoke, Avon
Printed and bound in Great Britain by Biddles Ltd.,
Guildford and King's Lynn

Contents

List of figures

List of tables

List of contributors

André Barcet is Associate Professor, University of Lyon II. Author of 'La montée des services. Vers une économie de la Servuction', *Economie et Humanisme*. Co-author (with Joël Bonamy and Anne Mayere) of 'Economie des services aux enterprises: approche empirique et théorique'; 'Les services aux enterprises: problèmes théoriques et méthodologiques', *Revue Recherches Economiques et Sociales*, La Documentation Française, 1984; 'Internationalisation des services: logiques, processus et structures en réseaux' (1989).

Peter Daniels is Professor of Geography and Director, Service Industries Research Centre, Portsmouth Polytechnic. Author of numerous articles and books on the location of office activities and on the geography of services: *Office Location* (1975); *Service Industries: Growth and Location* (1982); *Services and Metropolitan Development: International Perspectives* (editor, 1991).

Faridah Djellal is a research fellow at IFRESI (CNRS), Lille where she works as a member of the team CERIE (LAST).

Sven Illeris is Professor of Geography at Roskilde University, Denmark. On behalf of the European Commission, he supervised the studies on regional service development within the FAST programme. He was previously Director of Research at the Local Governments' Research Institute at Copenhagen. He published *Services and Regions in Europe* (1989).

Bruno Lanvin is a senior economist at the Cabinet Office of UNCTAD's Secretary General in Geneva. He was an economist at the UN Department of Economic and Social Affairs (1979–81) and a member of the Cabinet of the Director General of the UN (1981–83) in New York. He has published diverse articles on service economics such as 'Les services, clé du développement économique' (with F. Prieto), *Revue Tiers-Monde* and 'Services intermédiaires et Développement', *Revue d'Economie Industrielle*.

Flavia Martinelli is Associate Professor in Regional Development at the University of Reggio Calabria. She has published articles (*International Journal of Urban and Regional Research*, *Rassegna Economica*) and reports on the economic geography of producer services, branch plant economies and the relationship between producer services and regional development. She has worked as a consultant for international organisations.

Marie-Christine Monnoyer is Associate Professor at the University of Bordeaux I. She has published numerous articles, reports and books on regional economic systems (Alsace, Rhone-Alpes, Acquitaine), producer services and corporate information systems. She is co-author with J. Philippe and P.Y. Léo of 'PME, stratégies internationales' (1990) and 'Métropoles et PME: l'enjeu international' (1990).

Frank Moulaert is Associate Professor at the University of Lille Flandres Artois and senior researcher at IFRESI (CNRS) where he coordinates the CERIE (LAST) research team. He is the (co)author of articles and books on macroeconomics, econometrics, labour-market analysis, international migration, regional development and, more recently, producer services. Titles include: *Regional Development and the International Division of Labor* (edited with Patricia Wilson, 1983), *Regional Policy at the Crossroads* (edited with L. Albrechts, P. Roberts and E. Swyngedouw, 1987) and *C&C Industries in France and Great-Britain* (with P. Cooke, O. Weinstein, E. Swyngedouw and P. Wells, 1991).

Thierry Noyelle is Deputy Director of the Eisenhower Center for the Conservation of Human Resources, Columbia University, New York. He is the author and co-author of many books, reports and articles on services including *The Economic Transformation of American Cities* (with T. Stanback, 1983), *Beyond Industrial Dualism: Market and Job Segmentation in the New Economy* (1987), *International Trade in Business Services* (with A. Dutka, 1988), *Skills, Wages, and Productivity in the Service Sector* (editor, 1990), and *Employee Training and US Competitiveness: Lessons for the 1990s* (with L. Benton, T. Bailey and T. Stanback, 1991). Together with Penny Peace, he managed the preparation of volume I of the *Directory of the World's Largest Service Companies*, an effort involving nearly 20 researchers in six countries and published jointly by Moody's and UNCTC in 1990.

Pascal Petit is a CNRS Research Director working at CEPREMAP (Paris). His research on the links between productivity, growth and employment resulted in a sectoral approach toward economic growth, with a particular interest for the service sector. Publications include *Slow Growth and the Service Economy* (1986).

Jean Philippe is research engineer at the Centre d'Economie Régionale, Faculty of Applied Economics, University of Aix en Provence. He also teaches at the Institute for the Management of Enterprises and acts as a reporter for the CNRS Club for Anglophone Africa. He has published on regional industrial systems, business services, corporate information systems as well as on the Nigerian economy.

Olivier Weinstein is Professor of Economics at the University of Paris XIII. He is the author of *Lire la Crise* (with C. Barrère and G. Kebabdjien, 1983) and *C&C Industries in Great Britain and France* (with P. Cooke, F. Moulaert, E. Swyngedouw and P. Wells).

1 Advanced producer services: beyond the micro-economics of production

Frank Moulaert and P.W. Daniels

Introduction

The roots for the massive tertiarisation of production after 1945 were already present in the economic system at the beginning of the twentieth century. They became 'visible' in a limited way, for example, in the administrative apparatus of the large American and German firms in the 1920s, and in the telecommunication systems between factory complexes (such as in Spain during the Civil War of the late 1930s). The development of scientific methods (Taylorism, Fordism) for the organisation of work and production and the rise of the Business Administration System (see for example Chandler 1962; Hymer 1972) have promoted the growth of research, engineering, management and organisation consultancy, accounting and legal advice. These advanced services have been simultaneously using and producing complex information at an increasing rate and have created new modes of communication between production agents, different units of the production process and service users.

Large-scale visibility of producer services and their production has been manifest only since the 1950s in the United States and by the 1960s in the majority of West European countries. The main mechanisms underlying their rapid expansion are the accelerated internationalisation of production and trade as well as the revolution in the organisation and the management of large manufacturing and service enterprises, the principal agents of this internationalisation process. Moreover, the development of the 'serviced economy' has stimulated new and diverse interface services between state regulatory institutions and private as well as public production and distribution agents.

But more than half of a century of 'services to production' has not failed to generate an economic theory which adequately underpins the analysis of tertiary development. Only since the early 1970s has some theoretical work on the economics of services been seen. Important precursors can of course be found in the sectoral approach to the stages of economic growth; Fisher (1939) and Clark (1957) certainly laid the grounds for the first models that could be used to analyse the shift of demand towards services (Bell 1974; Gershuny 1978). Analyses of the development of multinational firms also led to interesting perspectives on links between administration and related services (accountancy, corporate planning, finance, insurance) (Hymer 1972; Chandler 1962). But these insights only loosely contributed to a theory of the production and circulation of services in the production system, that is producer services. The theoretical vacuum is not the result of neglect, but a consequence of the limitations of neoclassical economics and the overly strong empirical focus of services research. The first factor probably carries more weight than the second: service research is still too much embedded in traditional neoclassical economics and, therefore, suffers its limitations. But, at the same time, it cannot be denied that for the last 15 years the restricted financial resources available to social science research have been increasingly channelled towards empirical (judged to be more 'applied') rather than to theoretical analysis. Research on services, which began to develop during the same period has certainly suffered from this empirical bias. Researchers, even when they are convinced of the importance of fundamental research, do not have the financial resources necessary to conduct penetrating theoretical work that will lead to the improvement of analytical frameworks. Therefore, the lack of resources for fundamental research reinforces the first argument for the current theoretical vacuum, that is the inappropriateness of contemporary neoclassical economics for analysing the characteristics and dynamics of the tertiary sector.

The limited possibilities offered by neoclassical economics for the analysis of the production and circulation of producer services is illustrated in the first section of this chapter. Specific attention is given to the knowledge and human capital-intensive producer services, that is advanced producer services (APS). However, there is a danger that by criticising neoclassical economics in relation to a service production rationale, a polarisation between 'manufacturing' and 'service economics' will emerge. Such a polarisation, however, will actually restrict the prospects for improving the economic analysis of contemporary society. The 'tertiary' critique of economic theory will only be fully validated if it leads to the development of a theoretical framework that can be used to analyse the development of new use values and their new processes of production and circulation, irrespective of their manufacturing or service character.

The second section of the chapter examines the relevance of existing location and spatial development theories for the analysis of the geography of producer services. It will be suggested that the development of theories for explaining the spatial distribution of the producer services has not been constrained by the relativity of traditional economics. Because of its multidisciplinary predisposition, spatial analysis has combined the economic theory of agglomeration and the location of economic agents with elements of institutional economics and the theory of organisation. This combination allows analysis of the geography of the supply of APS to be conducted at different spatial levels (international, inter-regional and local).

1. Neoclassical theory: its relevance for contemporary production systems

The purpose of this section is not to review the sociological, institutional, neoricardian, radical or even internal critiques of neoclassical economics. Rather, the focus is on the weak points of neoclassical economics which become particularly visible when their analysis is applied to APS. These are:

(a) the mechanist character of the neoclassical production function;
(b) the definition of markets on the basis of a pairwise confrontation of supply and demand, each developed according to their own logic;
(c) the neglect of social relationships that structure the production and circulation of services;
(d) use values that are defined in terms of economic rationality only.

The mechanist character of the production function

According to Weinstein (Chapter 3) and Barcet (Chapter 5), the neoclassical production function would transform the notion of APS into complexes of outputs consisting of well-specified and, in terms of their origin, disconnected inputs. The transformation of inputs belonging to an input space into outputs belonging to an output space (goods or services) would then be determined by the requirements of the technology of production and by combinations of input quantities determined by their relative prices and by the required level of output. In reality, however, the production system for APS is more like an interactive chain between the input and output spaces and between the space of producers and users than a simple function mapping the input into the output space. Using this as the starting point, the model of the different stages of the production chain of APS can be modified (Moulaert in Ermes 1988, Chapter 10, Figure 1).

The notion of an APS production chain recognises that their key resource is complex knowledge and its implementation. We can define an APS as a combination of elementary or very specialised information into complexes of organised information (CI), procedures for the management and the transformation of information and implementation as well as application of CI to entrepreneurial functions. Schematically, we can divide the sequence of production of APS into four stages:

(R) Conception of the idea: what is the knowledge required to fulfil a certain objective? (research stage);
(D) How can this idea be made operational? Production methodology for APS (development stage);
(P: − CI   Production of CI and combination of information related to the objectives, along with implementation procedures (PROC);
     − PROC)

(I)   Implementation of CI and PROC to enterprise functions.

The different APS have sufficiently well-defined use values corresponding to production stages that are technically and institutionally identifiable. However, the use values are technically and institutionally determined, implying that they are not uniformly defined and that their production processes are not unique. In fact, many APS can be disaggregated or regrouped into 'new' APS with use values corresponding to user needs, to factors affecting levels of satisfaction or to the modes of delivery of suppliers able to satisfy those needs.

Within the constraints set by technology and economic and social determinants, the chains (R-D-P-I) can be interrupted at different points. This is quite characteristic of the production of knowledge and its application. Moreover, as Weinstein (Chapter 3) shows, the production of knowledge happens within a complex network with multiple entries and exits. This means that the trajectories of production and distribution are not simple to identify, since a multitude of possibilities can be put into practice according to the kind of APS and their links to the functions of the user enterprises, to their organisation and their history as well as to the strategies of suppliers and the institutional links between suppliers and clients.

Each stage of this chain can be accompanied or followed by evaluation of procedures and results. But every stage also requires a 'follow-up', enabling the transition from one stage to the next, applying the outcomes of the evaluation procedures (retroactive implementation). Few APS cover the whole chain of production: R-D-P-I. APS use values, by their nature, have a very specific content which sometimes corresponds to only one or two stages. This, for example, is the case for strategic technology or information technology consultancy, which is restricted to analysing technological systems and their modes of organisation as well as the design of new or modified technological systems. Such consultancy is not involved with the construction and implementation of technological systems. Limitation of tasks is also evident for financial audit and facility management: the former provides a financial evaluation of the operations and organisations of firms while the latter is confined to the management of processing systems, usually data-processing systems.

APS seldom deliver products resulting from a unidirectional flow, where the result of one stage constitutes a production factor for the next stage in the chain. High-technology consultancy, for example, results from the combination of knowledge and knowhow, existing or in the process of development, which in the course of its production is confronted with the result of the research undertaken in the context of the consultancy job itself. The same feedback mechanisms hold in the case of an advertising campaign: the advertising media as well as their mediate elements (symbols, images, texts, sounds) are adopted according to the reactions of the professionals conducting the campaign as well as those of the clients but also by taking into account the results of preliminary tests. In other words, elements of the result constitute an input for the utilisation or even the recomposition of the production factors.

Therefore, the image of the neoclassical production function based on a one-to-one correspondence between inputs and outputs should be replaced by that of a flexible correspondence between input and output spaces, whose separability cannot any longer be maintained. However, this flexible correspondence cannot be understood as an organised movement within the production and output spaces. On the contrary, it is governed by the idea of maximising the utility of created and utilised use values. The principal of one-to-one correspondence, the simple topological and algebraic character of the neoclassical production function, must make way for a complex network analysis or, in the terminology of Bonamy and others, a 'covalence'. This covalence is governed by the principle of optimisation of use values within a global complex of APS.

There are three corollaries to this observation:

(i)   it becomes practically impossible to define a production set in the way specified by neoclassical economics (cf. Debreu 1966);
(ii) the functionalities and behaviour of different agents are, in the majority of cases, not separable;
(iii) the model of the production of APS, combining several use values with complex content, has important consequences for the 'labour' production factor, in particular 'human capital'.

Let us first elaborate on the second corollary. The osmosis between 'inputs' and 'outputs' transforms a user, up to a certain level, into a co-producer and a producer into a co-user. It often becomes relevant to speak in terms of co-production and co-utilisation (Delaunay; Ermes *et al*. 1988). In consequence, the economic objectives of both types of agents as well as their behavioural models are no longer 'pure'. These agents and their behaviour should be analysed as two interactive systems. This, of course, does not correspond to the structure of the neoclassical model which, unless in its most sophisticated versions, respects the hypothesis of quasi-independence among the decision-making models of its agents.

The production and the circulation of APS (as it is expressed by Bonamy and Mayere, 1986; see also Monnoyer and Philippe, Chapter 8) correspond only exceptionally to a bipolar relationship between (two) agents, one being producer, the other user. Instead, this relationship is more like 'a multipolar relationship of producers and suppliers weaving stable and continuous relationships between them' (Bonamy and Mayère 1986). But this stability, which is often typical of the most standardised production of the least complex APS (say the 'infrastructure' of producer services), is not guaranteed for the more complex forms of production of APS. This is often the case for strategic management and communication advice, where the specific economic mission or the business culture and organisation of each client firm further complicates the relationship between supplier and producer. Still, at the level of the 'rules' of the game (the methodology) there remains room for standardisation.

The third corollary concerns the production of APS and labour inputs. APS is by definition intensive in specialised professional labour. The models of organisation of the work process no longer correspond to the divisions of labour as they characterise the large enterprises of the Fordist type. The Fordist segmentation of production tasks and labour market into primary and secondary, internal and external segments no longer corresponds to the division of labour in APS. In the new activities (productions based on new technologies' APS, new services to the consumers, reorganised public services), the segmentation of the labour process tends to follow the model of a hard-core labour force surrounded by a contingent labour force, with diverse skills and unequal socio-professional status. This strategy for the division of labour corresponds to the entrepreneurial model of flexible production. Vertical disintegration aims at the reorganisation of production and circulation tasks into operational units following technical criteria as well as cost and market criteria. These operational units follow the 'hard core/versus contingent labour' segmentation model. Some operational units constitute the hard core of the production and circulation system; the others play a more auxiliary or complementary role in the form of a subcontracting, a partnership or similar relationship. One finds variations of this model within the production of APS. The professionalisation of the labour force is very strong. If a need for contingent professional labour does exist in APS, most will be engaged on well-defined, short-term and lucrative contracts.

The definition of markets in terms of the confrontation between
supply and demand

The neoclassical theory of exchange and therefore of markets is partial (atomist) in its approach to the theory of production. The neoclassical theory of exchange derives from two behavioural models: one relates to supply and the other to demand. Of course, the market price works as a signal of willingness to consume by the users in confrontation with the availability of products offered by producers. Expectations about trends in revenues and prices make the use of indicators for the modelling of markets more realistic. But the interaction between suppliers on one side and users on the other, concerning essential issues such as co-production and the co-determination of use values (see below), remains absent from the theory.

In the case of APS it is not possible to model their transactions and markets in the form of a unique transaction or set of similar transactions on the assumption that any divergence only arises from price differentials, the level of market competition and total market scale. Both in co-production and co-utilisation of APS there exist a series of formal and informal transactions which are integral to their creation. This multiplicity of transactions is inevitable in an environment governed by economic decisions on whether to have internal and external recourse to producer services in general and APS in particular. These decisions originate from a multitude of strategic and operational factors, especially on the part of their users but also on the supplier side (see Martinelli, Chapter 11). Transaction costs are included among these factors which, following the nature and the functionality of the corresponding transactions, will have an operational or a strategic effect.

In any case, to model the exchange of an APS as a simple act involving a single demander, a single supplier and a unique (previously defined) use value within a completely contained market is some way from the reality. It is more realistic to view the exchange of APS as a transactional chain with multiple agents and partial use values that are prone to variations within the dynamics of production and exchange. This corresponds rather better to the way that activities such as engineering consultancy, advertising or management consultancy operate in practice. Moreover, consultancy and related studies, which are broadly comparable to R & D activities, are close to a situation in which the market is almost certainly not the only transactional vehicle. Public allocation and informal exchange play a part. The inevitability of the global product, the lack of anonymity and, to a lesser extent, the uncertainty of the result have fostered a multiplicity of transactional environments.

Social relations of production and circulation of services

As a consequence of its strictly mono-disciplinary approach, neoclassical economics has emphasised economic analysis of society at the microeconomic level. It assumes a social structure with a given socio-cultural and political substructure as well as predetermined physical and biological substrata. In this way, social relations are studied from a uniformly economic point of view: social relationships are reduced to economic relations that are governed by the pursuit of needs, satisfaction and profits. The origin and nature of use values is not analysed.

This reduction of the social variables inhibits recognition of a distinction between relations of co-production, co-utilisation and co-determination of service use values among producers, suppliers and users. Take, for example, work-process-organisation consultancy (an element of human-resources management as well as of organisation consultancy). This consultancy must take into account technological innovation, as well as the economic, social and political dynamics of the client enterprise whose work process is being evaluated. Its advice will only be economically useful to the client enterprise if it embodies non-economic factors within the work process: models of interaction between production and communication technology and organisation of the work process; the labour force and its professional hierarchy; power relationships between decision-makers and between units of the enterprise; the work culture and atmosphere or the modes of human interaction. If a consultancy study is limited to the man–machine interface in work-process organization and excludes the social and political dynamics of the enterprise, it will overlook a whole series of factors and mechanisms that affect the conduct of the work process.

Use values

As a consequence of reducing social dynamics to their economic dimensions it becomes impossible to define the intrinsic quality of the use values meant to satisfy specific needs. Consequently, any differences in use values are analysed objectively by using purely quantitative indicators such as price and income, elasticities-of-demand coefficients and coefficients of conjectural variation. The evaluation of these variables permits the classification of products according to sensitivity to market circumstances. But this evaluation does not actually contain a single element concerning the characteristics of the use values provided by these products.

For this reason, it is necessary to abandon the strictly economic framework and to adopt an approach which recognises the interaction between different levels of society, human behaviour and its codification. In this way (as explained by Petit in Chapter 4), the expansion of the banking system and the creation of new financial use values cannot simply be explained as a search by the banks for higher surpluses on the circulation of liquidities and quasi-liquidities. Rather, it results from the fundamental modification of the circulation circuits for goods and services, changing consumer needs, the management of uncertainty, the complementarity of multiple monetary and real use values and the regulation of the financial sector. As a result, the valorisation of banking products hardly follows the rules of productivity in manufacturing industry but is inspired much more by the transactional flexibility of commercial valorisation. The latter cannot be reduced to neoclassical price determination by market dynamics but must take into account the different factors just mentioned; and the role of each of these will vary for different financial products.

On the basis of the previous arguments there is a tendency to consider neoclassical theory as a theory for manufacturing rather than service analysis. The simplicity of the production and circulation of products in manufacturing is contrasted with the complexity of their service counterparts. The legitimacy of this approach is questionable and could lead the debate to a dead end. Such a polarised discussion of the differences between production–circulation of 'material' and 'immaterial' products is actually a very inefficient way to study new use values and the socio-economic structures within which they develop. For the contemporary economics of high technology and APS are certainly not the economics of antagonism between industry and services. On the contrary, they are the economics of a symbiosis between the 'hard' of the new technological engineering and the 'soft' of the new modes of production of knowledge, their management, their organisation and implementation. This symbiosis makes the distinction between new 'manufacturing' and 'tertiary' use values ever harder. More generally, analysis of the production and circulation of new products within the traditional setting of classification in branches and production processes will become more and more difficult and should be replaced by constructing *filières* of production and circulation, combining different intermediary and final use values, unique or complementary, with hard and soft components.

From this point of view then, the analytical challenge is not how to develop a new economic theory for services but whether an economic and social theory capable of analysing the dynamics of new products and processes of production and circulation, taking into account their technological and organisational aspects as well as the way they are incorporated into the institutional and social dynamics of contemporary society, can be developed.

2. The production geography of APS

From the analysis in the first section of this chapter, it appears that there is a strong need to develop a theoretical framework for analysing the production and circulation dynamics in APS and other new activities. Such a scheme must account for the complexity of interaction between supply and demand agents, the multiplicity of use values and their different functional destinations.

As indicated by Monnoyer and Philippe (Chapter 8), the 'relational necessity' is a key category for a good understanding of APS. Relational necessity is strongly determined by the particular use values of an APS or a complex of APS. This category is not a general theoretical category which would explain once and for all the tendencies in functional organisation of APS and their spatial configurations. On the contrary, the relational necessity defines the link between (co) suppliers and (co) users in terms of their *specific needs* and, therefore, in terms of the services which correspond to entrepreneurial functions such as production, circulation, management, logistics or R & D.

Within the context of this introductory chapter, it is impossible to list this entire population of functions and corresponding producer services. It suffices to defend the analytical thesis by stating that relational necessities and their geographical consequences can only be identified on the basis of theoretical schemes integrating aspects of the organisation, functions and behaviour of user and supplier firms within a broader framework of social and institutional dynamics. This corroborates the structural-realist thesis of the kind suggested by Storper and Walker (1983) and amended from an institutional point of view by Moulaert (1987).

On the demand side, Martinelli (Chapter 2) emphasises that such an analysis of demand and the modes of recourse to services by enterprises must necessarily be based on a theory of the organisation of large corporations. Such a theory must link the characteristic relational necessities of the services to the organisation of production and of the control system of corporations using them. Following the work by Chandler (1962), Hymer (1972) and Walker (1985), it seems appropriate to observe the relational necessities for the use of APS at the level of corporate headquarters. These headquarters are at the top level of the control system with a widely recognised need for APS to underwrite the efficient operation of their functions such as the central coordination of different administrative functions, strategic planning, treasury, economic cooperation and investment policy. It is especially for this type of APS that co-production and utilisation require close interaction between partners, often translated into spatial proximity and face-to-face communication. This explains the tendency for APS suppliers to locate in spaces where there is a relatively high concentration of corporate headquarters: metropolitan centres or large urban centres of national significance (Noyelle 1983, 1985; Daniels 1991).

On the supply side it is not only the presence of demand and the relational necessity between suppliers and users which generates centralised location patterns of consultancy, marketing or accountancy firms. The advantages stemming from agglomeration economies in terms of availability, productivity and an abundance of factors of production are also quite important. Professional human capital, data banks, libraries and documentation centres (human, scientific and cultural resources in general) strengthen the tendency toward spatial concentration of those activities demonstrating a high intensity of social, scientific and technical knowledge and knowhow as well as of highly skilled human capital (see Illeris, Chapter 7).

This structuro-realist approach, which has led to economically and socially logical conclusions concerning the spatial concentration of the supply of APS at the highest levels in the urban and regional hierarchy, further enhances most of these conclusions. In fact, such an approach is also capable of analysing and forecasting tendencies toward decentralised or even peripheral locations for certain APS activities. By making a distinction between different control levels and different operational and strategic functions, whether with reference to demand or to supply, it becomes possible to classify APS according to their functional destination in the user firms. In this way, the realm of APS goes beyond the strategic central coordination and other functions assumed by headquarters; there are also APS serving the management of a division or a national or regional operational unit as well as those producer services that are inputs to branch plant production activity. These correspond to activities at level II and III respectively in Lipietz's (1986) classification of economic tasks within large firms. This complementarity between producer services and control and production tasks of user firms is partly expressed in terms of the economic geography of APS supply structures.

The relatively decentralised location of a number of offices assuming Level II and III tasks is translated into a spatial deconcentration of certain APS (accountancy, legal advice, software services). However, this dispersal should not be exaggerated since it often only involves standardised and operational functions rather than complex and strategic services. Thus, Moulaert, Martinelli and Djellal (Chapter 9) find that high-level information-technology analysis and systems design consultants are strongly concentrated in top-tier agglomerations, whereas more standardised systems development is also located in second-tier urban centres (see also Moulaert and Djellal 1990). In addition, Daniels (Chapter 10) and F. Gallouj (Ermes 1988) show that the tendency towards spatial deconcentration is often part of a strategic reaction to saturating markets.

The institutional and structuro-realist approach to the organisation of agents in the 'covalent' system of production and utilisation of services allows different tasks or functions to be distinguished within user as well as within supplier firms. This approach allows the reconstruction, at a high level of disaggregation, of the spatial division of labour of APS firms in the way illustrated for information-technology consultancy firms in Chapter 9 and for accountancy and financial audit firms in Chapter 10.

Producer services and spatial economic development

Three chapters in the second part of this book explicitly establish links between the division of service labour and spatial economic development (Chapters 8, 9 and 11). Martinelli (Chapter 6) develops the thesis that the unequal distribution of service functions within the internal and external structure of large firms is reproduced within the system of regions and curtails the already limited development potential of peripheral regions. This is illustrated with a case study of the Italian Mezzogiorno (Chapter 11).

It is clear that the general tendency of regional economic development, as explained by service development linked to the productive system, results in the spatial concentration of producer services, especially APS supply systems (Martinelli, Chapter 6; Monnoyer and Philippe, Chapter 8; Daniels, Chapter 10). This concentration is reproduced in control centres and areas (high-level urban centres and regions) and is accompanied by spatial decentralisation of certain stages of production within the production chain of APS and of more operational and standardised producer services. The latter tendency is encouraged by factors favouring location in less-developed or even peripheral regions such as the emergence of local demand for producer services; the access of regional enterprises to new communication technologies; the existence of an appropriate human capital potential (Monnoyer and Philippe, Chapter 8). A policy of active regional penetration led by firms external to the region that are seeking to increase their markets is also important (Daniels, Chapter 10). It is evident that the effectiveness of each catalyst depends essentially on the level of development of the regional economy as well as on the existence of a trained and skilled labour force. Again, peripheral regions are worst off.

At a different scale, Lanvin (Chapter 13) examines the consequences of the globalisation of service markets and their ongoing deregulation for the development of economies in the Third World. This is complemented by Noyelle (Chapter 12) on the dynamics of the expansion of transnational business service firms with particular reference to their impact on host developing countries. A pure service development policy cannot substitute for manufacturing industrial policies even if the latter have recurrently failed in the development experience of different countries. A policy of economic development must combine manufacturing and service assets (Noyelle, Chapter 12) and should include an APS strategy which takes into account the existing economic structure of countries and regions. This structure circumscribes the locational possibilities for APS suppliers, but in any case the establishment of a service network will take time, implying that APS must be imported for a rather long period. As Lanvin (Chapter 13) notes:

One needs to be pragmatic, however. In most cases, developing countries are not in a position to develop rapidly enough the domestic capacities necessary to produce those services which will boost their overall international competitiveness. More often than not they even lack the basic infrastructures necessary to generate and transport such services (reliable telecommunication networks in particular). Thus, for a certain number of years such services will need to be imported.

In any case, the heterogeneity of economic structures in developing countries has created anxiety that the introduction of APS using modern technologies will lead to uneven economic and social effects on regions and countries.

3. Analytical traps to be avoided

The contributions to this volume form two distinct groups. The first group (Chapters 1–5) show that it is possible to bypass the framework of neoclassical economics and to develop different theoretical approaches that are useful for the analysis of the production and distribution of producer services in general and APS in particular. The second group of authors (Chapters 6–13), who are specialists in economic geography and spatial planning, have utilised various spatial levels to analyse tendencies toward centralisation or decentralisation at the different stages in the service production chain.

However, each of these chapters only examine one or two aspects of service development. They may therefore be susceptible to the criticism that they fail to accommodate the complexity of the service production process. Yet it could be argued that the contributions to this volume help service analysis to escape the reductionism of traditional economics and avoid the narrow spatial focus which often biases spatial analysis in social science. The collective result begins to surmount the traps outlined earlier in this chapter, that is the unilateral character of the micro-economic vision of tertiary development, the brutal polarisation between industry and services and the generalisation of tendencies toward spatial (de) centralisation.

References

Bell, D. (1974) *The Coming of Post-industrial Society*, London, Heinemann.

Bonamy, J. and Mayère, A. (1986) *Les services dans le systeme productif*, Economie et Humanisme, Lyon.

Chandler, A. (1962) *Strategy and Structure: Chapters in the History of Industrial Enterprise*, Cambridge, Mass., MIT Press.

Clark, C. (1957) *The Conditions of Economic Progress* (3rd ed.), London, Macmillan.

Daniels, P.W. (ed) (1991) *Services and Metropolitan Development: International Perspectives*, Routledge, London.

Debreu, G. (1966) *Theorie de la valeur: analyse axiomatique de l'equilibre economique*, Paris, Dunod.

Delaunay, J.C. (1988) 'Les facteurs generaux de la demande de services complexes par les enterprises multinationales' in Ermes, 1988.

Ermes (collective) (eds) (1988) *La demande de services complexes des firmes multinationales et l'offre correspondante*, UFR de Sciences Economiques et Sociales, Etude effectuée pour le Commissariat General Du Plan, University of Lille I.

Ermesceoll (1991) *Manager le Conseil*, Paris, McGraw Hill.

Fisher, A. (1939) 'Production, primary, secondary and tertiary', *The Economic Record*, June, pp. 24–38.

Gallouj, M.F. (1988) 'Les grandes "law firms" françaises et le service juridique destiné aux grandes enterprises' in Ermes, 1988.

Gershuny, J. (1978) *After Industrial Society? The Emerging Self-Service Economy*, London, Macmillan.

Hymer, S. (1972) 'The multinational corporation and the law of uneven development' in J.N. Baghwati, *Economics and World Order*, London, Macmillan.

Lipietz, A. (1986) 'New tendencies in the international division of labor: regimes of accumulation and modes of regulation' in A. Scott and M. Storper (eds), *Production, Work, Territory*, Boston, Allen & Unwin.

Moulaert, F. (1987) 'An institutional revisit to the Storper–Walker theory of labour', *International Journal of Urban and Regional Research*, **11**, 3.

— (1988) 'L'interaction de l'offre et de la demande de services complexes aux grandes enterprises' in Ermes, 1988.

— and Djellal, F. (1990) 'Les conseils en technologie de l'information: des economies d'agglomerations en réseau', paper presented at the Lyon Conference on Métropoles en déséquilibré.

— and Salinas, P.W. (1983) *Regional Analysis and the New International Division of Labor*, Boston, Kluwer Nijhoff Publishing.

Noyelle, T. (1983) 'The implications of industry restructuring for spatial organization in the US' in Moulaert and Salinas, 1983.

— (1985) *New Technologies and Services: Impacts on Cities and Jobs*, Monograph Studies no.5, University of Maryland, The Institute for Urban Studies.

Storper, M. and Walker, R. (1983) 'The theory of labor and the theory of location', *International Journal of Urban and Regional Research*, 7.

Walker, R. (1985) 'Is there a service economy? The changing capitalist division of labor', *Science and Society*, **49**, 1.

2 A demand-orientated approach to understanding producer services

Flavia Martinelli   L 89   R12

D24

Introduction

It is now just over ten years since producer services and their role in contemporary development began to gain pre-eminence with the concurrent publication of a few landmark works (Singelmann 1978; Lipietz 1978; Gershuny 1978; Stanback 1979; Momigliano and Siniscalco 1980). The service sector as a whole had already been studied by a number of pioneers (Fisher 1935; Clark 1940; Kuznets 1948, 1957, 1958; Stigler 1956; Fuchs 1968, 1969; Greenfield 1966; Braverman 1974; Bell 1973), but it is only during the last decade that the growing importance of these activities – in terms of both output and employment – has become widely acknowledged. A rich body of theoretical and empirical work has indeed arisen, contributing important changes in economic theory and undermining, in particular, the traditional notion of services as 'unproductive' activities.

In this literature a central position is held by producer services, that is those services that are inputs to other productive activities instead of being for final consumption. Their influence on productivity, innovation and competitiveness among firms, industries and regions is increasingly recognised. Producer services are gaining an important place in economic development theory.

A recent further impetus to the debate on producer services and economic development has been the GATT negotiations, which in the Uruguay Round have included services along with commodities. This event has forced developing countries to tackle the problem of services and development and has further enriched the debate with issues related to the location and tradeability of services as well as their impact on centre–periphery relationships.

In this and subsequent chapters by the same author in this book, the following theses are proposed: (i) producer services are to a significant extent an outcome of the increased technical and social division of labour *within* production; (ii) as such, their development within and across regions is a function of the extent and, more importantly, of the structure of their market, that is the productive system; and (iii) their development and location are, in turn, a new powerful determinant of the international division of labour and of regional inequality. As an illustration of this mechanism and particularly of (ii), a case study is also presented, concerning a peripheral European region (see Chapter 11).

The growth of service activities in contemporary society

Conflicting explanations?

In the general literature on services (for a review see Delaunay and Gadrey 1987), at least four major views can be identified about the causes and nature of service development.

First, many of the earlier scholars, more or less explicitly, viewed the growth of service activities and employment as a *function of economic growth* and, more precisely, of *per capita income*. This demand-based interpretation was fully theorised in the 'stages of growth' theory (Rostow 1966) and in the 'post-industrial society' thesis (Bell 1973), where the greater income elasticity of the demand for services, compared to goods, was considered a key determinant of services' growth.

A second view emphasised, in contrast, the *supply–push* character of a large part of services' growth, coupled with institutional factors. The linear transition through 'stages of growth' and the simplistic relationship between services and income was strongly criticised, whereas the role of *unemployment pressures* on the one hand and *social policies* on the other was stressed to account for the growth of certain consumer (for example retail) and public services (Sabolo 1975; Offe 1977; Singlemann 1978; Castells 1972; De Janvry and Garramon 1977).

Third, the consumption-based view was also explicitly denied by a number of other scholars who stressed how many goods were actually replacing services: for example washing machines, TV sets, etc. (Gershuny 1978) and how, more importantly, an increasing share of contemporary service activities are not for the final consumption of individuals and households but are intermediate inputs for other productive activities (see, among others: Gershuny 1978; Lipietz 1978; Stanback 1979; Stanback *et al.*, 1981; Momigliano and Siniscalco 1980, 1986; Gershuny and Miles 1983; Walker 1985). Although still demand-orientated, this approach underlined the production rather than the consumption-related character of most contemporary services and opened a major path for theoretical and empirical investigation.

A fourth and more recent position bypasses the above demand-versus-supply-determined discussion and proposes the development of services as a *policy* objective and a major sector of planned investment. The development of services must not be considered solely a 'product' of growth but one of its *preconditions* and, as such, an imperative area of policy action (UNCTAD 1985; Riddle 1986).

As pointed out elsewhere (Martinelli 1984), the existence of such contrasting views and the confusion that surrounded services for a long period stem from the great heterogeneity of the 'tertiary' sector which was originally defined in national accounting as a 'residual' group of activities. It includes, in fact, services as diverse as haircutting and legal assistance, electronic data processing and medical services, retail trade and maritime transportation, restaurants and R & D. Each of the above views, while referring to the whole sector, really concerns only particular services.

Indeed, a definition of services that encompasses all the activities included under this label is difficult to formulate. More importantly, a subsectoral classification of services is needed, both for theoretical clarification and empirical purposes.

Issues in defining and classifying services

In general, services can be defined according to three major interrelated characteristics, which distinguish this type of product from goods. In the first place, services are different from goods for their *immaterial* nature. They are a labour input or performance, which does not yield any immediate material transformation. Second, service transactions generally involve a *simultaneity in the production and consumption* of services which requires a direct interaction between the producer and the consumer. A corollary of this feature is the need for close proximity of services to their market. Consequently, services *cannot be stored or shipped on their own* but are embodied either in suppliers (in a 'potential' form), or in consumers, or in goods to which services are inputs.

However, several notable exceptions to and variations on the above general statements exist. A number of services can actually be embodied in some sort of physical support (for example digital impulses in electronic data transmission, paper in the case of consulting reports, pictures in advertising etc.). As a consequence, they can be stocked and shipped. Others do involve some form of material transformation (for example food preparation in restaurants).

This being said, important differences of a more structural nature emerge among service activities, and a number of subsectors can be identified which behave quite differently and whose development responds to different factors. Several classifications have, in fact, been tried. The most useful ones group services according to the *function/place* within the socio-economic system, the *type of demand* or the *form of supply*.

(1) The first criterion stems primarily from Marxist literature, although it has been adapted in a number of other works. In this perspective, services are grouped according to the 'sphere' they belong to: circulation (for example banking, trade); reproduction of the social factors of production (for example maintenance but also social services); reproduction of the social conditions of accumulation (for example government, defence); production itself; and consumption (Castells 1972; Lipietz 1978).
(2) The second approach looks at the market for services and distinguishes these activities as a function of the main macroeconomic

aggregates of national income accounting: intermediate consumption and final consumption (from which 'collective' consumption can be further distinguished). From this point of view, services are classified as 'producer' services, when they are inputs to other economic activities, and 'consumer' services, when they are consumed by individuals or households. (Among the first to point out this basic criterion we can mention Greenfield 1966; Fuchs 1968; Gershuny 1978; Stanback 1979; Momigliano and Siniscalco 1980).

(3) The third criterion is also rather important since it concerns the social and organisational form of suppliers and thus has relevance in explaining service development patterns on the supply side. Whether services are supplied by the government, non-profit organisations, private firms, or self-employed workers clearly involves differences in behaviour and strategies (Bhalla 1971; Lipietz 1978; Martinelli 1984).

Other classificatory perspectives include the content in human capital, technology or information (Frey 1975; Porat 1976; Martinelli 1989b).

The above approaches are not mutually consistent and do not lead to an unequivocal classification of service activities. The issue is further complicated by the 'industry' approach of most statistical classifications which identifies activities in terms of broad end-products, regardless of their function in the socio-economic system, their market or their productive organisation. However, some basic form of grouping is imperative when dealing with services in order to be able to account for the great variety of behaviours and trends.

A taxonomy of service activities

Despite the difficulties involved and compromising over theoretical and empirical constraints, an operational taxonomy of services is proposed in Table 2.1, based on the Nomenclature des Activités Economiques dans les Communautées Européennes (NACE) standard statistical classifications and some of the above-mentioned criteria. It partly relies on the classifications proposed by Singelmann (1978) and Stanback (1979). Accordingly, services can be placed in four main groups: *social infrastructure, consumer services, distributive infrastructure* and *business services*. The last two categories form the *producer services* group.

SOCIAL INFRASTRUCTURE

In this category are grouped all those services necessary to ensure and reproduce the social conditions of accumulation, that is the general functioning of the socio-economic system: defence and police, public administration (both central and peripheral), justice, social security, education, health services, social services. To these one can add international and non-profit organisations as well as business, union and other membership associations. They represent the institutional 'spine'

Table 2.1 A taxonomy of service industries based on the NACE classification

---

Social infrastructure
  Central and local public administration (including justice and military corps)
  Social security
  Education
  Health
  Social services
  Membership associations and international organisations

Consumer services
  Retail sales
  Lodging, eating and drinking places
  Cultural and recreational services
  Repair of consumer goods
  Personal services

Distributive infrastructure
  Banking
  Real estate
  Transportation and related services
  (Tele)communications
  Wholesale trade and commercial intermediation

(Public Utilities)

Business services
  R & D
  Insurance
  Non-banking financial services
  Legal services
  Accounting and fiscal consulting
  Technical and professional services
  Advertising and public relations
  Marketing services
  Organisational consulting
  Electronic data processing and related services
  Typing, photocopying and other paper processing services
  Rental of production equipment
  Other business services (cleaning, security etc.)

(Tourism)

(Construction)

---

of any nation. For this reason many of these activities are supplied or strictly controlled by the government or by non-profit organisations. Users are both individuals and organisations, that is society as a whole, and for this reason these services are also called 'collective' services. Their growth is a function of the level of national economic development and of political factors as determined by the particular history of any country. The growth of social services, in particular, is strongly influenced by the levels of unemployment, the amount of resources available and the political orientation of a country's government.

CONSUMER SERVICES

This category groups services mainly orientated to the final consumption of individuals and households: retail trade, hotels, eating and drinking places, sport, cultural and recreational services, personal services (laundry and cleaning services, barbers and hairdressers etc.), repair of consumer goods. The growth of these services, in line with the first view described earlier, is generally a function of per capita income. There are, however, exceptions and complicating factors to this assumption. A very important case is that of hotels, eating and drinking places. First, they do not cater exclusively to final consumers since they are often used for doing business and their value is thus included among firms' costs. Moreover, they are an important component of a growing sector of economic activity which has not found a clear place in statistical classifications: tourism. From this point of view, their development in many countries is not a function of 'local' per capita income but of tourist flows. In many of the studies spurred by the GATT negotiations in services they are actually considered an 'export' service industry (UNCTAD 1985). Another complication stems from the pressures of unemployment and the growth of 'marginal' employment in many consumer services (for example retail and personal services), even in the case of low per capita incomes.

DISTRIBUTIVE INFRASTRUCTURE

Together with business services this group forms the broader category of *producer* services, that is service mainly consumed by firms in the process of carrying out their production process. Distributive infrastructure includes all those services that ensure the circulation of capital, goods, information and people: banking, real estate, transportation, (tele)communications, wholesale intermediation and distribution. Theoretically, public utilities (for example electricity, gas, water) could also be included here, although it is unclear whether they are services or manufacturing industries. It must be stressed that most of the above services also serve the needs of individuals and households, but because of their strategic infrastructural role within the economic system they are generally included among producer services. For the same reason, in most countries they are operated or strictly controlled by the state (transportation, telecommunications, banking). Their growth is thus a function of both the level of productive development (the market) and political decisions. Also worth noting is the fact that many distributive services involve important investments in fixed capital in contrast with many business services.

BUSINESS SERVICES

This category groups all those services that are clearly directed to other firms, whether they operate in agriculture, manufacturing or other services: financial services, insurance, R & D, legal services, accounting and fiscal services, management consulting, engineering, architectural and other technical services, marketing services, advertising and public relations, electronic data processing (EDP) and related services, training services, photocopying and related services, special secretarial services, cleaning and security services. The growth of business services is most clearly related to the development of the productive system and its demand. The supply is largely private, either by firms or self-employed professionals. In contrast to distributive infrastructure, the amount of fixed investment required to carry out these services is generally lower than in distributive infrastructure, whereas human capital and information are more crucial factors.

As already mentioned, the above taxonomy is far from perfect. Much overlapping remains, especially with regard to consumer and producer demand. In the end, in order to be totally consistent, any study of services must narrow its focus on to individual service. Nevertheless, this classification is a useful starting point for identifying and understanding the different factors affecting services' growth as well as for conducting empirical research.

Producer services and economic development

Among the various service subsectors, it is with producer services that most of the recent literature is concerned. As already mentioned, these studies have stressed how, in contrast with the 'consumer society' perspective, a large portion of the recent growth of the service sector is accounted for by services directly or indirectly related to developments in production. Moreover, these services are increasingly recognised as a crucial element in economic development, as a factor that significantly influences the dynamics of growth, innovation diffusion, productivity increases and competitiveness across firms, sectors and regions.

They are defined as all those activities (that is labour phases) which do not involve direct material production or transformation but are necessary to carry out the full cycle of production in any type of industry. They include activities related to the mobilisation of resources (banking, finance, engineering, recruiting and training), the conception and innovation of products and processes (R & D, design, engineering), the actual organisation and management of production (business administration, management consulting, information processing, accounting, legal services etc.), production itself (quality control, maintenance, logistics), the promotion and distribution of products (transportation, commercial intermediation, marketing, advertising). They must therefore be considered production inputs in the same way as other intermediate goods: their value adds to the cost of production and is transferred into the price of final output in final markets. For many scholars they are merely an extension and transformation of production labour. Walker (1985) considers them as 'indirect' production labour. Momigliano and Siniscalco (1986) talk of 'tertiarisation' of production, against the thesis of de-industrialisation.

The determinants of producer services' growth

Precisely because of their close relationship to productive activities, the growth of producer services must be analysed and interpreted within the evolution of modern productive organisations. A major thesis of this contribution is that producer services' growth is demand-led, that is largely determined by changes in the way that production is carried out.

In particular, the development of such activities must be considered the result of at least four major interrelated processes: (a) the progressive *concentration of capital* and the *rise of the modern large corporation*, multiproduct and multilocational; (b) the growing *internationalization of markets and competition*; (c) the development of *new information technology*. These processes have engendered relevant changes in the organisation of production, accelerating the division and specialisation of labour typical of complex societies.

The existence of a trend towards growing technical and social division of labour as a feature of economic development was already stressed by classical economists (Smith, Ricardo, Marx). This trend, which can be considered organic to complex societies, has been accelerated by the progressive concentration of capital and the emergence of large corporations. In his analysis of Taylorism and Fordism, Braverman (1974) has, among others, most effectively described how large modern corporations have engineered a radical transformation of the organisation of production in the form of a growing separation and specialisation of tasks. Conception, control and executional functions have increasingly become separated. Activities previously performed organically by the same worker are progressively divided and attached to different personnel, giving rise, among other things, to a growing new salaried group: clerical, technical and managerial employees. Moreover, over the last century, firms have significantly evolved from the single-product, single-site type of organisation to the more complex multi-product, multi-locational corporate structure (Chandler 1977; Stanback *et al.* 1981). In order to monitor such complex corporate apparatuses, the weight of managerial, technical, professional and other service functions has become increasingly important. The need to control and coordinate enlarged and diversified operations has transformed the personal supervision of the traditional businessman into a sophisticated structure of 'scientific' management and services. The development of many producer services is thus the result of a growing separation between material production, conception, organisation, control, execution and distribution functions within the overall production process.

Parallel to industrial concentration, the growing internationalisation of markets has changed the forms of competition. Firms must keep pace with the growing pressures of oligopolistic and global competition. Inter-firm relationships (for both inputs and output) have intensified and greatly broadened their geographical scope. Firms must remain informed about sources and markets; they must innovate, diversify and promote their products; they must modernise production processes. Service functions such as telecommunications, information gathering and processing, R & D, design and engineering, marketing, advertising and public relations become crucial competitive factors. Strategic planning is indispensable.

Finally, one must consider the impact of new information technology. Generating, processing and transmitting information has indeed become a major and pervasive contemporary activity. The development of new information technology, in addition to revolutionising the way many services are produced and rendered, favouring both their specialisation and 'globalisation' (see Martinelli, Chapter 6; Moulaert *et al.*, Chapter 9), has also created entirely new sectors of service activity such as electronic data processing, software programming, systems engineering and the handling and maintenance of electronic machines in production itself (Moulaert *et al.*, Chapter 9).

At this point it is crucial to stress that the above process of progressive division of labour occurs *both within the firm*, through the establishment of in-house specialised functions and personnel (*technical* division of labour), *and across firms*, with the establishment on the open market of specialised, free-standing (cf. Stanback 1979) firms (social division of labor). Some producer services always existed on a free-standing basis (especially circulation services); others first developed in-house and then evolved into specialised independent activities (Daniels 1985); some have eventually been re-internalised (for example electronic data processing). Therefore, the study of producer services cannot be limited to the external activities traditionally classified as services in the tertiary sector (the industries listed in Table 2.1), but must necessarily take into account internal service activities, that is those carried out within non-service firms (Stanback 1979; Gershuny and Miles 1983).

As will be stressed later, although the prevailing trend observed over time is towards vertical disintegration (Porter 1990), i.e. the externalisation of services, there are also countervailing forces and the subject is far from settled. Nevertheless, whether services are provided in-house or by free-standing suppliers – whether the technical division of labour favours a deepening of the social division of labour – giving rise to new branches of economic activity has relevant implications in terms of regional economic development (see Chapter 11).

The effects of producer services on economic development

If producer services are a result of the growing division and specialisation of labour in contemporary productive organisation they, in turn, significantly affect the performance of the productive system itself.

It is now widely accepted that the development of producer services is strongly linked to productivity increases throughout the economic system, particularly in manufacturing (Kuznets 1971; Momigliano and Siniscalco 1980; Nusbaumer 1984; Porter 1990). Because of the difficulties involved in measuring and tracing the effects of producer services on economic growth, their role is actually far more important than suggested by their contribution to GDP (UNCTAD 1985).

Contemporary efficiency and productivity depends, to an ever increasing extent, on the links between different activities (UNCTAD 1985). Producer services have the peculiar role of integrating the increasingly differentiated and specialised parts of the economic system (Stanback *et al.* 1981). Moreover, many services have a highly innovative content and are often, in their own right, product or process innovations. They must therefore be considered basic carriers of innovation (Bearse 1978; Martinelli 1989a). Since many of them are associated with decision-making processes they eventually have a relevant strategic content and strongly influence directions of change.

For all these reasons, the development and diffusion of producer services must be considered a major determinant of *competitive dynamics* across firms, sectors and regions. The emergence of producer services in contemporary development is part of a structural revolution in the functioning of the economy, marked by a shift in management concerns from production costs to strategic planning (Stanback *et al.* 1981). As expressed by Walker (1985), the locus of competition has actually moved from the plane of direct production to that of indirect production labour.

The above considerations reinforce the point made earlier: although increasingly autonomous activities, services are an extension of the productive system and cannot be studied separately from the latter, and particularly from industrial production.

Technical and social division of labour: service demand and forms of supply

Having narrowed our attention to the producer services subsector and having posited that their growth is to a large extent a function of the increased technical and social division of labour, of organisational and technological changes and of the increased internationalisation of linkages and competition, we can now focus in greater detail on the specific *patterns* of producer services' development and diffusion among firms, sectors and regions. In fact, the technical division of labour giving rise to internal service functions does not occur uniformly in all firms, nor does it necessarily and everywhere evolve into a social division of labour resulting in the birth of specialised independent service firms.

The demand side, that is the structure of production and, in particular the extent and characteristics of the industrial system, along both organisational and the spatial dimensions, are again considered here a primary determinant of both the level and type of services demanded and the form in which they are procured.

Factors affecting the demand for producer services

We must distinguish among those factors related to the structure of firms, industries, and to regional economies. Among the most important determinants of service demand is the *scale* of both production and corporate organisation. We have seen how it is primarily in large firms that the technical division of labor giving rise to services has emerged. It is thus generally accepted that large establishments and/or firms demand a higher amount and a more diversified range of services than smaller firms. However, scale is neither a necessary nor a sufficient condition for a higher and more diversified demand, as the actual *structure, development phase* and *strategy* of firms further complicate the picture. In particular, firms covering several stages of the production process (vertically integrated) will demand a wider range of services than firms engaged in fewer phases. A firm organised as a conglomerate will probably have a different services' demand than a firm specialising in one product line. All other things being equal, firms involved in a restructuring process will need different services than firms just starting up their operations or firms having reached a stable regime.

The *type of industry and product* also significantly affects the demand for services. A firm manufacturing standardised products for mass markets will need more advertising, marketing and distributive services than a firm engaged in the production of customised products for a specialised market. All the same, the higher the innovation content of products and processes, the more important the demand for R & D, engineering and other technical services will be.

With regard to regional economic structures, the more diversified the productive basis, the wider will be the range of services demanded; whereas in areas of strong productive specialisation, the range of services will be narrower but also more specialised (cf. Martinelli 1989a).

Factors affecting the form of service procurement

Whether services are developed in-house or purchased on the open market from free-standing suppliers also depends on several factors. These factors are related to both the demand and the supply side. The size of establishments and firms, their structure and strategy, the characteristics of the service itself, as well as the actual existence of an adequate external supply, play a determinant role in the decision to internalise or externalise needed services.

Factors influencing the decision by firms to 'make or buy' given production phases (vertical integration versus disintegration) have actually been extensively investigated from a micro-economic perspective by the so-called 'transactional' school (see among others Coase 1937; Stigler 1951; Alchian and Desmetz 1972; Williamson 1980, 1986; Blair and Kaserman 1983; Casson 1986). Many of their observations can be adapted to the case of services.

On the demand side, size, again, plays a significant role. Large establishments and firms are certainly more likely to reach the scale necessary to support the costs of internal specialisation for given functions than small firms. But this general statement is again further influenced by the *structure and strategy of* firms. Howells and Green (1986) explicitly argue that cost criteria have a limited influence on firms' choices. A holding corporation or a conglomerate may not internalise as many service functions as a firm operating in one main line of products (Galbraith and Nathanson 1978). The internalisation of certain functions can also stem from a strategic choice, aiming at strict control over certain information (for example in R & D or marketing).

With regard to the *type of service*, Williamson stresses the importance of phase *specificity* in relation to firms' activities and strategies. Some functions are so specialised and tailored to a firm's needs that they cannot be easily found on the market. Stigler (1956) stated that functions that are 'complementary' are more likely to be internalised than 'rival' ones. Stanback *et al.* (1981) emphasise the difference between 'system maintenance' and 'system development' functions, the latter being more often externalised.

All the above factors, however, are in turn strongly influenced by *supply conditions*. A choice can actually only be made when an external supply does exist. If no services are available on the market the firm must either draw upon its own personnel or give up the service. On the role of the existence of an external supply see also Marshall (1982).

The complexity and variability of the above factors do not allow for a definite theoretical assessment and leave the subject rather undetermined (see Wood 1986). A double and contradictory movement of internalisation and externalisation can also be observed over time in relation to the developments of new information technology. Moreover, for many services firms develop both in-house functions and external procurement practices. However, the generalised growth of freestanding suppliers over recent decades suggests a prevailing trend towards externalisation.

Concluding remarks

As a result of the above discussion, some key theoretical points regarding the development of producer services can be emphasised. First, to study producer services and explain their patterns of growth, one must look at the structure and changes in the production system that is the market for such services. The existence of a developed and advanced market is of paramount importance in explaining the growth of producer services. As will be stressed later in this book, it is not by accident that the most significant growth of such activities has occurred in industrialised countries.

Second, the particular characteristics of the industrial structure (type of industry, structure and strategy of firms) further influence the range and specialisation of services, as well as the form in which they are supplied (in-house versus free-standing). In particular, the greater the scale of production and/or corporate organisation, the more the technical division of labour is likely to be extended and, hence, the demand for services. More importantly, because of economies of scale and scope, large firms can afford the internalisation of needed services to a greater extent than small firms which are instead extremely dependent on the existence of external suppliers.

The structure and form of services' supply has relevant implications in turn for economic development. We have stressed how service inputs are an increasingly crucial feature of competitiveness among firms, industries and regions. From this point of view, the development of free-standing services appears to have a far more relevant impact on regional development than internal ones. Free-standing services constitute a crucial catalyst for all economic operators. In areas where an external supply has developed, even small firms have access to advanced and specialised services.

Thus, the next questions to investigate are when, how and why does a technical division of labour occur and evolve into a social division of labour? According to the known theorem by Stigler (1951), this transition occurs when the market for a given internal phase of the production process reaches a sufficient size for an independent supplier to specialise in that activity and enter the market. But then, where do these specialised service firms locate and what is the spatial structure of their market? Chapter 6 in this book attempts to answer some of these questions.

References

Alchian, A. and Dermetz, H., (1972), 'Production, information costs, and economic organisation', *American Economic Review*, **62**.

Bhalla, A.S., (1971), 'Le rôle du secteur des services dans l'expansion de l'emploi' in *Essais sur l'emploi*, Geneva, ILO.

Bearse, P.J., (1978), 'On the intraregional diffusion of business services activity', *Regional Studies*, **12**.

Bell, D., (1973), The Coming of Post-industrial Society, New York, Basic Books.

Blair, R.D. and Kaserman, D.L., (1983), *Law and Economics of Vertical Integration and Control*, New York, Academic Press.

Braverman, H., (1974), *Labor and Monopoly Capital*, New York, Monthly Review Press.

Casson, M., (1986), *Multinationals and World Trade: Vertical Integration and the Division of Labour in World Industries*, London, Allen and Unwin.

Castells, M., (1972), *La question urbaine*, Paris, Maspero.

Chandler, A., (1977), *The Visible Hand: the Managerial Revolution in American Business*, Cambridge, Mass., Harvard University Press.

Clark, C., (1940), *The Conditions of Economic Progress*, London, Macmillan.

Clark, D., (1985), *Post-industrial America. A Geographical Perspective*, London, Methuen.

Coase, R., (1937)., 'The Nature of the Firm', *Economica*, **4**.

Daniels, P.W., (1985), *Service Industries: A Geographical Appraisal*, London, Methuen.

De Janvry, A. and Garramon, C., (1977), 'Laws of Motion of Capital in the Center–Periphery Structure', *Review of Radical Political Economy*, **9**.

Delaunay, J.-C. and Gadrey, J., (1987), *Les enjeux de la societé de service*, Paris, Presse de la Fondation Nationale des Sciences Politiques.

Fisher, A.G., (1935), *The Clash of Progress and Security*, London, Macmillan.

Frey, L., (1975), 'Aspetti di analisi economica in merito alla occupazione ter-ziaria: ulteriori spunti di riflessione', *Quaderni di Economica del Lavoro*, 2.

Fuchs, V., (1968), *The Services Economy*, New York, National Bureau of Economic Research and Columbia University Press.

— (ed.) (1969), *Production and Productivity in the Service Industries*, New York, Columbia University Press.

Galbraith, J.R. and Nathanson, D.A., (1978), *Strategy Implementation: the Role of Structure and Process*, St. Paul, West.

Gershuny, J., (1978), *After Industrial Society? The Emerging Self-Service Economy*, London, Macmillan.

Gershuny, J. and Miles, I.D., (1983), *The New Service Economy. The Transformation of Employment in Industrial Societies*, London, Frances Pinter.

Greenfield, H.T., (1966), *Manpower and the Growth of Producer Services*, New York, Columbia University Press.

Howells, J. and Green A.E., (1986), 'Location, Technology and Industrial Organization in U.K. Services', *Progress in Planning*, **26**.

Kuznets, S., (1948), 'National Income: A New Version', *Review of Economics and Statistics*, August.

— (1957), 'Quantitative Aspects of the Economic Growth of Nations. Industrial Distribution of National Product and Labor Force', *Economic Development and Cultural Change*, July.

— (1958), 'Quantitative Aspects of the Economic Growth of Nations. Industrial Distribution of Income and Labor Force', *Economic Development and Cultural Change*, July.

— (1971), *Economic Growth of Nations*, Cambridge, Mass., Harvard University Press.

Lipietz A., (1978), 'La dimension régionale du développement tertiaire', *Travaux et recherches de prospectives* **75**.

Marshall, J.N., (1982), 'Linkages between Manufacturing Industry and Business Services', *Environment and Planning* A, **14**.

Martinelli, F., (1984), 'Servizi alla produzione e sviluppo economico regionale: il caso del Mezzogiorno d'Italia', *Rassegna Economica*, 1.

— (1989a), 'Business Services, Innovation and Regional Policy. Considerations on the case of Southern Italy' in L. Albrechts *et al.* (eds.), *Regional Policy at the*

Cross-roads, London, Jessica Kingsley.
— (1989b), 'Problematics in Trade and Development of Services', notes for a discussion on GATT negotiations, UNCTAD, Geneva.
— and Siniscalco, D., (1980), 'Terziario totale e terziario per il sistema produttivo', *Economia e Politica Industriale*, 25.
— and — (1986), 'Mutamenti nella struttura del sistema produttivo e integrazione fra industria e terziario' in L. Pasinetti (ed.), *Mutamenti strutturali del sistema produttivo. Integrazione tra industria e settore terziario*, Bologna, Il Mulino.
Nusbaumer, J., (ed.) (1984), *Les services: nouvelles donnée de l'économie*, Paris, Economica.
Offe, C., (1977), *Lo stato nel capitalismo maturo*, Milan, Etas Libri.
Porat, M., (1976), *The Information Society*, Stanford, Stanford University, Center for Interdisciplinary Studies.
Porter, M.E., (1990), *The Competitive Advantage of Nations*, London, Macmillan.
Riddle, D., (1986), *Service-led Growth: The Role of the Service Sector in World Development*, New York, Praeger.
Rostow, W.W., (1966), *The Stages of Economic Growth*, New Haven, Yale University Press.
Sabolo, Y., (1975), *The Service Industries*, Geneva, ILO.
Singelmann, J., (1978), *The Transition from Agriculture to Services*, Beverly Hills, Sage.
Stanback Jr., T.M., (1979), *Understanding the Service Economy*, Baltimore, Johns Hopkins University Press.
— Bearse, P.J., Noyelle, T. and Karasek, R.A. (1981) *Services: The New Economy*, Totowa, NJ, Allanheld Osmun.
Stigler, G., (1951), 'The Division of Labor is Limited by the Extent of the Market', *Journal of Political Economy*, **59**.
— (1956), *Trends in Employment in the Service Industries*, Princeton, Princeton University Press.
UNCTAD (1985), *Services and the Development Process*, Geneva, United Nations.
— (1989), *Trade and Development Report 1988; Part Two: Services in the World Economy*, New York, United Nations.
Walker, R.A., (1985), 'Is There a Service Economy? The Changing Capitalist Division of Labor', *Science and Society*, 1.
Williamson, O., (1980), 'Transaction Costs Economics: the Governance of Contractual Relations', *Journal of Law and Economics*, **22**.
— (1986), 'Vertical Integration and Transaction Costs' in J.E. Stiglitz and G.F. Mathewson (eds), *New Developments in the Analysis of Market Structure*, London, Macmillan.
Wood, P.A., (1986), 'The Anatomy of Job Loss and Job Creation: Some Speculations on the Role of the Producer Service Sector', *Regional Studies*, **20**.

3 Production and circulation of scientific and technological knowledge: research and development as a specific economic activity

Olivier Weinstein $\overline{0}$ 3 2 $\overline{0}$ 3 3

Introduction

The present changes in the productive structures of advanced econo-mies are characterised by the development of new activities such as services to firms or the 'informational' activities, which do not come within the traditional framework of economic analysis because of the specificities of their nodes of production and dissemination. Analysing these activities involves complex issues on a micro-economic level as far as their characteristics and mode of organisation are concerned, as well as on a more global level as far as their implications with respect to the conditions of macroeconomic operation and regulation.

This chapter aims at raising some issues related to a particular activity: research and development (R & D), considered as the central form of production and circulation of scientific and technological knowledge. R & D may be analysed as part of the 'industry of knowledge' (Machlup 1962) or of the 'informational sector' (Porat 1976). It also may be con-sidered as a particular category of services, even as a category of services to firms dealing in industrial research and for a growing part of public research. Yet, in that context, R & D holds a particular place. We know its growing importance in industrial dynamics. Today, R & D holds a strategic position because of the volume of methods it mobilises and its effects on the structures of production. It tends to become as important – if not more important in some fields – as the investment goods sector. This is why it is important to understand the essential characteristics of the process of technological knowledge production and distribution, its specificities and the issues they raise.

This shift is revealed in a process of institutionalisation and professio-nalisation of research and in the constitution of what we may call a system of scientific and technical knowledge production (essentially the R & D sector).

However, this does not mean that the evolution of knowledge pro-duction has been realised under circumstances similar to those prevailing in the industrial sector. It is true that some analysts assert that the process of scientific production would have undergone the same kind of transformation as the industrial production process: a tendency towards marketing and packaging of output, to the industrialisation of production in which mechanisation (in the form of computers and other information technology hardware) is increasingly required, and of the division of labour (some authors even talk about a 'Taylorisation of research labour' or of 'intellectual labour'.[1] Knowledge production is apparently on the way to becoming similar to any other form of production.

Nevertheless, even if such tendencies explain some aspects of the R & D structures, the organization of forms of production and circulation of knowledge in general, and of technical knowledge in particular, demonstrate really original features compared to the features of material production. How to characterise and analyse this special factor is the problem that will now be considered.

Neoclassical micro-economics provides a specific way for analysing the characteristics of knowledge production and the market. Theoretical works on R & D have proliferated for some time but without providing us with a really unified and coherent vision.[2] Those works are led by the kind of issue they tackle: the conditions of existence and efficiency of market equilibrium. Nevertheless, confronting the standard microeconomic model with the features of the processes of production and circulation of technological knowledge allows us to point out their special features and already demonstrates some reasons why knowledge may not be considered like other commodities.

We propose here to examine how R & D may be analysed as an economic activity, and why, to understand its characteristics, it appears necessary to look far beyond the classical representation of the conditions of commodity production and circulation. To this end, we will first look at a neoclassic-inspired approach to 'knowledge' specificities considered as economic goods. Next, we will attempt to examine the characterisation of R & D activities and output. Finally, we will tackle some issues related to the organisation and regulation of R & D.

Knowledge as an economic good: indivisibility, appropriability and uncertainty

R & D may be analysed as a particular sector of knowledge production and more precisely as a set of institutions providing the production of new scientific and technological knowledge. As a starting point, we will consider the general definition of a 'knowledge industry' proposed by Machlup (1980): 'a group of bodies – firms, institutions, organizations and departments, or teams acting inside them, but also, under some circumstances, individuals and households – producing knowledge, information goods or services, for themselves or for others'.

To consider the production of knowledge, and especially scientific and technological knowledge as an economic activity, does not consist for us as a principle stipulating that any human activity can and should be analysed from a similar model of rational behaviour. The object is rather to take notice of some historical evolution in the social conditions of knowledge production and in the institutional forms prevailing at the present time. Without thoroughly tackling those questions here,[3] we may quickly note that, mainly during the twentieth century, scientific and technological labour has undergone an evolution similar to that of the industrial labour process: from a formal subsumption to capital – where capital uses knowledge without modifying its production and circulation forms – to a real subsumption overthrowing production and circulation conditions and tending to subordinate them to the logic and restraints of capital accumulation.

There are three classic reasons for 'market failures':[4] *indivisibility, uncertainty and inappropriability*, which appear as the three essential characteristics of the output, 'knowledge'. A piece of information or knowledge may be considered as an indivisible good, or as a public good, in so far as once produced, its use cost is low or even non-existent. If we consider more precisely this indivisibility, it appears to acquire a double nature: first, once produced, knowledge may be duplicated at no cost or at a low one; so, it may be appropriated by any user. Second, while being used, the 'quantity of knowledge' used to produce a commodity does not depend on the quantity of knowledge produced.

Consequently, 'the same amount of knowledge that is used to make m units of output will serve to make $m + 1$ units, and the same knowledge that is used by n persons (producers), can enable $n + 1$ persons to make the same product' (Machlup 1984). This does not necessarily imply that the costs of knowledge transfer or training are non-existent or low. On the contrary, one of the features of technical knowledge consists precisely in the importance of these costs. This is an essential aspect of R & D which refers to the exact nature of its 'output' and use conditions. We will reconsider that point later in this chapter. There is no contradiction in characterising technical knowledge as an indivisible collective good, but this shows that we have to search more deeply to grasp its specific qualities.

In fact, the *appropriation of knowledge* raises two questions: may knowledge, and in particular scientific and technological knowledge produced by R & D, be subject to some individual appropriation, and how far may this go? If it is possible, is it socially desirable? This second question has received the most attention in analyses and discussions, especially about patent systems. The problem may be considered as a dispute between static efficiency and dynamic efficiency: in so far as knowledge is a public good, its most efficient use will be obtained if it is dispensed free of charge. On the other hand, we may claim that in order to motivate researchers to produce new knowledge under the best circumstances, they must receive some profits and be able to appropriate this knowledge, at least partially. The dynamic efficiency implies an appropriation, or even a monopoly, at least temporarily, of knowledge by the producer (this is Schumpeter's opinion).

We are not going to discuss those theses here, except in so far as they lead to our first question: how may a private appropriation of this particular type of good be realised? As far as scientific and technical knowledge is concerned, the most common point of view consists in considering that on the one hand there is fundamental knowledge (the output of basic research), with the characteristics of public goods, freely available and mainly financed from public funds. On the other hand, there are R & D activities, the results of which may be the subject of a private appropriation or even of a commercial valorisation.[5] This appropriation is realised through the implementation of statutory and institutional forms: either through a system of legal protection (patents, copyright), or through secrecy, which implies the internalisation of the activity of knowledge production by the firms concerned. Let us note here that apart from public research (or research by non-profit institutions), internalisation is the rule. R & D in the industrial sector (industrial research) is mainly led by the industrial firms themselves, rather than by specialist R & D firms, providing the firms with a nearly complete monopoly of the knowledge produced.

But such processes are not sufficient for technological knowledge to be regarded as a commodity similar to common goods and services. Neither secrecy nor systems of legal protection may totally prevent information 'leaks'. In a way, taking out a patent consists in providing 'free' information, as does revealing the main points of some research drafts. Besides, appropriation, and especially merchandisation, do not often deal with knowledge itself but rather with material goods in which this knowledge is incorporated. This may of course be explained by the desire of the firm to appropriate the profits of its research but this is unlikely to be the only reason. Furthermore, the very complex circumstances of transfer and dissemination of R & D results make the integration of knowledge production and industrial production into the firm more efficient, enabling the firm to control the conditions of knowledge production and circulation.

Finally, we may observe that the appropriation of technological knowledge is not, as a rule, a way to establish a market (even less a competitive market). A firm has first to ensure its monopoly. The merchandisation of knowledge itself is only partially realised and under particular forms. We will reconsider this point further on.

Uncertainty is traditionally presented as the essential feature in the production of scientific and technological knowledge.[6] The links between uncertainty and research raise two separate questions. R & D output may be characterised as a 'reduction in uncertainty' in a specific field, or as 'an observation on the world which reduces its possible range of variation' (Arrow 1969).[7] Generally speaking we may consider (as Arrow did) that any production activity provides two kinds of answer: on the one hand, a physical output, on the other, a quantity of knowledge usable in the future for other production processes, and enabling a reduction in their uncertainty and improvements in their outcome. The former aspect is dominant in industrial production; the latter is, in a way, a by-product of it (learning by doing). As far as research is concerned, there is an opposite situation. Physical outputs may be obtained (technical appliances, prototypes, new equipment), but the essential part consists in a reduction of uncertainty in the prospects of achieving some outcomes and in the means of obtaining them.

The process of R & D production is itself characterised by a great uncertainty. This uncertainty presents several dimensions. As far as industrial R & D is concerned, the most common analyses emphasise the uncertainty in the matter of success or failure of R & D projects, as well as the cost and time necessary to obtain results. Then, we may differentiate the risk of technical failure (technical objectives not reached) from commercial failure (inability to implement industrially a process or output that is technically efficient) and from economic failure (innovation happening to be unprofitable) (Mansfield 1977). Generally, the probability attaching to these risks may be calculated.[8] But it is obviously necessary to add another type of uncertainty: the uncertainty about the nature and use of the results obtained. This uncertainty is emphasised by the fact that, in several cases, those results may be used as inputs both in an industrial process and in R & D itself. At each step, the process of knowledge production provides a field of potential uses more or less delimited rather than a 'product' which is well specified. The use value of the results is not strictly set. This aspect is tightly related to the unique and specific characteristic of each project and of each result as well as to the importance, the complexity and uncertainty of the interrelations between producers and users of knowledge. We may certainly consider that this last type of uncertainty essentially arises in the case of basic or exploratory research and much less in the case of finalised R & D (industrial or not). Nevertheless, even in this last case, uncertainty does not seem to be wanting.[9] Let us notice that unlike the previous types of risks, this one seems difficult to measure in probabilistic terms.

The most common approach to these issues is based on the use of probabilist models of decision and equilibrium under uncertainty. One may ask to what extent this type of approach may account for risks specific to research. Beyond that, the most interesting issues deal with the nature of institutional mechanisms enabling us to ensure the regulation and efficiency of the production and transfer of technical knowledge; we can only say that it seems necessary to leave the standard framework of the market mechanisms.

More generally speaking, here is the essential conclusion we may reach from the items broached above. From these characteristics – output indivisibility and particular conditions regarding its appropriation and uncertainty – we already understand part of the issues set by the R & D organisation, and more especially the limits to the 'classical' commercial forms, and the necessity for public forms (or of collective forms of another nature). But, to get the specific conditions of management and regulation of R & D activities, we have to look beyond the distinction between collective good versus individual goods and markets versus public institutions. These categories of analysis depend on the neoclassical approach and the kinds of issues it tackles. They aim at preserving what is essential in this framework, and at incorporating into it, as cheaply as possible, some 'disturbing' phenomena.

But it seems to us that some statements, notably in Arrow's work (1962, 1969) are more important and go beyond the limits of this framework. R & D gives rise to transactions that are different from the usual relationships in market–contractual relations or relationships closed to the sale of professional services. Personal relationships play an essential part in knowledge production and transfer. Interdependence between the various phases and various aspects of the inventive activity is important. These characteristics and others that we are going to consider now, lead us to deepen the analysis of the production and circulation specificities of technological knowledge, especially as far as the precise nature of the outputs and their use conditions is concerned.

Production, circulation and use of the R & D output: the specificities

Let us start from a general formulation of an economic activity (production of commodities) corresponding to the 'standard' conceptions of economic theory. A production process is represented by a shift from inputs to outputs such as:

$$(x_1 x_2 \ldots x_n) \rightarrow (y_1 y_2 \ldots y_n) \quad \text{or} \quad Y = F(X)$$

The specification of the F function is not important here. Even at this very high level of generality, essential hypotheses are found to be implicitly present:

— the existence of an area of products, inputs and outputs stated a priori (the classification hypothesis). The outcomes of the activity undertaken (as well as all its inputs) are supposed to be known and provided with perfectly determined characteristics. In addition, they are supposed to be quantifiable.
— the production and use of the outputs are clearly separated. The way of using an output and its use value are known and defined when it leaves the production process. This determines where the output is placed in the function of production or in consumption by the users.
— there is what we may call the 'anonymity' of an output, defined and assessed independently from the identity of the producers or users (and independently from its different uses). In other words, the relations between economic units, or between activities, may be reduced to the circulation of (material or immaterial) objects.

All this assumes that the activities studied provide outputs which have been normalised or standardised (this is also applicable to goods or services produced in small quantities or even by unit, and does not assume mass production, even if the model appears to exactly fit the situation). Finally, we can suggest that taking into account indivisibilities, uncertainty (about the volume of production obtained) or even the existence of externalities does not fundamentally modify this representation of the production process.

Is it possible to conceive the production and dissemination of scientific and technical knowledge as part of the same model? Some trends exist which aim to provide knowledge with a form corresponding to this model, that is a form adequate to the ideal conditions of commodity production, but it remains the case that R & D activity does not fit easily into this representation, particularly with reference to the characteristics of its output, its forms of circulation and use and the links between production conditions and use conditions.

In order to further this argument, it is useful to examine what R & D 'output' really is, and especially the output of industrial R & D. We know how difficult it is to answer this question because of the diversity of the types of 'objects' it produces, of the ways in which they are provided and in the multiplicity of the networks within which such objects circulate.

Product diversity: first, there are outputs in the form of structured, codified information (adapted to the areas in which it has to circulate):

- articles, or other works intended for the scientific sphere (working papers, notes, theses) or for the industrial sphere;
- patents;
- any kind of document (blueprints, software) designed to transfer outputs to industrial use. This type of output may circulate inside a firm, between firms in the framework of technological selling, or between research laboratories and industrial units, for example in the framework of contractual and cooperative relations.

Product diversity is complicated by the fact that these outputs are not only new scientific knowledge according to the common meaning, but may constitute expert appraisals on some specific technical problem faced by a firm or a production line, or even of trend forecasts of technological evolution in a particular field.

But the R & D outcomes, especially in industrial R & D, cannot be reduced to such pre-determined objects. They represent only part of the whole complex system of knowledge and skills R & D produces. The work of a laboratory mainly consists in experimentation and the perfection of new methods and technologies aiming at some new result or effect (Price 1984). This is achieved through new techniques and instruments, and through the formation of new job skills and qualifications. All such items may be transferred. Additionally, a great part of R & D output comprises non-formalised skills and abilities possessed by individuals or teams.[10] This aspect is essential and partly explains the specific conditions whereby the pieces of knowledge produced will circulate and be used (there is a problem in transferring knowledge from R & D to industrial units and a problem of R & D valorisation). Close relationships between producers and users of knowledge, or transfers of individuals or teams are often a vital means for transferring R & D outcomes. This gives rise to another factor: the nature of technical knowledge that is, in many cases, specific and differentiated (Pavitt 1986). This involves an R & D outcome that, generally, has to fit each user and each particular use. As such, it may not be formulated once and for all and be implemented without the intervention of the producers.

By further developing Arrow's formulation (1969), we may say that every activity of production provides three types of outcomes: a physical output and two types of information knowledge.

— formalised and codified knowledge taking the various forms we have previously listed (in the case of R & D) which may circulate (and be accumulated) autonomously;
— skills and abilities which are being developed throughout the production processes – under various conditions, especially with regard to learning and experience – without being precisely structured and formalised. As Machlup (1980) has stated, these pieces of knowledge are incorporated into individuals (or teams), or even into 'knowledge carriers'.

The main output of R & D activities consists in an arrangement of both these types of knowledge. In many cases, both forms are highly complementary: the former can only be used together with the latter. We may put forward the hypothesis that the more innovatory the pieces of knowledge produced are, the more important are the specific non-formalised skills held by research teams. Finally, a research output may be a specific material good, a new instrument for example.

The diversity of areas (where scientific and technological outputs are circulating) and of modes of circulation follow from the above. It is necessary here to take several axes of differentiation into account: a first axis is drawn between the scientific and the industrial fields. The inter-relations between both fields become tighter and tighter. (This differentiation does not cover any institutional opposition; at various levels, public research and industrial research take part in both areas.) But both fields keep their special features, especially as far as the finality and the form attributed to the outcomes are concerned. Their opposition may be analysed as the opposition between the scientific area and the economic area, each have their own rules and their own logic.

There are networks of informal relationships combined with networks of institutionalised and formalised relationships. The informal relationships cover interpersonal contacts – in the framework of scientific and industrial areas – or even non-strictly codified inter-institution relationships. They also cover the circulation of modes of knowledge of a completely different nature: the various procedures individuals or firms use as they secretly seek to appropriate various outcomes: spying, detailed examination of the outputs, patent infringement or headhunting. Such practices are obviously important in the spread of knowledge.

The institutional relationships themselves are varied. The purely economic relations take two essential forms:

— non-market relationships, internal to the firms or structured by networks of cooperation between firms and between laboratories;
— and market relationships: either direct selling of knowledge (patent transfer, licences), or selling of knowledge embodied in material goods (equipment, components) or in what we may call 'technological sets' combining various skills and abilities and, possibly, material goods.

The direct merchandisation of scientific and technological knowledge remains limited. Non-market circulation and circulation to captive markets are really much more important. A recent study of multinational firms (Bertin and Wyatt 1986) points out that for these firms:

— the main sources of technological knowledge are first of all internal R & D and then internal production;
— the modes of acquiring technical information are mainly: the published patents, congresses and technical meetings, from articles on scientific and business matters;
— the modes of appropriating technology are in the first instance know-how, and then patents.

Let us now try to delineate the essential characteristics of the production and circulation of scientific and technological knowledge, in relation to the traditional representations of economic processes. The specifics deal with the characteristics of the products, the production process and the relationships between production process and the 'consumption' (or use) process of the outcomes. As an hypothesis, we put forward four dimensions to explain the general problems of analysis and organisation of an activity such as R & D.

What we have so far described shows two aspects of the 'technological knowledge' product:

— its characteristic of specific indivisible good (each product is unique and collectively usable);
— its characteristic of being a multiform complex product. The 'research project' may be considered as the basic activity of the system of R & D production. The outcome of each project comprises a complex set of knowledge which can be 'objectivised' and circulated in the various forms previously discussed. More often than not a project will be a combination of structured and codified knowledge and non-formalised, tacit 'know-how'. But we will emphasise here another dimension of the R & D product we consider as fundamental: *the indetermination of its use value.*

The R & D product is used partly by R & D itself and partly by the productive system. Indetermination more particularly appears in the second type of use, especially as far as technological knowledge with industrial finality is concerned. Contrary to the common representation of production, it is not possible to provide the R & D outcomes – especially industrial R & D – with the characteristic of a well-defined product, the uses of which would be perfectly determined as soon as it 'leaves' the production process. The determination of R & D product uses will generally be the outcome of a long learning process linked with the diffusion of knowledge (and ranking with the production of a complementary knowledge). This has to be compared with the fact that, contrary to the classical presentation of the innovation theory, we may not strictly separate the innovation act which creates a new product or process from the diffusion process which deals with perfectly bounded objects.

As we have said, the process of technological knowledge production provides at each step a loosely bounded field of potentialities. Inside this field, the methods adopted actually depend on several factors either internal to R & D (its conditions of organisation and procedure, the securing of complementary outcomes) or external to R & D (the advance of complementary outcomes, the progress of demand and the productive structures, the modes of relationships between R & D and industry). It is useful to keep in mind that in most cases the technological innovation consists in conceiving some new use for existing knowledge, that is to say in *widening the field* of use. This is the very reason why the issue of research 'valorisation' (either public or industrial research) has to be tackled. This does not arise from the fact that R & D could be badly orientated or insufficiently finalised, but from the very nature of what R & D may produce. It is true that at the present time, almost the whole of industrial R & D and a growing part of university and public R & D is strictly finalised, in that it is dealing with projects aiming at outcomes with determined uses. But this generally does not prevent the outcomes achieved from having potentialities of use much wider than originally intended.[11]

In such circumstances, it is understandably difficult to assign some 'economic value' to the output, at a given time, from an R & D 'unit of production' (or to assess the profitability of a research project). This gives rise to some questions about what could guide the resourcing of this sector, or from a wider point of view, what could ensure its regulation. It also leads us to tackling the issue of the possibility of quantifying the R & D output. We will return to this point later.

A last essential aspect, related to the previous one, deals with the relationships between *production process and consumption (or use) process* of scientific and technological knowledge. The complexity and the multi-form characteristic of R & D outcomes, added to the difficulty of isolating a 'final' output at a given time, make it impossible strictly to separate production and use.

That is obviously another characteristic which may at least incorporate a wide range of services, especially the non-standardised services that require close integration with the users.[12] In the present case, the difficulties of implementing transfer operations between research centres and units of production, even when they take place in the same firm, and the important role always played by personal relationships, point out how impossible it is to take the mere process of circulation of an output as a basis for analysis (in the matter of market or non-market relationships).

Thus, the relations between an R & D unit and an industrial unit (or any other user) do not tend to take the form of a mere punctual process of output transfer, but rather of a sustained interaction between activities, and this implies a system of direct relationships between the working teams intervening in the knowledge production and the users of knowledge.

It follows that the institutional forms which enable the organisation and regulation of such relationships should be considered. These include merchant, quasi-merchant (contractual) relationships or any other relationships between autonomous units (cooperation for example) – especially between research centres and firms – as well as administrative relationships regulating, within firms, the relations between R & D units and production units.

There remain the quantifiable or non-quantifiable characteristics of the outcomes of R & D activities. Up to now, the most natural hypothesis has been to accept – as Machlup (1984) does for example – that these outcomes are naturally non-quantifiable. In other words, it is impossible either to define or to assess some 'production volume' for an R & D unit. All we have seen up to now about the characteristics of the 'technical knowledge' output leads to that conclusion. Except in some particular cases, it is difficult to conceive how it could be possible to reduce complex and specific knowledge (or sets of knowledge) to a 'quantum of knowledge units'.

Of course, it is possible to build various partial indicators in order to assess the activity of a researcher or of a research team. This is achieved either through articles (especially in basic research) or through patents and licences (in industrial research). Such indicators are really useful for analysing R & D activities, but it does not mean that they have the status of an R & D output assessment that can be compared with the assessments commonly used for industrial production.

Without claiming to resolve this issue here, it seems that it might be useful to examine the implications of the hypothetical non-measurability of the R & D outcomes, and more generally speaking, the implications of the co-existence of activities producing quantifiable outputs with activities producing non-quantifiable outputs within the same productive system. An important difference between both types of activity is that the former may be managed from calculations of outputs and productivity, while the latter will essentially be assessed on the basis of their costs.

That is why some observers uphold the thesis of an inevitable trend towards increasing costs of 'intangible' activities – especially the costs of R & D – compared to the costs of material production (Machlup 1984;

Baumol and Wolff 1983). This theory requires further discussion. It covers two different ideas:

— either the productivity or efficiency of R & D is, by nature, stationary (and non-measurable at the same time!) – this is a variant of traditional ideas about services;
— or the possible growth of the efficiency of R & D activities may only appear through its effects on material production, that is by its contribution to the visible productivity of the users. Hence, the increasing costs of R & D may not be explained by a differential growth of productivity but by the fact that information and knowledge are more and more important as a determinant of industrial productivity in comparison with the other factors (fixed capital and industrial labour).[13]

Whatever the situation, the issues concerned with the evolution of R & D efficiency or productivity (if we accept this notion as correct) can only be solved through the analysis of the particular characteristics of the R & D production process.

Analysis of the 'labour process' of R & D is dominated by two key factors that are closely connected. The first factor is the *determinant position of its highly qualified professional labour*. Even if it is true that at the present time, R & D implies the implementation of important and sophisticated equipment, the capacity and efficiency of a research centre is mainly based on the qualifications of its personnel as well as on the network of relationships and cooperation between researchers. This also implies organisational and operational conditions very different from those common to the standard industrial process.

The second factor is the *low codification degree of the working methods*. We cannot say that in a R & D unit there is a set of production methods or of well defined technique repeatedly used in the manner typical of an industrial process (or even of some services). This arises partly from the need for highly qualified professional labour, and especially from the fact that individual qualifications are not easily transferable (Nelson 1980). It also stems from the fact that the production of technical knowledge is generally not aimed at obtaining any standard well-defined result, repeatedly and within a determined period of time.

So, on the basis of Nelson's analysis (1980), we are led to distinguish the different productive sectors or activities according to the degree of codification of the production methods (undoubtedly – but not necessarily rigidly – related to the degree of codification of the outputs). In some sectors or activities, production rests on formalised and codified methods, mainly independent from the workers implementing them. Alternatively, there may be some separation between design (of products and processes) and production. In other sectors or activities, such as R & D, the production rests on the specific qualifications of individuals and teams. The effective conditions of operation are, in the latter case, much more difficult to grasp.

Nelson uses this to explain differences in productivity growth between sectors: where the methods are little codified, the process of perfecting the production conditions, and then the productivity growth, can only be slow. Once more, this is an hypothesis which requires further examination. But here, we will put forward a weaker hypothesis: according to the types of activities, the organisation and evolutionary form of the production process and the modes of obtaining productivity gains will differ, especially with respect to:

— the part played by the improvement and renewal of the codified techniques, when they exist;
— and in the opposite case, the prevalence of the processes of experiment and learning through practice.

But such a differential between two important forms of activities has surely to be modulated. On the one hand, it is obvious that non-codified items, individual and collective skills and the learning processes, take some part in every industrial process. On the other hand, it has to be considered whether some activities really are opposed by nature to any rigid codification and organisational form, or if the lack of such a situation is not a mere illustration of their relative 'youth' as economic activities, subject to profit restraints. Therefore, it is possible that R & D – either public or industrial – is only at the beginning of some 'rationalisation' process which could gradually be shifting its characteristics. It is obvious that the growing importance of R & D costs is leading in that direction.

Organisation and regulation forms: some issues

We will only tackle two issues here. The first deals with the limits of the merchant form in relation to activities such as R & D. The second deals with the problem of managing and regulating activities for which the outputs are not easily quantifiable.

Let us start with the three great institutional forms of economic activity: the market, the state and the firm from the point of view of Coase (1937), that is as the area of activity coordination. All we have observed leads us to doubt the ability of the market to direct the production and circulation of technological knowledge. So, the non-merchant forms may be considered from two points of view:

— following the logic of the collective good theory, the indivisibility of the output and the difficulties entailed in appropriating it lead us to emphasise the importance of the public form. The dualism of the R & D structures could then be explained: public research ensures the production of the most general and most difficult to appropriate knowledge (basic research), while industrial research concentrates on more specific and privately appropriable knowledge.

— some of the characteristics of the R & D activities – complexity and uncertainty of the outcomes, advantageous cooperation between producers and users of knowledge and the importance of *specific* skills – share similarities with the factors used to explain vertical integration: that is, the substitution of an administration coordination in the firm to market relationships; the importance of externalities and of cooperation gains, transaction complexity, and asset specificities. Then, the internalisation of R & D in industrial firms would be the main form for coping with these special qualities. Let us add that appropriation of the results and a stricter work control certainly are the essential reasons for research to be internalised.

It seems therefore that the main characteristics of R & D organisation – the importance of public intervention and the prevalence of internalised industrial research – have now been explained. Nevertheless, we cannot leave it at that. Such differences between the public sector and the private sector, and between merchant form and administrative form, can hardly account for all types of structures being constituted in R & D: a complex interpenetration between public institutions and private institutions as well as between public regulation and private regulation. We cannot rest with only the image of a distinction between 'free' public research and appropriated industrial research. Public research (or more generally speaking, 'non-profit-making' non-industrial research) is guided by its relationships with industry and by the evolution of the restraints it undergoes to fit in contractual relationships that we may call 'quasi-merchant'. On the other hand, industrial research is heavily affected by public financing which, jointly with public demands – especially military ones – has a privileged part in influencing the trend in the development of its activities. So, the R & D sector undergoes a particular system of regulation, combining specifically public forms with private ones.

Moreover, too strict an opposition between market relationships and administrative relationships inside the firm fails to account for the types of relations between production and exchange which are developing in research. For several years, various students of industrial economics have been pointing out the importance of relations between activities and between economic units which are, in a way, intermediate between pure market relations (the traditional selling contract) and the purely bureaucratic relations of integration in the same firm (relations which, additionally may take different forms). R & D is one of the fields in which such relationships become particularly important: these include complex contractual relationships, relationships of bilateral or multilateral cooperation dealing with more or less wide fields or relationships between institutions of different types (firms, university and public research laboratories, administrations). Analysing the content and logic of these institutional forms would enable us to grasp the conditions for the regulation of R & D, as well as the specific problems it tackles.

If the specific characteristics of technical knowledge production account for the role of the non-market forms and of 'intermediate' or 'mixed' forms, it is still questionable whether these forms can cover the R & D specifics and how they may do it. Those responsible for the management of research inside industrial firms point out that the answers are not obvious. This leads us to consider more particularly one of the specific characteristics of R & D – the difficulty, or even the impossibility, of quantifying its outputs.

The non-quantification of the output, the impossibility of defining and assessing a 'volume' of production of the R & D units, as well as a value, and consequently the impossibility of assessing its productivity – especially the productivity of labour – lead to two questions. We shall just raise them.

— the first question deals with the management and direction of the research activities themselves. What methods of labour management and control can be used, if we have no reliable assessments of individual and collective 'performances'? The steady growth of R & D costs, the various questions about its assessment and the attempts – under various guises – to control and direct public and private researchers more strictly, point out the reality of the issue. The problem is especially to know whether the regulation of R & D may finally be realised only through changes enabling some modalities to assess their output productivity.
— on a more general level, we have to tackle the question of the conditions of global regulation of an economy in which an important element provides outputs for which the volume/price partition and the calculation of productivity happen to be impossible. If we consider that the movements of productivity are the necessary basis by which the regulation and accumulation of capital – and more especially the regulation of wages – may be ensured, it appears that such regulation may be unrealisable (see Petit 1985).

The answer to these questions will only be achieved through regulating the growth of R & D, as well as the growth of other service activities in the context of more general transformations of the production structures (of which they are a manifestation) and by considering the transformation of the structural forms of organisation and regulation which accompany them.

Notes

1. See G. Ciccoti *et al.*, 'La production de science dans le société capitaliste avancée' in Ciccoti *et al.*, 1979.
2. See Guesnerie and Tirole, 1985.
3. See Weinstein, 1985.
4. See Arrow, 1962.
5. See Guesnerie and Tirole, op. cit.

6. See for example Arrow, 1969.
7. From this conception, we may attempt general formulations of knowledge production as part of the Bayesian methods, but we leave this aside here.
8. See Mansfield, 1977, who provides some examples. We may be doubtful about this approach being applicable to any research project, especially to the most innovatory ones.
9. Generally speaking, the degree of determination of outcome use varies considerably according to the type of research and the type of institution; it also varies according to the forms of organisation and the periods during the life of a technology. One of the main issues of R & D organization consists precisely in knowing how to provide some valuable definition and assessment of the results and how to adjust the output provided by the laboratory to the demand of the users.
10. A lot of articles appear as reports of experiments with their results. But effective means for carrying out the experiment are not included in the reports. This is one of the reasons why, in some cases, industrial laboratories allow their researchers to publish articles, without any fear of losing control over an essential part of their labour force.
11. This is illustrated, for example, by the issue of the repercussions on industry of military financed R & D.
12. See J. Gadrey, 1987.
13. It remains to examine the effect of this evolution, and more generally, the consequences of the speeding up of the renewal of technologies on all the productive structures and their global efficiency.

References

Arrow, K., (1962), 'Economic welfare and allocation of resources for invention' in R. Nelson, (ed), *The Rate and Direction of Inventive Activity*, Princeton, University Press.
— (1969), 'Classificatory Notes on the Production and Transmission of Technologic Knowledge,' *American Economic Review*, **59**, 4, pp. 29–39.
Baumol, J. and Wolff, N., (1983), 'Feedback from Productivity Growth to R & D, *Scandinavian Journal of Economics*, **85**, pp. 74–88.
Bertin, G. and Wyatt, S., (1986), *Multinationales et propriété industrielle*, Paris, PUF-IRM.
Cicoti, G. *et al.*, (1979), *L'araignée et le tisserand*, Paris, Seuil.
Coase, R., (1937), The Nature of the Firm, *Economica*. **4**, 386–405.
Gadrey, J., (1987), 'La productivité de la recherche universitaire', *Recherche et technologie*, La documentation Française, n.4.
Guesnerie, R. and Tirole, J., (1985), L'économie de la recherche-développement: Introduction à certains travaux théoriques, *Revue économique*, **36**, 5, pp. 843–71.
Machlup, F., (1962), *The Production and Distribution of Knowledge in the United States*, Princeton, Princeton University Press
— (1980–84), *Knowledge, its Creation, Distribution and Economic Significance*, 3 volumes, Princeton, Princeton University Press.
Mansfield, E., (1977), *The Production and Application of New Industrial Technology*, New York, W.W. Norton.
Nelson, R., (1980), 'Production Sets, Technological Knowledge and R & D, *American Economic Review*, (70), 2, pp. 62–71.
Pavitt, K., (1986), 'Avant-propos' in Bertin and Wyatt, 1986.

Petit, P., (1985), 'L'évolution du rapport salarial dans une économie tertiaire', Paris, CEPREMAP.

Porat, M. (1976), *The Information Society*, Stanford, Stanford University, Center for Interdisciplinary Studies.

Price, D.S., (1984), 'The science/technology relationship, the draft of experimental science, and policy for the improvement of high technology innovation,' *Research Policy*, **13**, 1, pp. 3–20.

Weinstein, O., (1985), Rapports entre science et production et recherche industrielle: quelques réflexions et questions, *Cahiers de CRMSI*, **11**, pp. 5–39.

4 Institutional changes and provision of market services: lessons from the banking sector

Pascal Petit   G 21

D 8 2

I. Questioning the adjustment of market organisations

The market provision of some services raises specific questions. Most of them concern the implicit contracts and externalities accompanying service transactions. The uncertainty about the precise content and quality of the services and their side effects must somehow be reduced and controlled for transactions to take place. This cannot be done by the buyer alone, who, for various reasons, cannot directly check the transaction and its effect. Either the service takes time and implies a long-standing relationship or it calls upon some special expertise which cannot be controlled. Furthermore, due to the overall uncertainty about the feasibility of what is required (be it medical care, a legal case or some economic or technical achievement), no commitment can be imposed which would assure a positive result. In addition, there are also the external effects of the transaction on the buyer or the seller side which remain mainly out of reach.

How then can the market provision for such services be organised? A priori, for such transactions to take place many problems must be solved. Some are known in the literature on principal agents as problems of 'adverse selection' or of 'moral hazard'. But problems also include cases of free riding or of 'prisoner dilemma', whereby the proper functioning of a whole market can be threatened by a few 'trespassers'. Finally the rules and practices concurring with the working of markets may themselves be subject to failures and breakdowns, independently of the intents of usual buyers and sellers. Such failures are due to major externalities and/or changes in the external conditions of the market.

Difficulties of this kind are a priori met in various types of transactions, especially when the product is not standardised, such as in the case of trade in equipment goods or business services. In fact, the quality of some new equipment, for example new computers, cannot be certified right away so that the buyer incurs some risk. Still, experiments can be done to test the new equipment and to facilitate the building-up of experiences. But at some point, if the learning process is too difficult and if servicing by the producer is repeatedly required, the sale of equipment goods is close to being a service transaction.

When allowing for such extended definitions of services, one has to notice, conversely, that some market services do not raise any question of the above type. Standard services whose quality can be easily checked and where externalities have no real incidence are perfectly allocated through the market. This has been the case for many years, without interference by any specific regulatory framework or recurring intervention.

Meanwhile, the provision of some services requires a proper organisation of markets, based on public regulation, on customs/practices or special market institutions. But all these forms of market organisation must evolve together with changing economic, social or technical conditions.

The need for such adjustments means a real challenge to economies. How are changes handled? To what extent do they correspond to the self-reorganisation and practice of markets, and what is the impact of state intervention? Economic theory provides only sketchy answers to such questions.

In the following section, we shall review the main concepts which can be used to address the three kinds of difficulties mentioned above (section II). In the third section, we will apply these concepts to the banking sector which is, a priori, one of the most problematic from the point of view of market allocation and adjustment. A last section seeks to extend the lessons gained from the banking sector to various kinds of services. An assessment of the expansion of the tertiary sector and how the future mix of manufacturing and services activities will feature in a world of more open economies undergoing large technical transformations is the main topic of that section.

II. Risks and failures in market provision of services

The market provision of services can run into difficulties at three levels: (i) the basic level of bilateral transactions; (ii) the overall system of allocation; (iii) the intermediate level of externalities and collusion between agents in the market itself. We shall review the various concepts used in the literature to address these issues.

1. Bilateral transaction under uncertainty

Services in this category are provided through a relationship that extends over some length of time and are realised on a more or less implicit contractual basis. From the buyer's point of view, such contractual relationship implies that some effort will be made by the producer according to well-defined conditions (either fixed by a preset timetable or on request), aiming at some objective, agreed with the user and at a price which may or may not depend on the result. Asymmetries of information between buyers and sellers can strongly bias these more or less implicit contractual arrangements.

Three types of conditions are generally considered to reduce such market imperfections in a given institutional context of bilateral agreement. First, motivations must be strong enough to ensure that contractors will respect their initial commitments during the time span of the provision of the service. Second, arrangements should be made so that the consequences of any change in external conditions as well as cases involving lack of competence (the adverse selection problem) can be dealt with. Third, the deal should be protected against moral hazards, that is malevolent behaviour by any contracting party or lack of effort and care. Above all it should be noted that many services within banking, consulting or insurance activities aim precisely at monitoring the functioning of markets to reduce the imperfections of market mechanisms. This has been stressed in the functional definition of services given in d'Alcantara (1986).

Nevertheless, the set of services which helps to secure the functioning of markets falls short of suppressing all market imperfections stemming from *the monitoring of their own market provision*. In practice, for such markets to exist, formal and informal institutions have been developed.

Holmstrom (1985) identifies four prominent market remedies to circumvent the shortcomings generated by informational asymmetries:

(1) contingent contracts, whereby payments will be partly based on the result and not on the effort of the seller;
(2) reputation, where an asset of good fame is backing the commitment and ability of the seller;
(3) signalling, where obvious signs of competence like educational level ensure the expertise of the seller;
(4) certification and monitoring, where regulations and rules are issued by public authorities or professional associations.

Most of the above concepts refer to cases of implicit contracts between two agents. The remedies suggested may well be of limited relevance for cases which involve externalities or interdependence at the level of the entire market.

2. Externalities and collusive behaviour

So far we have assumed that the provision of services can be regarded as a bilateral agreement, but third parties can be involved in many ways.

First, from the buyer's perspective, the quality of a service may be linked to the number and the quality of the other purchasers. The work of Veblen (1899) remains attached to the notion of conspicuous consumption. More recently, sociologists like Jean Baudrillard (1968) or Pierre Bourdieu (1979) have stressed that consumption behaviour is strongly influenced by the search for social status, by the need to conform with an ideal-type corresponding to a selected reference group. This applies even more to services where fashion and discrimination are quite effective. Markets are segmented and develop various kinds of signals identifying the various market segments. This segmentation will also favour collusion among users, on one side, and providers on the other. The networking which may follow will then act as a barrier to new entrants and to innovation. It reduces accordingly the pure market dimension of the service provision.

Similar market segmentation may occur for services delivered to firms. Competing firms may be reluctant to use the same business services when these are delivered in a long-standing relationship. Such exclusion is officially practiced in advertising for instance. But on the other side the reputation of some clients may act as a signal to attract new service practice. Such phenomena are linked with a shift in the mode of valuation which Keynes clearly identified as a move from a productive to a speculative logic. In the first case, the client firm takes products at their own face value, according to their role in the productive process. In the second case, products are valued by reference to the value they are expected to have for other firms. Such a system of reference is a process which strongly increases the risk of market instability. Markets must be organised to allow them to contain the risks brought forth by this speculative logic.

3. System risks

Even when all the previously mentioned biases have been covered by adequate organisation, the risk that external changes may provoke a collapse of the system remains. This risk does not depend so much on the behaviour of the economic agents or on the working of the system. A financial crisis leading to panic or a crash on the finance markets are standard examples: a generalised lack of confidence in the banking system launches a run on withdrawal which, by its magnitude, provokes defaulting and threatens the mechanism of lender of last resort in its operationality.

A general crisis of confidence can also occur with reference to the certification of expert reports, the reliability of some professionals, the efficiency of such institutions as justice, education or health systems. Such a crisis originates either from some external shock (war, prolonged stagnation and unemployment) or from some internal malfunctioning (overcrowding, extensive bribery, widespread misinformation).

Systems are more or less prone to such risks. This threat is enough to put some pressure on attempts to modify or redesign the whole system of market provision of the services under scrutiny. The case of the banking sector will help us to see how this pressure operates and how the various risks mentioned in this section combine to foster the renewal of the system.

III. The transformation of banking activities

1. On the nature of banking activities

Banking activities are commonly attributed with three functions:

— to run the payments system;
— to act as intermediary between lenders and borrowers;
— to be an adviser and a guide on all markets of financial products.

These three functions are interdependent although one of them, the intermediation function, has played a central historical role. The other two functions have developed as complementary to the intermediation function: potential borrowers and lenders are attracted and their means of payments are handled, while advice on their financial market deals is provided. Consequently, until recently, the services rendered under these last two headings were free or quasi-free. The main share of the banking product then came from the difference between interest paid and received as a result of the intermediation function.

Systems of national accounts divide banking activity in the production of various services (under the heading of cash management or of advising and operating on financial markets) and the net income from interest is tied to the intermediation function. This last item represents the imputed production of banking activities.[1] Table 4.1 illustrates the importance of this imputed banking production in relation to GDP or to the assets of financial institutions in the early 1980s. By comparison, the gains from other services (not linked with intermediation) remain small (less than one-fourth of the whole banking product; see Table 4.1) and cover only a small share of the operating costs.[2]

Table 4.1 Imputed product and fees in banking, OECD (average % 1980–84)

| | Imputed production related to | | Fees in relation to product | |
	GDP	total asset	(a)	(b)
United States	2.6	1.8	24.4	30.5
United Kingdom	4.0	1.8	–	31.5
France	4.1	2.1	15.4	14.8
Japan	4.3	2.0	15.1	20.6
Former West Germany	4.4	2.4	27.4	33.8
Italy	4.5	2.6	27.2	33.8

Notes: (a): all commercial banks; (b): big commercial banks
Source: Szymczak (1987), Table 1, p. 57 and Table 3, p. 61

Furthermore, imputed production, that is the difference between received and paid interest, still mixes net interest from financial investment realised for others with net financial results on the investments of the banks for their own account. This confirms the importance of the logic of speculation in banking.

2. The costs and advantages of handling the payment system

The history of the payment system shows how state interventions accordingly foster or hamper developments in private banking. In a first long phase, the state monopoly on the issuing of money was meant to favour increases in the number, the size and the places of transaction by providing state guarantees to the means of payments (cf. Vilar 1974; De Brunhoff 1976). At some stage, as stressed by Hicks (1969), the development of a monetary economy requires more autonomy to be given to the banking system in order to give it more credibility and to prevent government levies of any kind from interfering too heavily with the working of the monetary system.

Nevertheless, the management of the system of payment by the banks retains dimensions of a public good. In the first place, access to the system of payment is considered as a right. On this ground consumer associations claim that increasing fees (to pay for the cost of handling the system of payments) would discriminate against people with low or medium income. Second, a means of payment requires that a more or less dense network of economic agents use it. Therefore, excluding people from the use of one means reduces the effective power of this means of payment for the others. The advantage of a system with central money, as opposed to a system with many private issuings of means of payments is that it simplifies transactions. This is the argument that one can ultimately use (cf. Aglietta 1984) against analysts who contest the utility of central money (see Black 1970; Fama 1980; Hall 1983). In this respect, a system with diversified means of payment, freely accessible, is a valuable collective good. For private economic agents like bankers to be in charge of the production of such a good, it is necessary that they either benefit from it or have some kind of obligation to do so (either legal or customary). The management of cash and checking accounts offers a clear example of this combination. Banks are well aware of the characteristics of the clients whose short-term deposits and cash management are profitable, that is can lead to long-term deposits or loans. When needed, information technology has provided them with efficient credit scoring techniques, but they tend to refrain from the extensive discrimination that micro-economic rationale would suggest at first sight.[3] Current deficits (see Table 4.2) on these payment operations are thus balanced by some advantages in terms of restrictions set on deposits and loan markets (segmented markets, regulated interest rates on deposits, subsidised lending schemes). A complex of regulations and institutions helps to set this balance between costs and advantages of running the system of payments largely on a private basis.

But such a complex system has a poor capacity to adjust to changes in external conditions, be they innovations brought by information technologies, a sudden rise in real interest rates on world financial markets or new forms of competition issuing from the development of international trade.

Adjustments can follow several paths: from altering the regulatory framework; to shifting greater shares of the costs on to the users; by increasing fees for old products; or by pricing the new products more adequately.

From this perspective, we now review the deregulation movement which occurred in most countries during the last decade.

3. Adjusting the regulatory framework

Banking regulations are to control various risks and to establish the framework for a private provision of the 'public' service of handling the system of payments. For this purpose, regulations can separate the three functions of banking activities, introduce relays within the intermediation process, fix norms of handling, enforce guarantees and controls. These regulations vary from one country to another and from one period to another. The crisis of the 1930s led to a considerable reinforcement of these regulations, severely segmenting the markets (forbidding bank branching in the United States for instance, and separating commercial banks and investment banks in France). It follows that throughout the 1950s and 1960s, most banking systems were highly regulated.

The increase in external trade, the end of the Bretton Woods system of fixed exchange rates, the possibilities offered by information technologies which spurred innovations and competition among financial institutions all provoked in the 1970s a general trend towards deregulation. In fact, the regulatory frameworks had become rather obsolete as they had been bypassed by the world-wide extension of financial markets (the Eurodollar market was a first step in this respect), by the surge of new institutions beyond the range of control of banking authorities (like the Building Societies in the United Kingdom or brokers and big department stores setting up banking operations in the United States) or by the new handling facilities using information technologies. For example, in the United Kingdom the distinction between current account and deposit account was reduced by automated transfers and bookkeeping, so that the prohibition to provide interest on current accounts became meaningless.

The dismantling of the old regulatory frameworks stems from the recognition of this obsolescence. It facilitated the creation of new products and new markets, especially in financial futures. These transformations, together with the internationalisation of financial markets, led to a widespread 'disintermediation': the financing of industrial projects

Table 4.2 Running costs and current balance of national accounts in banking (% of GDP)

	Production of services		Running costs		Balance of current costs and receipts		Net interest received	
	1970	1980	1970	1980	1970	1980	1970	1980
United States	—	—	—	—	—	—	2.2	2.4
United Kingdom	—	—	−1.6	−2.1	−1.1	−2.7	2.5	4.5
France	0.7	1.6	−1.8	−2.9	−1.0	−1.4	2.4	4.1
Japan	—	—	—	—	—	—	4.1	4.1
Former West Germany	0.5	0.7	−2.0	−2.7	−1.4	−1.9	2.5	3.4
Italy	—	—	−2.3	−3.5	−1.6	−2.1	2.9	5.3

Source: Eurostat

was increasingly realised on financial markets and less through loans obtained from the banks.

All these changes have transformed the risks of banking activities more than they have eliminated them. Banks remain very active in financing industries as they intervene in financial markets, either through consulting or by offering their own financial products. Nevertheless, market power among financial institutions may have been reshuffled in the process. And banks are taking new kinds of risks in backing some financial operations which are often not registered in their balance sheets.[4] Financial markets are themselves open to speculative runs and are highly sensitive to events in the outside world.

For all these reasons, deregulation attempts should not be seen as a continuous decline in restrictions and controls. First, reregulation was on the agenda as early as the mid-1980s (cf. Pastre 1986), for example, when the financial crash of October 1987 made it clear that the new financial system was risky. Second, one should see the phase of deregulation during the 1980s more as a phase of readjustment of the regulatory frameworks. In most countries, we have just passed from one type of regulation segmenting markets, controlling interest rates, fixing prices of services and restricting external transactions to another type. The latter type of regulation is more market orientated on all previous dimensions but more compelling in terms of different kinds of internal control. There has been an extension of the range of control by authorities (to new institutions, to transactions off balance sheet, stricter definition of control procedures and greater frequency of controls, higher levels of requirements for risk provision and disposable capital (cf. Pecchioli 1987). To these can be added tighter internal controls linked with practices of auditing and of internal control of accounts. Furthermore, the international coordination of national authorities has improved, in particular through the action of the Bank of International Settlements in Basel.

It does not follow that all countries experience the same level of regulation and that adjustments just take place wherever they are required. The trend towards deregulation has been highly uneven and diversified, as have been the regulatory frameworks set up in the post-war period. In Canada, the United States and the United Kingdom, innovations by private agents spurred by competition ran over the regulatory frameworks and forced the reforms ahead while rendering regulations obsolete. In Japan, as in France, ministries coordinated the changes towards deregulation and favoured the introduction of financial innovations. In Germany, where the regulations were less constraining from the start, the central bank tends to limit the spread of financial innovations. In Italy, in contrast, the state wants to promote financial innovations which the agents have been rather reluctant to develop.[5]

It does not follow that all proper adjustment took place and reproduced an optimally functioning financial system. On the contrary, there are signs that the timing and magnitude of the adjustments might have been influenced by a bitter external constraint on the current balance of payments and by the pressure of competition among international world financial markets.[6] One is worried that this short-term pressure might have a detrimental effect on the overall competitiveness of the economy.

Financial systems will come out of this historical phase in a way which will condition the future dynamics of each national economy. It may be too early to tell whether or not a good mix of national and international dimensions has emerged. But clearly the overall working conditions of the economy have changed altogether in the process. Risks are different, macro-economic policies will be different,[7] and the provision of banking services has been transformed. The lessons we can draw on this subject can be of general interest to the market provision of some services.

IV. On the organisation of markets for complex services

Let us first recall that the market provision of some elementary services does not raise any specific question. In this chapter, we have mainly been interested in services in which strong externalities and asymmetries of information between buyers and sellers hamper the development of markets. More exactly, the development of these markets has been conditioned by the emergence of an adequate set of rules and institutions. In section II, we have stressed that such services were open to three types of risks and failures: those distorting bilateral transactions, those inducing intra-branch imbalances and, finally, those provoking the complete collapse of the market and of its basic institutions. We shall classify these services as complex services.[8]

As we observed in the case of banking services, a set of rules and institutions helps to organise at some point in time the functioning of the market, even if it is in a very limited and highly regulated way. How such regulatory frameworks adjust through time to changes in overall economic and social conditions tends to become the main issue in the market provision of complex services.

For the banking sector, the spread of information technologies, which enlarges greatly the capacity to store, to treat and to communicate information, as well as the opening of markets to external competitors have been the driving force behind the large-scale refurbishing of the basic regulatory frameworks.

But reforms did not occur as a smooth result of modernisation schemes, carefully planned and dealing extensively with the various asymmetries of information and externalities. Instead, adjustments often appear as a result of a process of trial and error where liberalisation trends are followed by a series of controls and restrictions. Furthermore, there is initial evidence that reforms are often made precisely when the constraints set by the changes are all the more biting. There is a strong historical dependency involved in this process of renovation of institutions. In such circumstances, the question arises as to the underpinnings of the steps taken towards the reform of some market institutions.

It is certainly difficult to appreciate the organisational efficiency of institutions for markets in a given economy. Still, at a time when economies tend to converge, and especially when the initial move to reform institutions was induced by an increase in external competition, the question is certainly worth asking.

This suggests that some law of entropy might be at work, directing the transformation of institutions. According to this general driving force, market organisations would tend to identify as free and independent products all those which can either be standardised or where asymmetries of information and externalities can be reduced by means of simple internationally agreed contracts. This may require new international institutions. Examples of these cases have been given in the field of international payments with such organisations as Visa or Eurocard. Similar examples of organisations concern copyright permissions for artistic works. It is a bit more complicated with other intellectual property like patents, where the system is still largely open to contests.

In some cases, institutionalisation is difficult, even at national levels. Such is the case for many business services where the limits of responsibility of the producer *vis-à-vis* the user are not yet clearly drawn. This is, as one example, the case in finance, consulting or legal counselling. Equally, all these activities will not reach a stage of mature market autonomy where competition can encourage innovation or where the barriers to entry, if any, remain below the level of contestable markets.

This is not to say that a market cannot flourish when linked with another market or when it is strictly dependent on an oligopolistic organisation which has gained some reputation of its own. Being tied with other activities, these specific organisations can effectively bring some synergy. The old national financial systems thus had values of their own. The problem is that the criteria to pick a winning combination of institutions are uncertain, a situation quite similar to the puzzling task of drafting an industrial policy. Everyone knows that such a policy can have very positive results (even if some agreed only recently on the potential efficiency of strategic policies); but no one can exhibit sound recipes for it.

Therefore, the tendency to adjust to external changes by following the law of entropy, whereby every product for which it is feasible can be organised separately on a straightforward market basis, will be predominant. Such a principle of market organisation has some similarity with the principle of 'subsidiarity' whereby the state should intervene only when no alternative private solution can be found. But it also has its drawbacks. The new markets may be more flexible, regarding innovations and external challenges, but also more unstable, being more open to speculative moves. Furthermore, the public provision of those services which will not have been liberalised could meet with great difficulties such as a lack of confidence, discrimination and so forth.

Such polarization could lead to some paradox since new private and new public services could turn out to be more difficult to provide on a separate basis than on a joint basis. In the long run, this would imply a return to some reregulation and financing arrangements to fit new forms of a mixed economy.

Notes

1. This treatment in national accounts is continuously debated. Arndt (1985) recalls the main steps of this debate. At first, financial institutions were mainly regarded as providers for handling the payments system (a public good), then banking services were regarded as being provided to lenders, that is mainly to households. Finally, the approach has been based on the consideration that services are provided to borrowers, that is mainly to firms for which banking services are intermediary uses.
2. It has been calculated that in France in 1983 the management of the payment system and financial consulting generated 49 per cent of running costs of commercial banks but brought in only 8.5 per cent of the product of the banks (cf. Szymczak, 1987).
3. This does not avoid restrictive practices (on checks delivery, on dates of value of payment documents) and concerted actions to raise fees and/or to discriminate among clients.
4. These new risks are far from being circumscribed (Raines 1986, 1987).
5. For a summary of these various experiences in deregulation see Métais (1986).
6. In effect, the first deregulations appeared in countries more subject to external constraints.
7. If only because monetary policies cannot rely on standard monetary aggregates to design stabilising policies since the meaning of these aggregates may well have changed with the new financial products and the ensuing changes in behaviours.
8. This qualification could also apply to the complex services to firms as illustrated in the Ermes study (1988), where much emphasis is put on the duration of the service and on the close relationship required between buyer and seller, conditions which tend to overcome asymmetries in information.

58   P. Petit

References

Aglietta, M. and Orlean, A. (1984), *La violence de la monnaie*, Paris, PUF.
— (1987), 'Structures économiques et innovations financières', *Revue d'Economie Financière*, No. 2.
d'Alcantara, D., (1986), *Concepts for the Improvement, Measurement and Formalization of Productivity in the Services*, Fast. Occasional Papers, 95A, July.
Arndt, H.W., (1985), 'Measuring Trade in Financial Services', *Banco Nazionale del Lavoro*.
Baudrillard, J., (1968), *Le système des objets*, Paris, Gallimard.
Black, F., (1970), 'Banking and interest rates in a world without money', *Journal of Bank Research*, 1, pp. 9–20.
Bourdieu, P., (1979), *La distinction*, Paris, Editions de Minuit.
De Brunhoff, S., (1976), *Etat et capital*, Paris, Maspéro.
Ermes, (1988), *La demande de services complexes des firmes multinationales et l'offre correspondante*, Lille, Groupe de travail du LAST-CLERSE, Université de Lille I, July.
Fama, E., (1980), 'Banking in the theory of finance', *Journal of Monetary Economics*, p. 39–57.
Hall, R.E., (1983), 'Optimal fiduciary monetary systems', *Journal of Marketing Economics*, **12**, 1, pp. 33–50.
Hicks, J., (1969), *A Theory of Economic History*, Oxford, Clarendon Press.
Holmstrom, B., (1985), 'The Provision of Services in a Market Economy' in Inman (1985).
Inman, R.P., (ed.) (1985), *Managing the Service Economy : Prospects and Problems*, Cambridge, Cambridge University Press.
Metais, J., (1986), *Innovations et dereglementations financieres: analyse comparative des experiences etranges*, Paris, Note Direction de la Provision.
Pastre, O., (1986), *La modernisation des banques françaises*, Paris, La Documentation Française.
Pecchioli, R.M., (1987), *Le contrôle prudentiel des banques*, Paris, OCDE.
Rapport Annual Mondial sur le Systeme Economique et les Strategies (Raines) (1986, 1987), Paris, IFRI, Editions Atlas Economica.
Szymcak, P., (1987), 'Eléments de comparaison internationale des coûts et marges bancaires', *Revue d'économie financière*, 1, pp. 51–74.
Veblen, T. (1899) *The Theory of the Leisure Class*, New York, The New American Library of World Literature.
Vilar, P., (1974), *Or et monnaie dans l'histoire*, Paris, Le Seuil.

5 Production and service supply structure: temporality and complementarity relations

André Barcet L 80 L 89

D24

Introduction

An analysis of service production and supply shows that service firms have collectively built up a set of relations forming a specific service supply structure. Of course, economic analysis has been dealing with the whole of industrial relations for a long time, especially thanks to the IO-matrix. Qualitative analysis of these relations was originally based on the traditional relationship of customer to supplier; more recently, the notion of subcontracting, or even of co-contracting, was developed in order to designate a more particular relation that at the same time implies a degree of permanence and a hieracrchy.[1] Analysis of the relations among service firms can undoubtedly be developed in the same way.[2] However, notions like supplier, customer, subcontracting relations are not sufficient to express the specific nature of service relations.

I am going to try to show that the majority of services have specific characteristics that require a corresponding response from supply. Then, these forms of the organisation of supply bring to mind the conditions of the creation of value, the conditions of competition, the long-term vision that we can have of the system. If a specific supply structure is really developing in some services, we can wonder whether the whole supply structure in the productive system is being modified in order to fit, in a new way, a long-term transformation of the conditions for the generation of outlets, for competition and for profitability. This approach has been developed for service activities. But it can undoubtedly be applied to industrial activities too in so much as they produce goods that increasingly are specific to their customers (so-called 'customised goods') and in so far as the 'service' dimension is becoming an integral part of their strategy. As with other fields, an examination of service activities can reveal the underlying trends of the evolving economies that become 'service economies' and that the market relation is established on the basis of a good, a service or their combination. This can be illustrated using contemporary examples showing the transformation of the service supply and particularly of the weakening of the frontiers between the sectors. But in my view, deregulation is only a revealing factor of the potentialities of a specific supply structure that already exists – even in highly regulated, indeed closed professions.

1. The constraints of service production

Traditionally, service analysis recognised three main characteristics for distinguishing services from goods: immateriality, immediacy, partici- pation. Each of these characteristics seems to be applicable in different degrees to each kind of service. However these features are not import- ant in their own right, but because of the consequences they may have and the problems they pose for sales and production organization (Barcet *et al.* 1984). If services are actually specific in comparison with goods, it seems to me that this specificity should in fact be understood with regard to the relation they have with material. In other words: services can only be said to be immaterial because their relation with material is different from the relation the good has with material. For a good, the form is a finite set; in a service, a movement, an act in connection with material. This kind of service relation with material is important in so far as it determines the way in which services are inserted in the productive system. This point requires a clarification of three aspects and their consequences: the service as an act, the temporali- ity of insertion of services, the service in connection with a system.

The service as an act

Following Hill (1977), the most general definition of service consists in defining it as an act, as a process. This definition is interesting because it sees the service as a movement, meaning that the result of a service, since it does not possess a storable or material form, has strictly speak- ing no meaning. According to this point of view, the output notion traditionally used in economic theory would not be directly applicable. It can only be used by analogy with goods or only in the form of an amount of money which is paid, from which follows the hypothesis that both the real output and this amount of money are equal. In the case of a good, we have the following sequence:

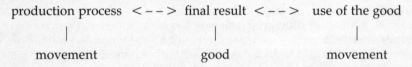

production process < – – > final result < – – > use of the good

| | |

movement   good   movement

In the case of a service, there is an act going on which effectuates the service; the effect of this act concerns the user. Both aspects, production movement of the service and the effect of the service, are closely linked together, even if the form of this link is different. Thus, the result of the service is its effect, but this effect is, strictly speaking, neither synony- mous with the result of the production process, nor with an amount of money. For a good, the materiality of the good and the effect of this good have never been confused.

Such a situation has several consequences, especially for the question of measuring production and subsequently that of productivity, as well as for the question of the value of a service (Barcet 1990). We will insist on a precise consequence of the sales act. A simple trade operation specifies that the sales contract is an agreement for the transfer of ownership of a thing in return for a payment. Furthermore, the exchange is normally based on a relation of transparency, in as much as the object of the transaction is perfectly known. Strictly speaking, it cannot be said that a transaction involving a service corresponds to such a definition. Indeed, there is no real transfer of ownership of anything; the buyer expects an effect and the seller undertakes to employ some specified means. At the very moment of the signing of the contract, the buyer cannot control the nature and quality of the result. Thus, such a situation is not a real sales contract. It then becomes necessary to admit that in the market sphere of the economy there is room for a type of relation that is neither a sales relation in the strict sense of a giving up of an object, nor a lending or hiring relation – this other relation is a 'servuction' relation (Barcet 1987). It has as a distinguishing character-istic the fact that it implies a particular risk: for the service producer, an undertaking whose limit is sometimes difficult to know, and for the beneficiary the problem of estimating and anticipating the real effect of the service.[3]

In the case of a service, demand is always preliminary to the service act (and this is also true in the case of complex goods); moreover, it is not possible to control, at the time of delivery, conformity of the result obtained with the expected result. The service act is performed; any necessary correction can only be made through an additional service act.

The condition of materiality of a service

If the service is an act, it is necessarily directed towards something or somebody. In other words: the nature of a service requires that it be integrated into a whole – into an object, into a person. The service does not achieve finality by itself. Its finality is determined by the finality of the system to which it belongs. Using biological theory or the theory of robotics, we can then characterise a service as an effector.[4] Therefore, services are not directly consumed, but concern the functioning con-ditions of a system; this notion must be considered in the broad sense of the word. Then, it is possible to classify services either according to their 'support', that is following the nature of that 'something' at which the service act is directed or in accordance with their functionality, their way of acting in the system.

The consequences of such an analysis differ, depending on whether the service must be steadily repeated so that the system in which it is integrated can keep functioning in normal conditions or whether the service only has a function at a precise moment. This distinction concerns among others the nature of the job being undertaken. In the case of a 'one-off' service, it is undoubtedly possible to determine what will be the committed means and consequently to estimate the 'necessary cost' of the service. In contrast, in the case of a repeated service, it becomes a regular activity flow which has to reoccur under rather precise conditions. The undertaking of the service producer consists not only in performing an activity, but above all in assuring the normal functionality of the system. However, an undertaking may imply an activity flow which is not directly foreseeable in its entirety. The activity flow may sometimes be reduced to nothing at all, or conversely be extremely busy. Therefore, there is not necessarily a strict proportionality between the activity flow and the production action since this action is of a probabilistic nature. Thus, an analysis in terms of risk is more necessary than an analysis in terms of production. The consequence of this point is obviously important in determining the price of the service, depending on whether it functions according to a production cost rationale or a probable risk rationale.

Between a merely irrregular service whose activity flow is short and whose production cost can be estimated without error margin and the service whose effects are improbable but anticipated, there is a whole set of activities in which the logic of production cost and of risk coexist. The analysis allows us to make a distinction between two kinds of consequences. On the one hand, there are consequences which correspond to the terms of administration and management of service firms and which are suitable for an irregular supply. In this case, there is a preoccupation with the 'materialisation of an intangible supply' for services like air transport, fast-food restaurants and so on. On the other hand, there are consequences which concern the risks connected with the use or functioning guaranteed by the service (Giarini 1986).[5]

The temporality of services

The engagement which is represented by any act will have different consequences according to the temporality of the service. Nothing allows us to assume that the temporality of the production process is equal to the temporality of the expected effect. Indeed, a service can require a short production process and yet have an effect spread over a long period. In other words, the undertaking agreed by the producer cannot necessarily and exclusively be estimated on the basis of the time required by the production process as foreseen when signing the contract.

A second point must also be considered: the conditions in which the service will have an effect, namely the condition of materiality of a service. The reproduction of a service as the necessary condition of the functionality of a system necessarily puts this service in the scope of a long time-frame. Generally speaking, we can wonder whether the production conditions of a service and the problems linked with its profitability lead to a search, through 'servuction', for a long-term relation. In fact, we may ask whether service production firms ought to seek a certain durability in their service supply as the condition for controlling their markets but above all for securing relatively steady production and productivity conditions.[6]

In this way, services become differentiated from goods by their prime process characteristics. Services are an act that simultaneously incorporate finality and a time component implying that the question of the involvement of the producer is crucial.

2. The service supply structure

The analysis of the specificity of the servuction relation has important consequences for the service supply organisation. First of all, there are consequences regarding the internal organisation and the spatial location of service firms. That point will not be dealt with now (Bonamy and Mayère 1986). There are also particularities characterising the relationships between service firms. This kind of relation, based on complementarity and what I shall call 'covalence', is a search for a specific answer to the question of the nature of the engagement and of the temporality that services imply.

The service production as a system: the principle of covalence

The notion of service integration mentioned previously leads to the conception of service supply as a system in which different elements have a precise and determinate place. Of course, not every service supply is 'a service system', as De Bandt (1985) says. But as far as a service tends to fit into the scope of a duration and of a precise undertaking, it tends to be enmeshed in a whole series of relations that permit appropriate answer to the existing constraints. Thus, if the service must have a certain durability, we can show that it obtains this durability through the more or less permanent mobilisation of goods, services or labour. This mobilisation implies that it appeals to the outside world in a more or less explicit way. The service considered as a system and as a 'complex' solution implies a multitude of relations with other firms, with other economic agents strictly speaking, the input of a service is not something which is processed but something which is mobilised, used, associated, integrated. One part of the service production work is precisely the realisation of this organisation, of this complementarity between elements of a different nature. Service production is a combination of different flows, of different acts.

The following scheme, which is based on J. Bonamy and others (1988), shows this combinational activity in a distinct way. Indeed, the servuction relation is rarely a bipolar relation (see Figure 5.1). As Figure 5.2

---

64   A. Barcet

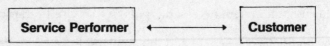

Figure 5.1 Servuction as a bipolar relationship

shows, it is more often a multipolar relation in which service performers and suppliers who establish stable and steady relations among themselves take part. We suggest that this kind of relationship may be characterised by covalence. This notion is used in chemistry to point out the connections which are made between atoms (or between ions) in order to obtain a combination or a chain whose value is determined by the different elements, knowing that, independent of their nature, each one has an essential place. Thus we can use this notion, in the form of an anology, but drawing out two further aspects. First of all, there is the simple idea that the service is obtained through the combination of several acts. But, above all, it is a matter of circulation of money and, more generally speaking, of formation of value. In this 'service system', there is an entry point of money coinciding with the moment when the interaction with the beneficiary takes place. This entry point has a rather fundamental function in the whole monetary movement: it redistributes money to every agent involved, to every link in the service production. Of course, such a relation may be analysed in terms of the economic notion of subcontracting as used in the field of industrial relations. However, the service relationship does not involve the power relation that can exist between the principal and the subcontractor.

Above all, the notion of subcontracting involves a choice by the principal firm, a choice that can theoretically be revoked. In the case of a

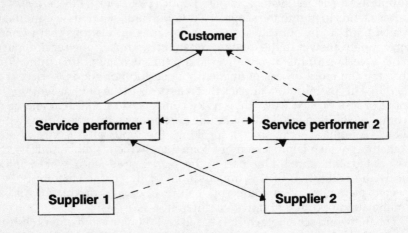

Figure 5.2 Servuction as a multipolar relationship

'service system', every link is absolutely necessary from an economic point of view. The concept of a 'service system' allows for the main constraints of service production, particularly the questions of location and temporality. Moreover, the flow of money which circulates is not necessarily and strictly determined by the instantaneous activity flow. The flow of money appears to function as a 'flat rate' whereas the service-activity flow itself is determined by the daily conditions of the service performance. Of course, if a gap between the two flows is sustained, the flat rate will normally be renegotiated, but this adjustment is not instantaneous. Consequently, all the monetary flows that are built up in such a relation are often difficult to detect from outside or by the use of traditional accounting documents. It is only when considering the service in its entirety that the added value may be comprehended. What counts at this stage is to obtain a satisfactory service. The complexity of the production, the spatio-temporal specification of the concrete production of each service may imply production acts which are different in time and space, without changing the service either from the point of view of the customer or from the point of view of its price. But an act may not necessarily add any further value to the final result of the service. This point directly introduces the question of the formation of value in such a service system. In other words, what is the role and function of each link? Does each link have exactly the same place in terms of value?

This last question is undoubtedly one of the most difficult to solve. Some activities of professionals are a challenge to economics. Indeed, there is a distinction in some professions between services with a value added and the others. It is clear that this usage of value added is not totally synonymous with the traditional accounting definition in economics. In my opinion, this distinction can be justified as follows: some services in a service system aim simply at providing the basic means required by service production; they aim at creating and managing the material framework without which the service cannot be effected. As examples we can cite the management and creation of advertising media, a hotel building management, the creation of the framework of a network within a telecommunications system. The setting up of these means is a necessary condition of the service, but it is not the service itself: it is a service potentiality that must be activated. From this point of view, this setting up does not create any value and only adds its cost to the final value added of the service. Along with these services, others will incorporate the concrete element which will activate the basic means: intellectual design activities shape the setting up of the means; it is the act which turns a potentiality into a service. In this context may be cited television programmes; the organisation of a hotel service (reception, maid service etc); the programme for a visit; the comfort, speed and punctuality of a train journey. This notion of service with a value added is perfectly illustrated in the field of telecommunications (IDATE 1986) in which the value added (that is what can be valorised and has a price) is the benefit which is passed on. Of course, this question to a large extent also covers the goods linked with most new technologies. The value of these goods combined with services is then sought fundamentally in their intellectual content and their 'servicelike' content.

Theoretical consequences: a competition–complementarity supply structure

If some services are produced within a form of a division of labour that involves this covalence relation, it follows that the analysis of competition and of supply cannot be made using the traditional concepts of economic theory. Undoubtedly, we can identify the form of the competition which exists in several service sectors as ologopolistic. Indeed, most sectors are characterised by the existence of few big firms which have a great influence on a national and even international scale. Along with these firms, and often engaging in more or less permanent relations with them, there is a relatively important number of small-sized firms which often have few plants but with more localised influence and markets. This structure can probably be explained by a rather significant segmentation of the market according to categories of revenue, in the case of services for households, and according to the nature of the firms, in the case of producer services.

If such an analysis is largely correct, it nevertheless overshadows the other aspect of the relations between firms. Sector-based analyses would be required to show this phenomenon, that is the covalence relation that implies complementarities and solidarities between firms. This point is as important as the competition among them. The example of insurance companies is the most illustrative. No insurance company alone can incur the risk involved in insuring: it necessarily takes the risk with other companies. It is the only solution in order to face future risks.[7] We can also find such complementarities in the field of advertising. The impact of an advertising campaign is not only the power of the message (which is the result of the design) but also its mode of relation with the public. This mode of relation can be multiple, using all media. The management of the campaign can be made through the mobilisation of competitive advertising agencies each having a specific role for a specific medium or in a specific country or region. Relations that organise this complementarity appear.

We understand that the main function of this form of competition–complementarity is to make it possible to fulfil what is undertaken by any service firm when taking action. The engagement consists in producing an effect which one never knows in advance either how it will occur or how long it will last. Thus, the competition–complementarity form which appears tends to lower the risks, to make sure the probability of the effect is important. Such a conception should mean that sooner or later, every firm must become extremely competent in a particular field. Moreover, as soon as it has a market, it will try to find complementarity with the very firm which, for a given aspect and a given time, is the most competitive. Of course, this complementarity implies a transfer of revenues. This is necessary for the firm to keep its position in the market and to assure its survival in the long term. The central idea of such a conception of competition is not that of an immediate but of a long-term profit. In such a conception, the problem of the price of an irregular service which is performed at a precise moment is not important. What becomes fundamental is the monetary flow which is the result of the sharing-out of money; and this flow tends to be continuous. It is here that, in my view, the specificity of the 'servuction' relation and of what this relation implies for the structuring of supply is to be found.[8]

3. Conclusion

If services have some specific qualities, it is undoubtedly and above all, because they possess a proper spatio-temporal logic. This implies the involvement of the service producer over a period that tends to be long; and not all the characteristics of this involvement are known. This specific constraint tends to shape the service supply in a service production organization in which activities of a different nature are mobilised. Some of these activities provide the framework, the materiality, to the service; others create the immaterial dimension. This service supply in which several firms participate – sometimes firms that have the same nature or that work on similar activities – tends to create complementarity or solidarity links. Sooner or later, this will modify the facts and forms of competition. This modification is undoubtedly linked with the ways the value is obtained and with the modes of circulation of money. The hypothesis that seems to emerge is that services tend to disconnect the monetary from the real flow, that is the global long-term flow rendering the profitability of the activity flow. There is no longer a strict correspondence, at least not in the very short term. Therefore the flows, like the competition, can provoke problems over a longer period and solidarity tends to lower some of the pressure stemming from the very short-term competition. It can provide a certain form of stability which is more favourable to the long-term profitability of capital. One wonders whether the long-term emergence of this problem is not potentially one of the important trends of the whole productive system, in so much as industrial firms themselves are faced with more important uncertainties in which exacerbated forms of competition tend to have dominant negative effects on the sector leader as well. From then on, the whole productive system would potentially be submitted to the servuction logic: the logic of an undertaking over a period, allowing at the same time a better control over demand but also giving an answer that is more qualitative. As such, new forms of relations between firms will arise and set up new complementarities.

Notes

1. I refer to research in industrial economics.
2. This brings to mind the precursory but, because of its sector-based point of view, limited work of D.F. Channon (1978).

3. The risk factor is an explanation for the development of the judicial environment of the company within the content of a service economy. The American example is particularly typical; see *Business Week*, November 1986.
4. For more details, see Bouchut (1984), Laborit (1980) and Millot (1980) who use equally the English word 'effector' and its translation into French *effectueur*.
5. The growing importance of maintenance in industrial production is an example of the rationalisation of the management of this risk and of service integration (Barcet and Bonamy 1988).
6. From this point of view, analysis of the externalisation factors of service functions made by firms remained insufficient. From my point of view, the cost saving would only be an element of a behaviour searching for the objectivisation of the service production process, of its internal productivity, of its effect and of its quality (CGP 1983; Barcet 1990).
7. The case of banks is also interesting as far as the principle of credit-association is a means of facing the more and more important solvency risk to a country or a large-sized firm.
8. A great number of examples that would illustrate the obvious transformation of the supply structure could be developed. The current disappearance of the frontiers between services is noticeable only because it provokes large-scale strategic and financial movements (in the field of financial services one can cite the movements between banks, non-banks and insurance companies; in the field of consulting and in the field of industry services of the association between industrial engineering and software and hardware producers; or speaking more generally of the by-passing of the non-tariff barriers to international trade through direct investment or the development of partnership practices). But, more fundamentally, these examples reveal the specificities of the service supply structure. Statistically, we have been able to bring to the fore the importance of these competition–complementary relations (Bonamy *et al.* 1988; Barcet 1987).

References

Barcet, A. (1987), *La montée des services, vers une économie de la servuction*, Ph.D thesis, Lyons, CEDES.

Barcet, A. (1990), 'Productivité et valorisation des services', in Jacques de Bandt (ed.) *Les services, productivité et Prix*, Paris, Economica.

Barcet, A., Bonamy, J. (1988), 'Les activités de services et la tertiarisation de l'économie' in *Traité d'économie industrielle*, R. Arena *et al.* (eds), Paris, Economica.

Barcet, A., Bonamy, J. (1988), 'Services et transformation des modes de production', *Revue d'économie industrielle*, **43**.

Barcet, A., Bonamy, J. and Mayère, A. (1984), 'Les services aux entreprises, problèmes théoriques et méthodologiques', *Recherches économiques et sociales* No. 9, Paris, Documentation Française.

Bonamy, J. *et al.* (1988), *Ressources de la base de données de l'enquête annuelle d'entreprises de services*, Lyons, Economie et Humanisme.

Bonamy, J. and Mayère, A. (1986), *Les services dans le systeme productif*, Lyon, Economic et Humanisme.

Bouchut (1984), *Choix d'investissement*, Lyons, PUL.

Channon, D.F. (1978), *The service industries, strategy, structure and financial performance*, London, Macmillan.

Commissariat Général du Plan, (CGP) (1983), *Services consommées par le secteur productif, travaux pour le 9ème plan*, Paris, Documentation Française.
De Bandt, J. (1985), *Les services dans les sociétés industrielles*, Paris, Economica.
Giarini, O. (1986), 'Coming of age of the service economy', *Science and Public Policy*, **13**, 4.
Hill, J. (1973), 'On goods and services', *Journal of World Trade Law*, March–April.
IDATE (1986), 'Les services de communication du futur', *Bulletin de l'Idate* **25**, Montpellier.
Laborit, H. (1980), *La nouvelle grille*, Paris, Gallimard.
Millot, R. (1980), *Dix leçons sur la robotique*, Lyons, PUL.

6 Producer services' location and regional development

Flavia Martinelli   L89 O̅ 12

R12

R32

Introduction

Where services are located has relevant implications for regional economic development. It is thus important to attempt a theoretical assessment of the locational trends of such activities. In the first part of this chapter factors affecting the geography of producer services will be reviewed and the spatial polarisation of service production highlighted. Subsequently, the consequences of this unequal distribution of service activities on different regional economies and the emergence of a new international division of labour based on producer services will be stressed.

It should be mentioned at the outset that the term 'regional' is used in a broad sense, meaning large portions of territory, characterised by a particular economic structure, whether at the international level (groups of nations such as developing versus industrialised countries) or at the intra-national level (lagging regions within advanced countries). Most often, a stylised 'peripheral' region will be contrasted to a similarly stylized 'central' region. Although regional characteristics vary greatly and significant differences exist between international and subnational regions, the above simplification proves a useful pedagogical device.

The argument developed in this chapter runs as follows:

1. Several factors account for and tend to reinforce the current *spatial polarisation* of producer services, despite some recent trends to deconcentration. The production of such services is, indeed, overwhelmingly concentrated in advanced economies and, within these, in a few metropolitan regions. In accounting for such a spatial polarisation, the characteristics of the demand, that is of the industrial structure, play a major role. In particular, the spatial division of labour carried out by multilocational and multinational corporations and the spatial concentration of advanced production and headquarters in a few regions must be considered determinant. On the supply side, the need for physical proximity and agglomeration economies involved in the service production/delivery process reinforce spatial concentration.

2. Developments in new information technology, while providing new locational 'opportunities', do not inherently involve any deconcentration of activities, particularly of producer services. Although the new technology provides the possibility of interacting at a distance and hence the opportunity to separate functions and phases of production, only certain activities have decentralised, while others have concentrated. For given technological paradigms, the structure and strategy of firms is much more important in explaining locational trends.

3. In the last decade some growth of service supply has been observed outside central regions. This is partly due to a diffusion of service demand from the more advanced regions to others and, hence, the growth of a local supply. But to an important extent it is also due to development and locational strategies on the supply side, that is by service firms themselves. Having grown and specialised on the basis of central regions' advanced markets, these firms are now expanding their operations and reaching for new markets. In many cases this is achieved through the opening of peripheral service branches. As will be stressed, however, this trend should not be overemphasised.

4. The polarisation of service production and delivery has important consequences for the development of regions. Producer services contribute an increasingly important share of total value added. The use of advanced services is also an increasingly strategic competitive factor, across firms and regions. Consequently, the presence of a developed service supply has at least three major beneficial consequences for a regional economy: (a) creation of value added; (b) increased productivity within the entire productive system; (c) growth of employment and skills.

   In central regions, a virtuous circle of growth and synergies between services and production has developed which has also engendered relevant economies of scale and specialisation. In peripheral regions, where the industrial structure is weak or independent from outside decision-making centres, a vicious circle unfolds, where the scarce demand for services does not support the development of a local supply. This in turn limits the modernisation of the industrial base. Furthermore, when a demand eventually develops, it may actually increase the region's dependence on various service imports since local service firms must compete with more advanced firms from central regions.

5. The current geography of producer services thus gives the advantage to industrialised countries and regions which thereby appropriate a large portion of world value added in services. Peripheral regions are instead left with the lower segments of the value-added chain (for example more standardised or lower value-added production). A new international division of labour emerges, based on producer services.

The location of producer services

Underlying assumptions

In early definitional efforts (see Martinelli, Chapter 2, crucial distinctive characteristics of services in contrast to goods were considered: (a) their *immaterial nature*; (b) the *close interaction* needed between suppliers and users; and (c) the fact that services cannot be *stockpiled and shipped*. To these one can add a fourth feature: (d) many producer services are also 'tailored' to the user's particular needs, or *customised* (cf. Stanback 1979; Grubel 1987). Spatial corollaries of such peculiar transactional characteristics are: (a) service producers have to locate *near their market* (in this case productive activities, especially manufacturing) and (b) the structure of their supply is quite *atomistic* (low economies of scale) and *diffused* (local markets).

It has already been stressed how the development of producer services is symbiotic with the evolution of productive organisation. Emergence of demand from the industrial structure is the primary engine of a virtuous circle of services' growth, and the characteristics of the productive structure significantly influence the type and forms of services which develop (in-house versus free-standing and relative specialisations).

Using this perspective and in accordance with the above assumptions, the geography of producer services should then simply reflect the geography of production. As postulated by Stigler (1951), free-standing service suppliers develop wherever the market for such specialised functions becomes large enough. And indeed, on an international scale, producer services are overwhelmingly concentrated in industrialised countries and do reflect regional industrial specialisations (Porter 1990) and structures.

However, not all of the above assumptions are completely accurate, and the related theoretical statements therefore require modification. First of all, the services' production/delivery process comprises different phases which do not necessarily involve physical proximity to one another and may have different locational requirements. In other words, the intensity and patterns of interaction with the client vary across production/delivery phases. In many business services, for example, part of the service is carried out at the client site, part at the supplier site, part in other locations, often by different specialised personnel (see Moulaert *et al.*, Chapter 9 and Noyelle, Chapter 12).

Second, although services consist mainly of immaterial labour phases, requiring a rather direct interaction between supplier and client, this does not necessarily imply physical proximity. Services can to a certain extent be stored and moved, and trade in services does indeed increasingly occur, even across long distances, although in very specific forms. There are three broad ways in which services or segments of their production/delivery process can actually travel (Grubel 1987): (i) the *movement of service output*, that is services or parts therein that are embodied in some forms of material support such as tapes, paper, digital signals, etc. (for example pictures and tapes in advertising; technical reports, drawings and documents in professional consulting; or information codified into magnetic impulses in data transmission) and, thereby, shipped; (ii) the *movement of suppliers*, for example consultants temporarily moving to the client site or transportation carriers travelling between different client locations; (iii) the *movement of buyers*, for example personnel from the client firm travelling to get training in another region or transportation carriers stopping to get maintenance services in particular locations.

Third, the development of new information technology has further altered the conventional locational constraints attached to services' production and delivery. A large portion of service inputs and output is made of information (computerised reservation systems in the transport sector, the electronic processing of deposits or bills in banking and insurance, the electronic processing of data in engineering etc.). Such information can now easily be codified and transmitted over long distances, provided the necessary equipment and infrastructure are available.

Finally, it is not entirely true that no economies of scale exist in the production and delivery of services. The increased distance allowed by the movement of services and by telecommunications provide enlarged market opportunities for suppliers. Moreover, not all services are necessarily of a fully customised nature. Large portions of their production process can be standardised and do not require high levels of skills (for example data entry and record processing). Even in the most customised phases, codified procedures and tools have been developed ensuring some form of standardisation (Moulaert *et al.* 1990). Finally, economies of specialization also develop, as firms build up increasingly specific know-how (Stanback *et al.* 1981).

All the above counter-features significantly complicate the simplified picture of producer services geography provided earlier. But while they relax the need for proximity to markets, they still reveal nothing about the actual spatial concentration or dispersal of service activities. In the following pages factors affecting spatial concentration and dispersal are reviewed in detail.

The spatial concentration of services

Despite significant variations across individual activities, up to the late 1970s producer services displayed a distinctive aggregate trend towards spatial concentration, whether at the international or intra-national level. Producer services are overwhelmingly located in industrialised countries, in a few central metropolitan regions. In part, this phenomenon reflected the unequal spatial distribution of production, particularly of manufacturing. But the spatial concentration of producer services observed in this period is significantly greater than that observed for manufacturing, especially in those service activities with a higher strategic and innovative content. This has been shown in a number of national and international analyses (see, among others, UNCTAD 1985, 1989 for the international level; Marquand 1979, Daniels 1985 for the United Kingdom; Martinelli 1984, and Del Monte and Giannola 1984 for Italy; Lipietz 1978 and Monnoyer and Philippe 1985 for France; Stanback *et al.* 1981, Noyelle and Stanback 1984 and Clark 1985 for the United States). This trend towards spatial concentration of services is particularly striking when contrasted with manufacturing which, over the last four decades, has experienced a significant decentralisation from 'core' to more peripheral regions. Two major arguments have traditionally been proposed to explain this trend (cf. Martinelli 1984): (a) the *hierarchical structure of large corporate organisations*; and (b) the peculiar *agglomeration economies* linked to service transactions.

CORPORATE HIERARCHY AND CONCENTRATION OF IN-HOUSE SERVICES

The first explanation looks at the corporate characteristics of the industrial structure and, in particular, at the organisational and locational structure of large multilocational corporations. It focuses mainly on in-house services. We have already stressed the crucial role of large modern corporations in developing a demand for diversified and specialised services and how many of these are secured in-house. What is important to stress here is that the hierarchical organisation of activities within modern multilocational corporations translates into a correspondingly hierarchical locational structure. As was first noted by Hymer (1972) and further developed by others (Westaway 1974; Lipietz 1980; Cohen 1981), the functional separation of activities within modern corporate structures – particularly that between management and material production – is reflected by a hierarchical spatial division of labour, enabling each different function to respond more exactly to its specific locational factors (Massey 1984). At the lowest and more spatially dispersed level of the hierarchy are generally found more or less standardised material operations, whereas more advanced and innovative types of production, as well as all strategic and decision-making functions tend to concentrate in the upper 'nodes' of the hierarchy. Since strategic producer services increasingly concern phases before and after material production (Martinelli and Schoenberger 1991), in the growing separation and specialisation of corporate functions they tend to be located at the headquarters' level. Therefore, the majority of in-house service production is concentrated in a few central metropolitan areas.

As will be stressed later, this hierarchical spatial structure of in-house services has very negative consequences on the development of peripheral regions hosting decentralised operations.

AGGLOMERATION ECONOMIES AND THE CLUSTERING OF
FREE-STANDING SERVICES

The second argument stresses one of the basic assumptions about
service production and delivery – that is the need for rapid and direct
communication between suppliers and users, especially in the case of
services with a high strategic and innovative content – and concerns
free-standing services. As early as the 1960s, Hoover and Vernon had
stressed the role of agglomeration economies in explaining the clustering of office activities and other services in the New York region. Later
authors stressed the role of fast communication as a more specific type
of agglomeration economy. Both the early quantitative studies on
communication flows (Thorngreen 1970; Tornqvist 1970; Goddard 1971)
and later work on corporate motivations in office locational choices
(Westaway 1974; Goddard 1975; CHR 1977; Goddard and Pye 1977;
Daniels 1977, 1979) stressed how 'face-to-face' contacts, speed of information, proximity to other specialised services, as well as the availability
of a skilled labour force (Illeris 1989) were of primary importance in
explaining the concentration of office and service activities in central
urban locations.

Since headquarters of large corporations' represent a major and
sophisticated market for services – because of both a 'Stigler effect' and
'Marshallian' agglomeration economies, particularly 'face-to-face' communication – free-standing services develop and cluster in those same
central areas to form what have been called 'corporate headquarters
complexes' (CHR 1977). In these areas a dynamic integration between
demand and supply, in-house and free-standing, advanced and 'ancil-
lary' services develops (Cohen 1981; Polese 1983; Friedmann 1986),
giving rise to the classical synergies of a 'virtuous' circle of development.
A new urban hierarchy emerges, based on services (Pred 1977; Noyelle
and Stanback 1984), where modern corporate organisation and agglomeration economies reinforce each other.

Trends towards a spatial dispersal of producer services?

Although the spatial concentration of services, especially those of a
more innovative and strategic nature, remains substantial, recent
studies stress that some deconcentration of service employment has
occurred during the 1980s, even in advanced consulting services (Lazzeri 1985; Monnoyer and Philippe 1985; UNCTC 1987; Moulaert *et al.*
1991).

Three explanations are generally given for this possible trend: (a) the
diffusion of demand from core to more peripheral regions which spurs
the development of a local supply; (b) developments in new information
technology; (c) trends on the supply side, that is the expansion strategies of service firms from core regions.

THE DIFFUSION OF DEMAND

According to a classical model of innovational diffusion (Hägerstrand 1967), as changes in the organisation of production spread through various mechanisms from leading firms, industries and countries throughout the economic system, a growing demand for services should emerge also in more peripheral regions. This demand should then support the growth of a local supply, featuring the same dynamics observed in core regions. But radical economic geography has by now made clear that economic dynamics do not repeat themselves at different times and places and that economic inequality relations dominate development patterns. Even when a demand for services eventually arises in peripheral regions, it does not necessarily activate the development of a local supply. It can actually support the growth of suppliers located in other regions. This certainly happens with intra-corporate service flows from headquarters to peripheral branch plants in the case of large multilocational corporations. Moreover, local suppliers may find it difficult to compete with service firms in advanced regions which have already gained competitive advantages from scale and specialisation. Beyond this 'epidemic' approach, other factors must be discussed.

THE ROLE OF NEW INFORMATION TECHNOLOGY

'Energy experts from Tokyo to Athens trace oil shipments by consulting a computer data base in Houston. The fire brigade in Malmo, Sweden responds to a fire alarm by consulting a computer data base in Amsterdam on the most efficient route and the closest fire hydrant. Lawyers in the U.S. consult a computer data base containing abstracts of American law cases summarized in South Korea' (Feketekuti and Aronson 1984, p. 63). This quotation neatly exemplifies what the development of new information technology can do.

The term 'new information technology' generally refers to one or more of the following activities: generation, conversion, storing, processing and transmission of information. Its impact on the organisation and location of services is quite relevant. In fact, a distinctive feature of the new technology is that it profoundly affects non-production activities, that is management and services or all those activities concerned with flows and processing of information. This is in distinct contrast with other major technological innovations which have mainly affected material production (Stanback et al. 1981). Among other things, new information technology has dramatically reduced transaction costs and enhanced the interdependence of the economic system.

Two major consequences of the new technology for the production of services can be mentioned: (a) an increase in their 'transportability' (UNCTAD 1985) and (b) a further increase in scale economies of production (Stanback et al. 1981). New information technology has in fact significantly relaxed one of the key properties of service production: the fact that production and consumption had to be carried out simultaneously and in the same place. The possibility of storing a significant part of intermediate service inputs in the form of information and quickly transmitting them in response to demand has allowed the separation of significant segments of service production from the time and place of delivery. By increasing the scope for the coordination and timely bringing together of diverse inputs in order to deliver the final product, between and at different locations, new information technology has also enhanced economies of scale in production. Service firms can cover wider market areas and exploit economies of specialisation. But precisely how these developments influence the spatial organisation of services' production and delivery, and whether they are conducive to the diffusion of service supply or to a further concentration, is still controversial.

In contrast with a generalised belief, the development of information technology and the subsequent improvements in communication technology do not necessarily involve a spatial dispersion of activities. In this regard it is interesting to note that even Coase (1937) suggested that the diffusion of telephone communication might actually lead to greater spatial concentration of industry. It will be argued here that concentration or dispersal of activities depends on the structure and strategy of firms rather than on technological innovation *per se*.

As has been stressed (Dosi 1988), technological innovation is seldom an independent event, as its developments are closely linked to firms' objectives and conduct. New technologies offer a range of new strategic opportunities, which must be exploited by firms according to their individual structure and strategy. In other words, new information technology must be considered, if not a thoroughly neutral, certainly only an 'enabling' factor (Illeris 1989) rather than a univocal determinant of location.

In fact, new information technology has been exploited for decentralization in particular industries and by particular firms. It has actually influenced large multilocational, often multinational corporations to decentralise their operations, whether in pursuit of market penetration or cheap factor-sourcing strategies. So far, information technology has thus assisted the separation of management and related services from production operations – especially those of a highly mature and standardised nature which have partially decentralised to peripheral regions – by facilitating the rapid transmission of information, pictures and decision-making (cf. next section on branch plants). Even within service activities themselves a decentralisation of the most routine and standardised functions has been observed (Daniels 1979, 1985).

In many instances improvements in telecommunications have actually helped in further reducing the autonomy of manufacturing subsidiaries and branches (UNCTAD 1985). The introduction of 'on-line' telecommunication linkages between headquarters and branches has in fact permitted the 're-concentration' at headquarters level of many management functions previously performed at branch level (for example accounting, inventory control, payroll etc.) (cf. Martinelli, Chapter 2).

Keeping in mind Thorngren's (1970) taxonomy of contacts – 'programmed', 'orientation', and 'planning' – a number of studies suggest that decentralisation has so far mainly affected 'programmed' types of contacts and 'man-machine' communications. In contrast, 'man–man' communication and both 'orientation' and 'planning' contacts in decision-related and creative functions prove rather resilient to the replacement of face-to-face contacts and synergies available in 'core' service areas by long-distance communications (Pye 1979; Illeris 1989; Monnoyer and Philippe, Chapter 8).

Throughout the 1970s the developments in telecommunications and information processing, while allowing the separation of functions, seem to have favoured the concentration of strategic and advanced services but the diffusion of more standardised activities, mostly material production.

It should finally be noted that new information technology, while dramatically reducing transaction costs, nevertheless costs. Important investment in infrastructure and equipment are needed, even to plug into a telecommunications network. In terms of telecommunication operating costs distance still matters. For the same service, firms in peripheral regions thus incur significantly higher costs than firms in central ones.

THE SUPPLY SIDE: THE GROWTH OF LARGE SERVICE PRODUCERS

The growth of large multilocational service firms and their expansion strategies, through the opening of dispersed branches, certainly contribute to a partial deconcentration in the location of producer services.

An implicit consequence of the early definition of services was what has been called the 'misconception' of low-scale economies (Stanback *et al.* 1981), the idea that service industries had necessarily to be fragmented in structure and spatially diffused, owing to the need for close interaction and physical proximity between suppliers and buyers. But while this may be true for certain, especially consumer services, the industrial stucture of producer services is quite diversified with regard to both the level of product specialisation and corporate structure (Daniels 1985; Taylor and Thrift 1984). Alongside small firms with a prevailingly local market, large service corporations have always existed in some circulation services. More recently they have also developed in newer technical and professional consulting services (Stevens 1981; Noyelle 1989 and Chapter 12; Ermes 1988; Gadrey 1988; Moulaert *et al.*, Chapter 9).

In the latter activities, heavily based on information processing and specialised know-how, relevant economies of scale and specialisation do exist. Although highly customised activities, business service firms have worked out a form of 'standardisation' in methods, tools and procedures (Moulaert *et al.*, Chapter 9). New information technology has enlarged their markets and made it easier to transmit and process information rapidly, a major factor in service production. Free-standing firms established in central metropolitan areas to serve large corporations' headquarters have developed know-how, standardised methods, and have specialised. They have started to grow and look for new markets, In activities such as financial services, accounting, management consultancy and advertising, a number of very large firms have emerged, serving the needs of their multinational clients throughout the world.

Part of this business is carried out over long distances through telecommunications and the movement of personnel to the client's site, or vice versa. However, despite new information technology and the possibility to sell significant parts of services at a distance, physical proximity to the market still proves an important requirement. In order to establish their presence in distant markets, transnational service corporations are increasingly opening branches (Sauvant and Zimny 1987; UNCTC 1987, 1988; Noyelle 1989). The concentration recorded by the accounting and management consulting business in the last couple of years (from 'Big Eight' to 'Big Five') and the parallel proliferation of branches both in peripheral regions of industrialised economies and in less-developed countries confirms a new trend. Both trade and foreign direct investment in services, although still a small share of totals, are in fact recording the highest rates of growth among industries (Sauvant and Zimny 1987). Moveover, direct investment appears to significantly exceed trade in services. For example, in 1982 American exports of non-factor services amounted to $32 billion, compared to $183 billion in sales by American service affiliates abroad (excluding wholesale trading) (Whichard 1987).

However, the decentralisation trend sketched above should not generate too optimistic views about the diffusion of advanced producer services to peripheral regions. A hierarchical spatial division of labour similar to that implemented by large manufacturing corporations emerges for large transnational service firms as well. More routine and less-skilled operations have been separated and decentralised to cheap labour regions, whether within industrialised or developing countries. This is the case with certain data processing functions which have been decentralised to suburban areas around metropolitan service centres (Nelson 1986; Baran 1985) or data entry that has been decentralised to developing countries (Feketekuti and Aronson 1984; Lall 1986). On the other hand, a hierarchical division of labour exists between branch service offices and central headquarters, where most of the R & D, strategic planning and marketing is concentrated (see Moulaert et al., Chapter 9). Branch offices are often operational agencies or just 'sales' branches, where most 'intermediate' service inputs are imported from headquarters. This, again, generates little local contribution to the final service value added.

* * *

In sum, the locational dynamics of producer services are quite complex, contradictory and themselves evolving. So far, several factors have accounted for a generalised trend towards spatial concentration, especially in the most innovative and strategic services. The growth of large service firms together with an emerging demand in more peripheral regions are now generating a countertendency towards decentralization. Developments in new information technology, while providing one more degree of freedom, must be considered an 'opportunity' variable rather than a univocal determinant of location.

Producer services and regional development: a new international division of labour

How does the location of services affect the development of regions? If the development and location of services is a function of the industrial and corporate structure of regions, the existence of a regional supply of services – both internal and external but particularly the latter – significantly influences the performance of the local economy. Services production affects a region's development from at least three points of view: (a) the creation of value added; (b) the competitiveness of the local economic system; (c) the labour market.

As already stressed, producer services contribute an increasing share of total value added, as suggested by the steadily growing value/weight ratio of commodities in contemporary production, that is the value of embodied work relative to materials (Nusbaumer 1987). The increased division and specialisation of labour feature a complex value added chain in which services – whether internal or external – begin to prevail over material transformation. Such a trend is only partially explained by the share of producer services in GDP, since a large portion of intra-firm service transactions whether within national economies or across borders goes unrecorded (UNCTAD 1985). Moreover, producer services represent a crucial locus of innovation and a major determinant of competitiveness (Walker 1985; Damesick 1986; Martinelli, Chapter 2; Porter 1990). Their existence and use thus has relevant consequences for the modernisation of the productive system. Finally, the development of such activities has positive implications for the labour market, both in quantitative and qualitative terms. In particular, it provides new jobs, in partial substitution for declining manufacturing employment, and contributes to the upgrading of skills and know-how (Wood 1986).

Consequently, it does make a difference where services are located, despite the significant mobility observed in their production/delivery process and the development of telecommunications.

Impact on regional economies

In *central* regions, a 'virtuous' circle of services' development is nourished by the continued interaction between services and advanced centres of decision-making and production. The existence of external suppliers, in particular, constitutes an 'externality' for the whole productive system, especially for small firms which would otherwise be unable to secure certain services. In central metropolitan areas, where a concentration of large-firms' headquarters exists, service firms have also been able to first reap economies of scale and specialisation, and are now exporting services – through various forms – to more distant locations. They have thus evolved into service-base economies, appropriating the highest value-added segments of the contemporary division of labour. The development of services also provides ample labour opportunities in highly skilled and semi-skilled occupations, thus contributing to an upgrade of the local labour market. Moreover, the creation of local know-how and capabilities further reinforces the competitiveness of the region's firms and industries.

A different situation arises in a number of *less central regions* where large firms' headquarters are not dominant but where strong local productive specialisation and interfirm integration may be found, for example in 'industrial districts' or other advanced industrial regions. Although large centres of decision-making may be absent, an extended social division of labour has none the less developed in these areas, fostering, often with the help of local authorities, the development of a local supply of 'sector-specific' services (cf. Martinelli 1988 and 1989a for Italian industrial districts). Here, as well, the development of such services contributes to the region's appropriation of important segments of the value-added chain, to the greater competitiveness of firms and industries, as well as to employment generation and upgrading.

Peripheral regions are the most disadvantaged. The limited development of an industrial base is generally a first bottleneck for the spontaneous development of producer services. But even when a significant productive basis exists, its often dualistic and scarcely integrated structure is a further obstacle. In fact, in many peripheral regions, the most relevant and advanced operations are 'branch plants', that is productive units dependent for most of their inputs on exogenous centres of decision-making (see next section), whereas indigenous capital strives to take off and is generally characterised by its small size of operations, local markets, and a loosely integrated structure. A classic 'vicious' circle unfolds, whereby the limited overall level of regional demand does not stimulate the development of a local supply. The absence of external services in turn depresses the demand, especially for small firms. The scarce use of services further limits industrial growth; overall stagnation worsens the employment problem. The consequences of this cumulative mechanism are multiple.

In the first place, the regions do not produce or control an increasingly crucial portion of contemporary value added but are left with lower-value agricultural or manufacturing activities. Moreover, these regions most often import services needed to carry out their production from outside the region – whether via intra-corporate or inter-firm flows. In both cases their dependence on specialised know-how and information inputs from central regions increases. In the case of less-developed countries, to this 'technological' form of dependence must be added a worsening trade and capital deficit. And even when a demand for services eventually emerges, competition coming from central regions may prevent the formation of local suppliers.

Second, the absence of an advanced and diversified service base slows down or prevents altogether the modernisation of the regional productive basis, particularly of the indigenous component, thereby increasing the competitive lag. In central regions, the existence of service firms and organisations constitutes an externality which, via mechanisms of imitation and competition, favours the diffusion of organisational and technological innovation throughout the economic system. In peripheral regions, local firms are not exposed to this environment effect and must rely on extra-regional service suppliers, incurring all the costs and uncertainty associated with distant transactions.

Finally, the underdevelopment of producer services negatively influences regional employment opportunities. This effect is particularly severe at a time when the growth of service activities compensates for the stagnation or decline of direct production labour. Moreover, it also retards the formation of a human capital adequate for modern organisational needs.

Branch plants and regional development

An important and special role in the current spatial division of labour and in the underdevelopment of peripheral regions is played by large, multilocational, often multinational corporations. As was mentioned earlier, in recent decades large firms have implemented a strategy of decentralisation of operations to more peripheral regions, both within industrialised and developing countries. The rationales for such a strategy are either market penetration (where barriers to trade of various kinds exist) or cheap factor sourcing (cheap labour).

On the economic impact of branch plants in peripheral regions there now exists quite a large body of literature (see among others Gilmour 1974; Firn 1975; McDermott 1976; Dicken 1971, 1976; Hoare 1978; Thwaites 1978; Townroe 1975; Britton 1974, 1980). Although the typology of branch plants is quite diversified (Lall 1978; Massey 1984), most of these analyses have shown how peripheral production branches generally possess little decision-making power, are quite vertically integrated and not very innovative. Most importantly, they keep privileged linkages with the parent firm for their material inputs and the marketing of their outputs. Therefore, they show a low aggregate propensity to establish local backward and forward linkages and generate limited effects on the development of local firms, the productive integration of indigenous capital and the diffusion of know-how in the host region.

The majority of the early studies concerned 'material' transactions and the issues related to technological 'spin-off'. Only at a later stage, were service transactions considered (Marshall 1979, 1982; Martinelli 1984; Rugman 1987). Indeed, the 'short-circuited' (Britton 1980) nature of branch-plants' operations concerns service flows to an even greater extent than material linkages.

The headquarters of multinational industrial corporations transfer to their subsidiaries a great deal of firm-specific know-how and information, in the form of financial, managerial, technological and marketing services (Lall 1986; Rugman 1987). These transfers are 'hidden', first because they are internal to firms and second because these firms are often manufacturing companies. Only quite recently have statistical agencies started to tackle the problem of intra-corporate service flows. Recent data for the United States show that in 1984 previous manufacturing companies sold to their foreign affiliates selected services worth about $2.5 billion, more than half the total sales of those same selected services by both American service (excluding banking) and manufacturing firms to their foreign affiliates (Whichard 1987). But in general, this type of data is not available. Using return on foreign direct investment as a proxi for the value of service and technology transfers, Rugman (1987) estimated that intra-corporate international transfers of services by American firms amounted to 34 per cent of total American service exports. A partial assessment of intra-corporate service flows to peripheral regions within industrialised economies has been made by Marshall (1979) for the north of England and Martinelli (see Chapter 11) for the south of Italy.

It is important to stress that within such a corporate, supra-regional system of service transactions, branch-plant service demand bypasses the host regions and diverts a substantial part of regional service demand from the local economy. Such a demand does not contribute to, or even prevent the development of, a local supply. Moreover, the internal system of services and information flows only benefits operations within the corporate structure and does not constitute an externality for the host economy. Knowledge and information, two major factors in the current technological and organisational paradigm, are made unequally available. This proprietary use of innovative resources can even include physical infrastructure (think of corporate-owned satellite communication channels). Finally, although unrecorded, intra-corporate service flows are indeed a form of import, which worsen the dependence of peripheral regions.

The intra-corporate division of labour led by multinational corporations is thus a major determinant of the spatial polarisation of producer services and of uneven regional development.

A new international division of labour

In conclusion, the spatial polarisation of services is a new, very important key to explain uneven regional development, as it represents a vehicle of dependency and a constraint to the diffusion of innovation and to self sustained development in the periphery. A new international division of labour emerges, based on producer services (Martinelli 1989b), in which large, multinational corporations play a relevant role, both on the demand and the supply side. The increased division and specialisation of labour in contemporary productive organisations display an increasingly complex value-added chain in which services – whether upstream, onstream or downstream – begin to prevail over the material production phases. This pattern concerns both in-house and free-standing services, suggesting, among other things, that the current share of producer service value added (which only concerns free-standing operations) largely underestimates the actual extent of this transformation.

The international division of labour, based originally on industrial versus primary production and subsequently on advanced manufacturing versus labour-intensive/mature industries continues to change. Because of their lead in producer services, central regions create, control and retain within their borders a large portion of the world value-added chain. Not only do they appropriate the highest value-added segments of the chain, but also the most strategic – those that affect innovation (R & D, strategic planning, design, engineering etc.) and those that allow control over markets and terms of trade (marketing, distribution). Peripheral regions, to different degrees, are thereby left with the least value-added and least competitive activities in the primary and secondary sectors. Because of their limited and scarcely integrated industrial structure, the division and specialisation of labour within these regions is poor. Moreover, in order to remain competitive, they must import at least some services from central regions. Many peripheral regions are thus captive suppliers of given products and phases, in an international division of labour which they do not control.

However inadequate, statistics on trade in services show that the majority of developing countries, although they use many fewer producer services than industrialised countries (cf. the analysis of input/output tables for 26 countries by Park and Chan 1989) indeed run important trade deficits in these activities (cf. UNCTAD 1989). Shipping is a good example: although developing countries ship 46 per cent of world loaded goods (in tons), their merchant fleet contributes only 21 per cent of world tonnage; the ratio is much worse when the few leading shipping countries such as Korea, Singapore and Brazil are excluded (GATT Secretariat 1989).

Thus, internal disarticulation and dependent integration are the most important problems faced by peripheral regions, whether at the national or international level. With regard to services, these areas are faced with a dilemma: if they want to retain a competitive position in their productive specialisation and further diversify and integrate it in the world economy, they must increase their use of specialised service inputs. Since a local supply does not readily develop and is also faced by competition from central regions, they might need to import services and increase their technological and financial dependence.

Some policy considerations

How to break the vicious circle and how to protect developing countries is at the heart of current GATT negotiations on services. Several policies in support of services' development have been tried in certain peripheral regions of advanced countries. This is not the place for a thorough review of these issues, but a few general recommendations in the light of the arguments developed earlier can be made.

In the first place, any service policy must have an integrated, micro-economic, and strategic perspective. As already mentioned, producer services exist and prosper where there is a demand from the productive system. To address them as independent activities, without taking their market into prior consideration, is a widespread mistake. It is not sufficient to state, 'producer services must be developed', but one must ask, 'which services should be developed, for which industries?' This means that the industrial structure of the region must be carefully assessed and that any service policy must be strongly integrated with industrial policy. To do so, macroeconomic policies are not sufficient and a microeconomic approach, geared to specific sectors and firms is needed. Moreover, inputs to producer services are different from those to manufacturing. In addition to capital, technology and infrastructure, producer services have a relevant know-how and information content, often very specific to given market sectors. A careful assessment of the availability of such factors and of the opportunities for supporting their development must be made. Finally, such policies must be strategically designed: regions and countries must identify potentials and priorities, as well as constraints and bottlenecks, in both their demand and their supply of services; strategic choices must be made.

Three basic options are available to peripheral regions: (a) importing services; (b) supporting local supply as a form of import substitution (and possibly export base); (c) allowing and sustaining extra-regional direct investment in services.

The first option – to buy services from central regions – is only possible for certain services (for example, transportation, some types of consulting). It involves the short-term benefits of quick access to both services and technology and hence rapid improvements in the competi-tiveness of existing production. It has, however, several drawbacks: (a) it increases the import dependence of the region which may not be offset, in terms of trade balance, by the gains from improved exports; (b) procured services may not be 'appropriate' to the products and pro-cesses of the country, thereby having a lower impact than expected; moreover, they certainly involve additional costs because of the distance involved; (c) this strategy does not change the structure of the inter-national division of labour, implying a worsening in the relative position of the region in the value-added chain. On the other hand, in many countries and for many services, there may not be sufficient or appropri-ate local resources to support a domestic supply; imports may be the only available strategy.

The second option – promoting domestic development in services both as an import substitution and possibly an export strategy – is a longer-term endeavour, more desirable, but also more time and resource consuming. The main advantages would be: (a) a supply of services more closely geared and fitted to the local needs and conditions; (b) an improvement in competitiveness in existing production together with an increase in the domestic share and control over the value-added chain; (c) a development of infrastructure and human capital adequate to modern production, apt to spread over several sectors and able to control further technological and organisational progress. However, such a strategy involves a lengthy and difficult process. Resources may not be readily available (especially know-how and skills), slowing down gains in competitiveness. Moreover, the import content requirements of such a strategy, in terms of for example technology, could at least initially, be very high. Finally, and this is rather important for an export strategy, know-how in services does not develop in a void and it may take quite a time to catch up with or bypass comparative advantages by advanced regions.

The exogenous direct investment option – supporting the establishment of service branches from other regions – has contrasting features. Permitting extra-regional companies to open service branches can ensure the ready provision of services to the host economy without major domestic capital outlays and without an a priori worsening of the import dependence. Services would actually and at least partially be produced in the host region, thereby increasing its share of world value-added service. Moreover, in contrast with manufacturing branch plants, service branches would actually produce services *for* the local market, thereby creating an 'externality' for the overall region. Finally, local people employed and trained by the foreign branch might build up know-how and skills which could lead to future spin-off effects. On the other hand, service branches, via the greater competitive advantages derived from know-how and information accumulated at the parent company level, could prevent the development of a domestic supply. Moreover, they can attract the scarce domestic human capital and subtract it from domestic ventures. Finally, they can impose their own organisational and technical models, thus indirectly contributing to increases in technology imports.

In all three options, which are not mutually exclusive and can be adapted to different services, the role of the state is crucial. Whether through direct intervention or by promoting and regulating firms and activities, government policy is needed in order to correct unbalanced market trends.

References

Baran, B. (1985) 'Office automation and women's work: the technological transformation of the insurance industry' in M. Castells (ed.), *High Technology, Space, and Society*, Beverly Hills, Sage.

Britton, J.N.H. (1974) 'Environmental Adaptation of Industrial Plants: Service Linkages, Locational Environment, and Organization' in F.E.I. Hamilton (ed.), *Spatial Perspective on Industrial Organization and Decision Making*, London, Wiley.
— (1980) 'Industrial Dependence and Technological Underdevelopment: Canadian Consequences of Foreign Direct Investment', *Regional Studies*, 14.
Clark, D. (1985) *Post-industrial America: A Geographical Perspective*, London, Methuen.
Coase, R. (1937) 'The Nature of the Firm', *Economica*, 14.
Cohen, R.B. (1981) 'The New International Division of Labor, Multinational Corporations, and Urban Hierarchy' in A.J. Scott and M. Dear (eds), *Urbanization and Planning in Capitalist Society*, London, Methuen.
Conservation of Human Resources (CHR) (1977) *The Corporate Headquarters Complex in New York City*, New York, Conservation of Human Resources.
Damesick, P.J. (1986) 'Service industries, employment, and regional development in Britain', *Transactions Institute of British Geographers*, 11.
Daniels, P.W. (1977) 'Office Location in the British Conurbations: Trends and Strategies', *Urban Studies*, 14.
Daniels, P. (ed.) (1979) *Spatial Patterns of Economic Growth and Location*, London, Wiley and Sons.
Daniels, P.W. (1985) *Service Industries: A Geographical Appraisal*, London, Methuen.
Del Monte, A. and Giannola, A. (1984) 'Imprenditoria locale e sviluppo del terziario nel Mezzogiorno d'Italia: una nuova politica per il Sud?', *Rivista di Politica Economica*, 10.
Dicken, P. (1971) 'Some Aspects of the Decision-Making Behavior of Business Organizations', *Economic Geography*, 47.
— (1976) 'The Multiplant Business Enterprise and Geographical Space: Some Issues in the Study of External Control and Regional Development', *Regional Studies*, 10.
Dosi, G. (1988) 'Sources, procedures, and microeconomic effects of innovation', *Journal of Economic Literature*, 26.
Ermes (ed.) (1988) *La demande de services complexes des firmes multinationales et l'offre correspondante*, Lille, Faculté des Sciences Economiques et Sociales, Univ. Lille I.
Feketekuti, G. and Aronson, J.D. (1984) 'Meeting the challenges of the world information economy', *The World Economy*, 7, 1.
Firn, J.R. (1975) 'External Control and Regional Development: The Case of Scotland', *Environmental Planning*, 7.
Friedmann, J. (1986) 'The World City Hypothesis', *Development and Change*, 17.
Gadrey, J. (1988) 'Stratégie et structure des grandes entreprises et modes de recours aux services complexes' in Ermes (ed.), 1988.
GATT Secretariat (1989) *Trade in Transport Services*, New York, MTN.GNS/W/60, United Nations.
Gilmour, J.H. (1974) 'External economies of scale, interindustrial linkages, and decision-making in manufacturing' in F.E.I. Hamilton (ed.), *Spatial Perspectives on Industrial Organization and Decision Making*, London, Wiley.
Goddard, J.B. (1971) 'Office Communications and Office Location: A Review of Current Research', *Regional Studies*, 5.
— (1975) *Office Location in Urban and Regional Development*, London, Oxford University Press.
— and Pye, R. (1977) 'Telecommunications and Office Location', *Regional*

Studies, **11**.

Grubel, H.G. (1987) 'All traded services are embodied in materials or people', *The World Economy*, **10**, 3.

Hägerstrand, T. (1967) *Innovation Diffusion as a Spatial Process*, Chicago, University of Chicago Press, (Swedish edition: 1953).

Hoare, A.G. (1978) 'Industrial Linkages and the Dual Economy: The Case of Northern Ireland', *Regional Studies*, **12**.

Hymer, S. (1972) 'The Multinational Corporation and the Law of Uneven Development' in J.N. Bhagwati (ed.), *Economics and World Order*, London, Macmillan.

Illeris, S (1989) *Services and Regions in Europe*, Aldershot, Avebury Gower.

Lall, S. (1978) 'Transnationals, domestic enterprises, and industrial structure in host LDCs: a survey', *Oxford Economic Papers*, **30**, 2.

— (1986) 'The Third World and comparative advantages in trade services' in S. Lall and F. Stewart (eds), *Theory and Reality in Development. Essays in Honor of Paul Streeten*, New York, St. Martin Press.

Lazzeri, Y. (1985) 'L'interaction entre les prestataires de services et les PMI', Vol. 2, Aix-en-Provence, CER.

Lipietz, A (1978) 'La dimension régionale du développement tertiaire', *Travaux et Recherches de Prospectives*, **75**.

— (1980) 'Inter-regional Polarization and the Tertiarization of Society', *Papers of the Regional Science Association*, **44**.

Marquand, J. (1979) 'A Locational Analysis of the U.K. Service Sector', *CES Occasional Papers*, **9**.

Marshall, J.N. (1979) 'Ownership, Organization, and Industrial Linkages: A Case Study in the Northern Region of England', *Regional Studies*, **13**.

— (1982) 'Linkages between Manufacturing Industry and Business Services', *Environment and Planning*, **14**.

Martinelli, F. (1984) 'Servizi alla produzione e sviluppo economico regionale: il caso del Mezzogiorno d'Italia', *Rassegna Economica*, **1**.

— (1988) *Productive Organization and Service Demand in Italian Textile and Clothing 'Districts': A Case Study*, MTN/RLA/CB.6, Geneva, UNCTAD.

— (1989a) 'Business Services, Innovation and Regional Policy. Considerations on the case of Southern Italy' in L. Albrechts *et al.* (eds), *Regional Policy at the Cross-roads*, London, Jessica Kingsley.

— (1989b) 'Problematics in trade and development of services. Notes for a discussion on Gatt negotiations', Geneva, UNCTAD.

— and Schoenberger, E. (1991) 'Oligopoly is alive and well. Notes for a broader discussion on flexible accumulation' in G. Benko and M. Dunford (eds), *Industrial Change and Regional Development: the Transformation of New Industrial Spaces*, London, Belhaven Press.

Massey, D. (1984) *Spatial Divisions of Labor*, London, Macmillan.

McDermott, P.G. (1976) 'Ownership, Organization and Regional Development', *Regional Studies*, **10**.

Monnoyer, M.C. and Philippe, J. (1985) *L'interaction entre les prestataires de services et les PMI et le développement régional*, Aix-en-Provence, CER.

Moulaert, F., Martinelli, F. and Djellal, F. (1990) *The Role of Information Technology Consultancy in the Transfer of Information Technology*, The Hague, NOTA.

— Chikhaoui, Y. and Djellal, F. (1991) 'Locational Behaviour of French High Tech Consultancy Firms', *International Journal of Urban and Regional Research*, **15**, 1.

Nelson, K. (1986) 'Labor Demand, Labor Supply and the Suburbanization of

Low-wage Office Work' in A. Scott and M. Storper (eds), *Production, Work, Territory*, London, Allen and Unwin.

Noyelle, T. and Stanback Jr, T.M. (1984) *The Economic Transformation of American Cities*, Totowa, NJ, Rowman and Allaheld.

— (1989) 'Professional/business services and the Uruguay Round negotiations on trade in services' in *Trade in Services: Sectoral Issues*, New York, UNCTAD, United Nations.

Nusbaumer, J. (1987) *The Service Economy: Lever to Growth*, Norwell, Mass., Kluwer Academic,.

O'Farrell, P.N. (1980) 'Multinational Enterprises and Regional Development: Irish Evidence', *Regional Studies*, **14**.

Park, S.-H. and Chan, K.S. (1989) 'A Cross-Country Input–Output Analysis of Intersectoral Relationships between Manufacturing and Services and their Employment Implications', *World Development*, **17**, 2.

Polese, M. (1983) 'Le commerce interrégional des services: le rôle des relations intra-firme et des facteurs organisationnels', *Revue d'Analyse Economique*, **59**, 4.

Porter, M.E. *The Competitive Advantage of Nations*, London, Macmillan.

Pred, A. (1977) *City Systems in Advanced Economies*, London, Hutchinson.

Pye, R. (1979) 'Office Location: The Role of Communication and Technology' in P. Daniels (ed.), *Spatial Patterns of Office Growth and Location*, Chichester, Wiley & Sons.

Rugman, A.M. (1987) 'Multinationals and trade in services: a transaction cost approach', *Weltwirtschaftliches Archiv*, **123**, 4.

Sauvant, K. and Zimny, Z. (1987) 'Foreign Direct Investment in Services: The Neglected Dimension in International Service Negotiations', *World Competition*, **31**.

Stanback Jr, T.M. (1979) *Understanding the Service Economy*, Baltimore, Johns Hopkins University Press.

— Bearse, P.J., Noyelle, T. and Karasek, R.A. (1981) *Services. The New Economy*, Totowa, NJ, Allanheld Osmun.

Stevens, M. (1981) *The Big Eight*, New York, Macmillan.

Stigler, G. (1951) 'The Division of Labor is Limited by the Extent of the Market', *Journal of Political Economy*, **59**.

Taylor, M. and Thrift, N. (1984) 'Business Organization, Segmentation and Location', *Regional Studies*, **17**, 6.

Thorngren, B. (1970) 'How do Contact Systems affect Regional Development?', *Environment and Planning*, **2**.

Thwaites, A.T. (1978) 'Technological Change, Mobile Plants and Regional Development', *Regional Studies*, **12**.

Tornqvist, G. (1970) *Contact Systems and Regional Development*, Lund, Lund Studies in Geography.

Townroe, P.M. (1975) 'Branch Plants and Regional Development', *Town Planning Review*, **46**.

UNCTAD (1985) *Services and the Development Process*, Sales No. E.85.II.D.13, Geneva and New York, United Nations.

— (1987) *Role of Transnational Corporations in Services, Including Transborder Data Flow*, E/C.10/1987/11, New York, United Nations.

— (1988) *Foreign Direct Investment, the Service Sector and International Banking*, London, Graham and Trotman.

— (1989) *Trade and Development Report 1988. Part Two: Services in the World Economy*, TDR/8/Offprint, New York, United Nations.

Walker, R.A. (1985) 'Is There a Service Economy? The Changing Capitalist Division of Labor', *Science & Society*, **1**.

Westaway, J. (1974) 'The Spatial Hierarchy of Business Organizations and Its Implications for the British Urban System', *Regional Studies*, **8**.

Whichard, O.G. (1987) 'U.S. sales of services to foreigners', *Survey of Current Business*, January.

Wood, P.A. (1986) 'The Anatomy of Job Loss and Job Creation: Some Speculations on the Role of the Producer Service Sector', *Regional Studies*, **20**.

7 Location of services in a service society

Sven Illeris   L 80   R 12

R 30

We live in an exciting period where one of the main revolutions in the history of mankind is starting. Earlier fundamental changes were from hunter economies into agricultural societies and from agricultural into industrial societies. The shift which is now occurring in the most advanced industrial societies seems to be just as fundamental.

The purpose of this chapter is to discuss the regional implications of this shift. Where do service activities – now becoming the most important sector of the economy – locate? What are the consequences for regional development? What can be done to influence these developments? I can only suggest some broad answers – grossly simplified – to these questions, and many reservations must be made. The service society is only just being born. The tendencies observed today are complicated and sometimes contradictory. The chapter should be understood as a scenario focusing on those developments which in my judgment are the basic and lasting ones. I do not take my point of departure in any particular academic school but find it more constructive to combine elements from many sides.

When I postulate that we face revolutionary change in industrial societies, it is of course something which cannot be shown in a traditional positivist way. Societies have always changed. Especially during the most recent centuries, the changes have been so fast that it is difficult to distinguish the revolutionary shifts. That can only be done with certainty afterwards, when things have stabilised.

The service society

The most important characteristics of the 'service society' will be outlined in this part of the chapter. Other labels are 'the third wave', 'flexible production systems', the 'meta-industrial society', the 'information-', 'knowledge-' or 'communication-society'. ('The postindustrial society' is a misleading label, however, since manufacturing will remain an important activity).

Table 7.1 shows how fundamental the shift is. It characterises some of the changes in production, markets, the organisation of work and the structure of firms. It should be stressed that the suggested changes are net tendencies in the total economy. The complicated world in which we live will easily show examples of developments in the opposite direction.

The hammer and the sickle may symbolise the prevailing economic activities around 1917, namely the production of agricultural and industrial goods. Chaplin's *Modern Times* is another symbol of the industrial society, in which the prevailing mode of production was mass production of long series of identical goods. The assembly line had economies of scale which minimised costs and prices. The capital laid down in machines formed the decisive factor of production. Work was organised according to Taylorist and Fordist principles, each worker monotonously performed the maximum number of a minimum of different operations and only needed a minimum of skills. Production was carried out by men, while women took care of the reproductive work in the households. Firms merged into large corporations with a vertical integration of production chains.

Now the most important activity is the production of household and producer services. The modes of production have changed. Even if economies of scale still exist (only big corporations can establish R & D units), the series of production tend to become short. On the other hand, economies of scope become important. Competition parameters are quality, adaptation to the demand from different market segments, and service contents, rather than price. While routinised operations are automated, the labour force is occupied in such service functions as development, planning, management and marketing. It must be stressed, however, that these producer services are complementary to physical production. The interaction between producer services and industrial production becomes the driving force in the creation of economic values.

Production gets increasingly complex: a hammer is simple to produce and to sell compared to a computer which must be accompanied by programs, instructions and error finding before the buyer can use it. At the same time production gets more flexible and easier to change. This is made possible by information technologies allowing the machine programs to be changed quickly. And it has been made necessary by the frequent market changes. Markets become international, but require adjustment to the special characteristics of different countries. Even national markets become increasingly segmented. Competition makes it a must to be able to differentiate the production. Small enterprises become competitive through quality and flexibility. Large corporations must give more independence to their divisions in order to avoid bureaucratic rigidity. Some firms become 'hollow': frameworks for the organisation, coordination and marketing of goods and services produced by independent sub-contractors.

Inside the individual firms hierarchies tend to become flatter. Complex and flexible production makes it necessary to make individuals or groups responsible for different tasks. New technologies break the earlier information monopoly of the management. The industrial army

Table 7.1 The industrialised society and the service society: a comparison

Industrial society	Service society
Mass production	Differentiated production
Long series of production	Short series of production
Standardisation	Flexibility and complexity
Economies of scale	Economies of scope
Capital most important factor of production	Knowledge and creativity most important factors of production
Goods production most important function	Development, planning, management, marketing most important functions
Cost minimisation	Quality maximisation
Price competition	Product competition (quality, service, adaptation to customer needs)
Stable and homogeneous markets	Turbulent and segmented markets
National markets	International markets
Mass consumption	Individual consumption
Monotonous routine work	Automation
Standard qualifications	High and diversified qualifications
Job specialisation	Job enrichment
Standardised labour market	Flexible employment
Hierarchical organisation	Flat hierarchies, network organisation
Vertical integration	Sub-contracting, externalisation
Large corporations	Small and medium enterprises, divisionalisation
Nation states	International cooperation, local and regional self-government
Division of labour among persons	Division of labour among firms

of slaves is reduced, while the number of planning and decision-making jobs increases. The knowledge, creativity and cooperative abilities of the staff become the most scarce and most important factors of production. Material values get lower priorities compared to environment, quality of life and self-realisation. Generally, increased skills are needed, and the education and training systems are enlarged. But instead of the traditional class antagonisms we observe a polarisation between a qualified majority on the labour market and an unskilled, low-waged, often unemployed minority. This is sometimes described as 'the two-thirds society'.

The need for higher qualifications has repercussions on production. The labour force – not least the women – demand more interesting work. A mode of production which needs all human resources tends (slowly) to reduce discrimination of gender. It remains a problem that more and more jobs exclusively use the intellectual qualities of human beings, abilities of abstract thinking etc. Thus the changes in production cannot be described in purely economic terms.

Not only in firms but also in societies at large is the recognition that centralistic management from the top is too ineffective in a complex and turbulent world. Almost all dictatorships in southern Europe and Latin America have disappeared over the last fifteen years. The general cause must be found in the modes of production and societal development. Clearly inefficiency is also behind the fall of the centralised East European regimes. It is the irony of history that the Communists had forgotten the most basic statement of Marx, that the suprastructure of society must adapt to the productive basis. The internationalisation of production makes international cooperation between nation states necessary. At the same time, the increasing need for innovation, flexibility and differentiation makes regional and local self-government more important.

The changing division of labour

The division of labour among individuals – the sometimes quite absurd Taylorist specialisation – is reduced in order to make reasonable decisions under complex and turbulent conditions. Today sociologists of work talk about the end of the division of labour. But the division of labour among firms, sectors and regions still progresses, in spite of some tendencies opposed to the do-it-yourself idea. Specialisation causes a growing need for exchange of information, goods and persons.

The pre-industrial society may be shown in a simplified way in Figure 7.1. Households or at least local communities were largely self-sufficient. Figure 7.2 illustrates the division of labour in industrial societies: a chain from primary production over manufacturing to distribution and consumption. Service activities are limited to trade and transport, a little bit of government regulation (increasing under Keynesianism) and some services tied to consumption (for example barber shops and laundries). We have all grown up with this image of the economy.

Figure 7.1 The subsistence society

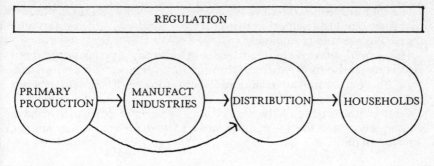

Figure 7.2 The industrial society

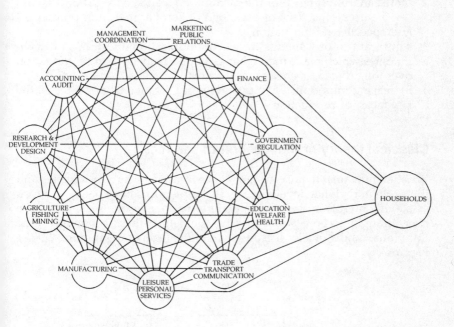

Figure 7.3 The service society

Figure 7.3 suggests an image of the far more complex society which is now emerging. Producer services – performed internally or bought externally – are necessary for the performance of producers. They are also responsible for innovation and dynamism – for instance R & D, design, new organisation and management methods in sum, for the productivity gains that can be obtained in the total productive system.

The East European economies functioned reasonably well in the industrial phase, but the neglect of these services was largely the reason why they have recently crumbled.

Household services are important, too, not only for consumption but also because the (re)production through education, health services etc. of a qualified, innovative and fit labour force is a *sine qua non* for production.

Four characteristics of the service society seem in particular to have consequences for the location of services and for regional economic development:

1. rapid growth of the share of services (in particular of sophisticated information services and producer services) in total production and employment;
2. increasing importance of interaction between service-producers and service-users and thus of exchange of complicated, non-programed and specialised information;
3. significant improvements in telecommunication and transport technologies which make the exchange of goods, people and information over long distances cheaper and faster;
4. increasing importance of a qualified and creative labour force as the key factor of production.

Classical theory of the location of services

We shall now turn to the question of the location of service activities and their role in regional development. Just as services have been perceived as playing no role in the development of national economies, they have been thought to be a totally passive element in local economies. The traditional model of a local economy had the form of the number '9' (see Figure 7.4).

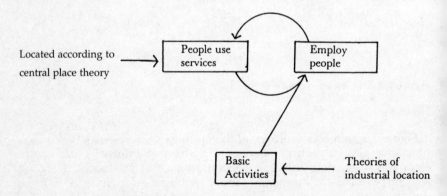

Figure 7.4 The economic-base model

It was thought that the basis of a local economy was the production of goods in agriculture, mining or manufacturing. The goods could be sold elsewhere and thus bring money into the local economy. Some of this money was used to pay the people who worked in the basic activities. These people spent some of their money on services – private services like retailing and public services like schools – which had to be provided locally, since retailing and school-teaching cannot normally be sold over long distances. Such service activities employed other people who in their turn bought still other services locally. Thus all service activities and incomes depended on the money which the 'basic' activities brought into the local area. Therefore, local and regional development policies could ignore the services. They would automatically follow, if only the policies aimed at manufacturing growth were successful.

What was 'the local area'? That would depend on the type of services. Widely used services, for instance non-specialist lawyers, could get sufficient business from a quite small town and its immediate surroundings. More specialised services, like consulting engineers or management consultants, could be based only on a larger area and were located only in medium-sized or large towns. The most sophisticated producer services would only be found in national capitals or other major cities, from where they served entire regions or whole countries. Thus a hierarchy of service centres, or 'central places' on different levels, served smaller and larger 'local areas' in such a way that distances between service suppliers and customers were always as short as possible.

New hypotheses about the location of services

It is clear that the emerging service society with its growing service sector and its increasing inter-regional and international trade in services undermines the classical theory of the location of services. How can we provide it with a new theory? In this chapter, some hypotheses are suggested. They are summarised in Table 7.2.

The structural effect

The first hypothesis is concerned with the effect of the increasing share of services – in particular of high-quality services – on the economy. It states that service activities with high growth rates tend to be geographically concentrated in large metropolitan areas. Examples are highly qualified business services. On the other hand, service activities with low growth rates tend to be more evenly distributed (for example retailing). The effect of this structure is an increasing concentration of service activities into the major metropolitan areas.

Regional statistical data from West European and North American countries in the 1970s and early 1980s (Illeris 1989) show that it is largely true that the most rapidly growing service activities are over-

Table 7.2 Changes in society, in service activities and in service location

Societal changes	Service activities concerned	Locational forces	Locational impact	New locational role of service activities
Increasing share of high-quality services in total economy	All	Structural changes	Increased concentration of economic activities in big cities	
	Household services and some producer services	Proximity to customers remains important	Growing consumption, reduced economies of scale cause decentralisation. Vice versa	Remain non-basic
Increased exchange of complicated information	Qualified information services	Need for face-to-face contacts. Growing agglomeration advantages	Increased concentration in big cities	May become indirectly basic
Improvements in communication and transport technologies	Qualified information services	Reduced travel time-costs and agglomeration advantages	Many locations become possible	Basic
	Routinised information services	Telecommunications relax need for proximity	Many locations become possible	Basic
Increased role of knowledge and creativity as factors of production	Information services	Human resources decisive (education, labour market, environment)	Individual qualities of localities become decisive	Some services become indirectly basic

represented in large metropolitan areas and that slowly growing service activities are better represented elsewhere.

Some authors stop their analysis at this point and conclude that the service society will be characterised in increasing geographical concentration, but clearly that is not warranted. It is necessary to look at the locational changes which may take place inside each sector, too. In shift-share terminology, not only the share component, but also the shift component must be taken into consideration.

According to the above-mentioned data, in most countries both the rapidly and the slowly growing services showed lower growth rates in the metropolitan areas than elsewhere. As a result, total service growth rates were lower in big-city regions than elsewhere. In all countries, the shift component was heavier than the share (or structural) component. The following sections will discuss these shifts in service location.

Proximity to customers remains important

The second hypothesis is concerned with a large part of the service activities for whom the societal changes do not seem to cause major revolutions. The central place theory remains valid. This hypothesis is supported by multiple regression analyses made in Italy, in Belgium and in the United Kingdom in order to examine the variables that could explain the observed regional development of service activities (summarised in Illeris 1989). In all three cases, the regional distribution of population was the most important explanatory variable. Why?

In spite of all modern technologies, it is still costly to overcome distance, especially if it has to be done frequently. Therefore proximity to customers remains important for many services. If retailers need not locate quite so close to us as previously, now that we have private cars, they must still avoid being too far from us if they are to attract our custom. Proximity remains important in cases where the service production normally requires that service producer and service user are present at the same time and place:

— service activities which affect persons (education, health, childcare);
— service activities which affect goods (repair, retailing, restaurants), although goods may in some cases be transported to the service firm;
— in some cases, service activities which affect information in an individual way (bank branches).

The central place theory was developed with large numbers of ubiquitously distributed customers in mind, typically households. It may also be valid for producer services which supply a large number of firms with rather similar service products, for instance simple accounting and audit services to retail shops and small manufacturing firms. It should be noted, however, that producer service firms, even if they are located in the same region as their clients, rarely agglomerate into central places in the same way as household services do. The reason is that while households are able to reduce their travel costs through visits to centres which offer a variety of services, producer service firms usually travel to their clients and thus cannot make similar economies in transport costs. Producer service firms with few and scattered customers cannot possibly locate in a central place pattern, even if they try to minimise the distances to their clients.

Central place theory has a static character, but of course the parameter values may change which means that a process of adaptation towards a new equilibrium of the central place system starts and contributes to the regional dynamics of services. For instance, a changed distribution of customers may cause such processes. The Danish regional shift of manufacturing firms and households out of the Copenhagen region during the last two decades has been followed by a redistribution of service activities. Furthermore, changing consumption patterns may trigger off a change in the location of services. When in the 1960s it was decided to expand public service activities in Scandinavia this first took place in universities, specialised hospitals and similar institutions located in a few big cities. In the 1970s, however, the growth mainly took place in local welfare services and secondary education, spread over a large number of small towns. The internal economies or diseconomies of scale in service firms may also change, causing the minimum threshold to increase or decrease, which again means geographical concentration (retailing) or decentralisation (mental care).

Increased need for face-to-face contacts

The third hypothesis concerns the increasing exchange of complicated information which seems to be an essential aspect of the emerging information society. Such exchanges involve sophisticated producer services and other strategic or controlling units in society, corporate headquarters, government offices, pressure organisations etc. Experience shows that personal meetings (face-to-face contacts) between these actors remain necessary. Business travel and especially the lost working time of highly salaried staff are costly. Thus proximity remains an important advantage. Since we are talking here of information services which are used by relatively few firms not forming a ubiquitous market, this factor pulls service producers and users towards agglomeration in big cities. Examples of producer services with high needs for personal contacts are information services such as management consultants, computer services and consulting engineers.

Many authors (for example Andersson & Strömqvist 1988) claim that since firms increasingly use such information services, the advantages of agglomeration are growing. Hence producer services should concentrate more and more in big cities where face-to-face contacts are cheap and easy. Medium-sized cities could, however, also offer advantages of agglomeration, if they specialise within one economic sector in such a way that firms can find all necessary contact partners locally. This is the rationale behind such specialised industrial districts as the textile areas of Prato (Tuscany) and Herning (West Jutland).

Relaxation of proximity constraints

The fourth hypothesis is based on the revolutionary developments in telecommunication and information storage technology, as well as on the fundamental improvements in long-distance personal travel connected with cars, airplanes and high-speed trains. These changes have led to the question of whether the traditional need for service activities to locate close to their customers will disappear. Will the notion of distance become meaningless, if distances can be overcome without costs?

The increasing possibilities for transmitting data by relatively cheap telecommications have reduced the problem of distance. Today, even rather complicated information can be transmitted, provided of course that the necessary infrastructure is present. This fact has allowed many service activities to locate independently of their customers. For instance, 'back offices' of banks which calculate and distribute financial information, as well as VAN service producers, are not tied to proximity to their customers.

As already indicated, face-to-face meetings remain necessary in many cases, but meetings between distant partners have also become much easier and cheaper, thanks to airlines, cars and high-speed trains. Even if travel costs have not disappeared, they have been reduced, especially in terms of lost working time. People come together in meetings and conferences more than ever. Distances still matter, but they are shrinking. Consequently, another group of authors (Toffler 1980; Planque 1983; Claval 1989) argue that agglomeration advantages are decreasing. The handicaps of peripheral locations diminish. 'There is everywhere', as Pascal (1987) says.

Data on the location of sophisticated producer services highlight this hypothesis (see Tables 7.3 and 7.4.) In the literature, it is often said that the fast-growing sophisticated producer services increasingly concentrate in big cities (for example Kelly 1987). Tables 7.3 and 7.4 show that this is not the case in Denmark and France. Though employment in business services has been growing in the capital regions of these countries, the growth rates have been below the national averages. On the other hand, the growth rates of provincial regions were rather uneven. We observe fast-growing and slow-growing regions. They do not form a simple centre/periphery pattern but rather a complicated mosaic.

Table 7.3 Employment in business services in Denmark 1981 and 1987(%)

	Computer services		Management consultants		Consultant engineers	
	1981	1987	1981	1987	1981	1987
Copenhagen region	65	61	72	71	58	53
Zealand, Lolland, Falster, Bornholm	1	3	1	4	5	6
Funen	4	5	6	5	6	6
East Jutland	18	19	16	12	15	17
South, West, and North Jutland	12	12	4	8	16	18
Denmark	100	100	100	100	100	100
= thousands	8.9	13.9	1.0	1.4	10.3	14.8

Source: Danmarks Statistik

Table 7.4 Employment in high-tech consultancy in France, 1976 and 1987 (%)

	Technical studies		Consultancy services		Data processing	
	1976	1987	1976	1987	1976	1987
Ile-de-France	60	50	71	62	41	43
Rhône-Alpes	10	12	7	9	16	9
Provence-Alpes, Côte d'Azur	5	9	3	6	5	6
North & West	12	17	9	12	22	21
East & Centre	9	9	8	7	13	14
South	4	3	2	4	4	6
France	100	100	100	100	100	100
= thousands	101	136	15	81	15	35

Source: F. Moulaert *et al.*

Another kind of empirical evidence is formed by data on service flows. Such data have been gathered in surveys in many countries (see Tables 7.5 and 7.6). They show that although many services are bought from the nearest centre of the relevant order – as predicted by the central place theory – considerable amounts are bought from other regions or even from abroad. Thus service firms usually have 20–40 per cent of their turnover outside their own regions.

Table 7.5 Provision and location of producer services (%)

	Provision of producer services				Location of externally bought services			
	Respon- dents	Internal	Parent firm	External	Own area	Capital	Rest of country	Abroad
Esbjerg	40	45	9	46	58	9	32	2
Estrie	34	29	20	60	58	22	17	3
Ireland	56	34	13	53	46	46	2	6
Merseyside	58				71	17	36	1
Rhône-Alpes	34		38		62	82	18	0	0
Switzerland	91			54	91		9	
5 Swiss regions		38	10	52	53		47	
Sweden				36	64	13	23	
United Kingdom		56		44	79		21	
Valencia	32	66		34				

Source: Illeris (1990)

Table 7.6 Service sales (%)

	Local	Other regional	Rest of country	Abroad
Bari	40	24	27	9
Estrie		70	30	0
Netherlands	32	48	16	4
Puget Sound	44	17	34	5
2 Swiss towns	47		49	4
UK	42	35	19	4
Vancouver	71	12	10	7

Source: Illeris (1990)

The development of service flows over time is illustrated by Stabler and Howe (1988). They show that service trade among Canadian provinces is rapidly increasing – even 'exports' from regions without major central places.

In Figure 7.5, an attempt is made to illustrate how these findings must modify central place theory. The thick arrows represent the service flows predicted by classical central-place theory. The thin arrows show the increasing service flows that cross the traditional hierarchy: flows from low-level to high-level centres, among centres on the same level and 'diagonally' to centres which are not the nearest ones.

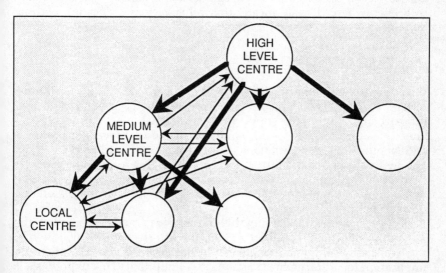

Figure 7.5 Modifications of central place theory

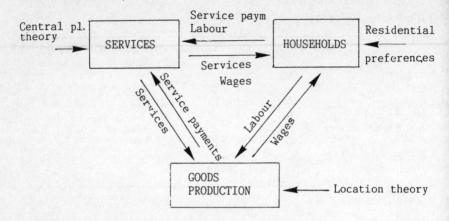

Figure 7.6 A model of mutual dependence

It may be concluded that there are forces which increase the advantages of agglomeration, and thus pull towards a more concentrated pattern of location, and forces which pull in the opposite direction. It is possible to talk of a race between these forces, where in different cases different forces may gain and lose. This perception may contribute to an understanding of the widely differing regional development tendencies observed in West European countries recently.

However, decreasing needs for proximity between service producers and service users does not mean that service firms can operate equally well everywhere. It only means that other factors of location become decisive.

Local conditions

There are several 'other factors' which may constitute local conditions, different from place to place. There are variations in equipment and infrastructure, and in the support which regional policies or local economic policies offer. There are variations in the cost levels of premises and labour. There are variations in the structure of local markets: independent enterprises and strong local governments form better markets than branch plants and centralised public systems, and a good local market retains some importance as a good basis for later remote market development.

However, there is little doubt that the supply of qualified people is the most important local condition. Thus, the fifth hypothesis will be that the availability of human resources is a significant factor of location. By implication the attractiveness of a place is important. This hypothesis is clearly related to an extremely important quality of the emerging society, namely the crucial importance of knowledge and creativity as key factors of production. Indeed, from a locational point of view many recent studies (for instance Illeris and Jakobsen 1990) point towards the local possibilities of recruiting and retaining an adequate staff as an extremely important factor. This means that the traditional notion in regional theory – that the man must come to the job – may be reversed. Now the job must often come to the man or put another way, the firms which are where the men prefer to be have an advantage.

As regards the recruitment of qualified personnel, big cities have several advantages: that is where most educational institutions are, thus ensuring supply; that is where there is a large labour market for people with specialised qualifications. (The labour market forms another kind of agglomeration advantage which according to Illeris & Jakobsen is more important than contact opportunities). Finally, many people prefer to live in big cities with their cultural and professional services etc.

But clearly some other regions, too, are able to attract people because of their physical or social environment. Old university towns are examples, and so are the 'sunbelts' of southern France, Germany and the United States. The establishment of educational institutions in small or medium towns leads to an increased supply of qualified people. On the other hand, old industrial and mining areas are often reported to be unattractive. And it seems that the local labour market must attain a certain size. If these conditions are met provincial firms may find that their personnel is more stable than that of their metropolitan competitors who often experience a high and costly staff turnover. Thus, the variation in local conditions may explain why some provincial areas display growing service activities and others not.

The role of services in regional development

To conclude, let us summarise the role of service activities in regional economic development. Would it be possible to accelerate regional development through influencing the service development? Some answers are suggested in the last column of Table 7.2. First, to some degree the economic base model and central place theory, which attribute a passive role to service activities, remain valid. Many household services keep a non-basic character. There is no point in considering them in a regional development policy.

Turning to producer services that need to locate close to their customers, it is not easy to define their role in regional development today. Do they passively follow the location of their customers, as stated by the economic base model? Or have their services become so important for the competitive capabilities of their clients that their presence is now a necessary condition for the location of the latter? In other words, have they – although indirectly – become the true economic base of their region? Already in 1955, Blumenfeld claimed that this was the case. If he is right, regional development policies should encourage such producer services.

Producer services which are no longer required to locate close to their customers, and which sell their services all over the country and even internationally, clearly contribute to the economic base of their region. Such services obviously should form a target for regional development policies. According to Beyers (1990), they even have higher local multiplier effects than manufacturing firms since, per dollar of export sales, they import less input from other regions than manufacturing firms.

Finally, it is important to note that a number of household services contribute to the supply of human resources in an area and thus indirectly to its economic development. Educational services is an obvious example, but also cultural and leisure services may make an area more attractive for qualified people. Once such people have been attracted, the area derives a higher chance of attracting firms which need qualified staff and local quality firms obtain a competitive advantage. The labour market expands, making the area even more attractive for qualified people etc. In recent years, several European towns and regions have adopted development policies including measures to make the environment, in a broad sense, attractive.

In sum, it may be stated that producer services directly and indirectly contribute to the economic development of the regions in which they are located: through regional exports and as necessary conditions for the performance of other firms. Furthermore, the quality of certain household services contributes indirectly to the regional dynamics by making the region more attractive.

Thus the classical economic base model, as shown in Figure 7.4, must be changed into a model of mutual dependence between goods production (formerly the only activities considered basic), households, and service activities (see Figure 7.6). Households depend on jobs, but firms also depend on the availability of good labour. Service activities depend on households and firms as customers, but firms also depend on services and so does the supply of good labour. Policy-makers should be aware that in this triangular chain of mutual dependence no link must be missing. However, it should be stressed that today these views can only be regarded as hypotheses, and much work needs to be done to substantiate them.

References

Albrechts, L., Swyngedouw, E. (1989) 'The challenges for regional policy under a flexible regime of accumulation' in L. Albrechts, F. Moulaert, P. Roberts and E. Swyngedouw (eds), *Regional policy at the crossroads*, London, Jessica Kingsley.

Andersson, Å. and Strömqvist, U. (1988) *K-samhällets framtid*, Stockholm, Prisma.

Blumenfeld, H. (1955) 'The economic base of the metropolis: critical remarks on the "basic–nonbasic" concept', *Journal of the American Institute of Planners*, **21**, pp. 114–32.

Beyers, W. (1990) 'The contemporary role of producer services in the economic development of advanced economies: United States evidence', in S. Illeris and L. Jakobsen (eds), *Networks and Regional Development*, Copenhagen, NordREFO.

Christaller, W. (1933) *Die zentralen Orte in Süddeutschland*, Jena, Gustav Fischer.

Claval, P. (1989) L'avenir de la métropolisation, *Annales de géographie*, **550**, pp. 692–706.

Delaunay, J.-C. and Gadrey, J. (1987) *Les enjeux de la société de service*, Paris, Presses de la Fondation Nationale des Sciences Politiques.

Giarini, O. (1986) 'Coming of age of the service economy', *Science and public policy*, **13**, 4, pp. 209–15.

Hirschhorn, L. (1987) L'économie post-industrielle: quel travail, quelle compétence pour un nouveau mode de production? *Economie et humanisme*, **295**, pp. 25–43.

Illeris, S. (1989) *Services and regions in Europe*, Aldershot, Avebury.

— (1990) 'Local and distant service provision: a survey of quantitative studies in S. Illeris and L. Jakobsen (eds), *Networks and Regional Development*, Copenhagen, NordREFO.

— and Jakobsen, L. (1990) 'Computer services and the urban system: a case study in Denmark', *Acta geographica lovaniensia*, Leuven, KUL.

Kelly, T. (1987) *The British Computer Industry*, London, Croom Helm.

Kern, H. and Schumann, M. (1984) *Das Ende der Arbeitsteilung*, Munich, C.H. Beck.

Lambooy, J.G. (1988) Intermediaire dienstverlening en economische complexiteit, *Economisch en sociaal tijdschrift*, **42**, pp. 617–29.

Moulaert, F., Chikhaoui, Y. and Djellal, F. (forthcoming) 'Locational behavior of French high tech consultancy firms, *International Journal of Urban and Regional Research*.

Noyelle, T.J. (1986) *New Technologies and Services: Impacts on Cities and Jobs*, College Park, The University of Maryland Institute for Urban Studies.

Pascal, A. (1987) 'The vanishing city', *Urban studies*, **24**, pp. 597–603.

Pedersen, M.K. (1988) 'Service i det postmoderne samfund' in O.W. Anderson, J.S. Pedersen, J. Sundbo, *Service og erhvervsudvikling*, Roskilde, Samfundsøkonomi og planlægning.

Planque, B. (1983) Une nouvelle organisation spatiale du développement in B. Planque (ed.), *Le développement décentralisé*, Paris, Litec.

Scott, A.J. (1990) 'Flexible production systems and regional development: the rise of new industrial spaces in North America and Western Europe' in S. Illeris and L. Jakobsen (eds), *Networks and Regional Development*, Copenhagen, NordREFO.

Skolka, J. (1987) 'Wissen, Arbeitsteilung und Strukturwandel', *Wirtschaft und Gesellschaft*, **13**, 2, pp. 245–70.

Stabler, J., Howe, E.C. (1988) 'Service exports and regional growth in the postindustrial era', *Journal of Regional Science*, **28**, pp. 303–16.

Toffler, A. (1980), *The Third Wave*, London, Pan.

8 Localisation factors and development strategies of producer services

Marie-Christine Monnoyer and Jean Philippe*

Introduction

Spatial analysis of producer services implies taking into account the features of the production of services compared with the production of industrial goods. The first feature lies in the absence of total non-contact between the service producer and the user, between the act of production and the act of consumption. For certain services which are absolutely non-stockable, the acts of production and of consumption run parallel. A second feature arises from the service buyer's participation in its production process. This participation is more or less marked or necessary according to the type of service, but it intervenes as an input or a modifier in the production process. These particularities translate immediately in terms of space: in order to become merchandise, services need a meeting place between producers and consumers.

The success of this interaction often requires that information and advice be supplied, and it also depends on environmental contexts, as has been shown by marketing theories (Eiglier and Langeard 1979), interaction studies (Valla 1982; Flipo 1984) and servuction processes (Veys 1981; Eiglier and Langeard 1987). This means that if industry and services have a certain number of factors in common such as labour and capital, information technologies and communications, the degree of competence of the service producer and the participation of the client will be of particular importance for services. For the production of goods and the localisation of industries it is necessary to take into account the cost and the availability of the workforce, ease of access to raw materials and sources of energy, the quality of the economic and socio-cultural environment and the cost of transport in the total cost of the products. For those theories of localisation which include these constraints two key determinants in the choice of localisation are the cost of transport and labour, to which since Weber (1909) the economies of agglomeration have been added. This is a localisation factor that has been successively

* The authors are grateful to Mrs Moya Jones for her translation of the original manuscript.

analysed and incorporated into the concepts of industrial clusters or 'poles of development' and which more recently has been incorporated into the concepts of innovatory districts and technological poles.

The economies of concentration are also particularly important for service activites: they allow them to minimise transport costs, to reduce the uncertainty concerning markets or else to establish commercial relationships with other producers. However, if it is easy to perceive their impact on the development of businesses, it is more difficult to explain their formation and the observable irregularities in the geographical distribution of these groups of services. As far as services to consumers are concerned, Christaller's theory of central places and its derivative models (Barcet *et al.* 1983) offer a framework for analysis which is still largely valid. Services and businesses come together in certain places because this way they can meet a demand that is sufficiently large in volume and with buying power at a reduced transport cost. Each service therefore has a minimum service area. The most common consumer services are characterised by small market areas, their large number and the regularity of their localisation. More specialised services with a larger market area are to be found less frequently. The degree of specialisation of services and the importance of their market area also corresponds to the rank that the town where they are localised holds in the hierarchy of towns classed according to size. On the other hand, the inequality and often the irregularity of the spatial distribution of business services is a characteristic that has been observed in all the developed countries. Among the different causes that explain this spatial configuration it seems to us that the need for contacts between the supplier and the demander of services should be at the forefront. We will analyse this first before showing how information technologies modify the functions of the supply of services and sanction new spatial development strategies for firms.

Contact need: a structuring element in services offered and an explanatory factor in the spatial concentrations of business services.

It seems to us that it is not possible to explain the choice of localisation for business services without referring to the dominating role played by the contact need that links service suppliers and consumers.

Contact needs and the head offices of businesses

The considerable expansion of producer services during the past twenty years is mostly due to the decisions taken by large industrial companies (Barcet, *et al.* 1983) to externalise their demand for services. This externalisation was originally motivated by reasons of cost (sub-contracting productivity) and then because of a real division of tasks between suppliers and demanders owing to the creative and original content of new services (agencies for surveys, recruitment, advertising, etc.). Supplying a service therefore proved to be dependent on the strategic choices implemented by large industrial companies (Valeyre 1985). It is linked within these firms to the development of Taylorist forms of work organisation and the automation of administrative and commercial tasks.

The contact need is situated at the level of the negotiation betwen the person who decides on the externalisation of the demand for services and the supplier, that is geographically between the head office of the individual business which centralises the main service needs of regional branches (Polese 1983) and the business service. Thus the concentration of tertiary-sector industry in urban centres has favoured the concentration of business services. Daniels (1985) insists on the symbiotic character of the development of industry and of services: industry does not precede services because industrial development would not have been possible without the help of financial services, transport, warehousing. etc., but the development of internal services precedes the appearance of an external offer.

Numerous geographers have studied these findings and have concentrated their analysis on businesses' head offices. Pred (1977) especially has shown that the localisation of business services could be better interpreted if the constraints of seeking information and the way in which this information is circulated throughout contact networks were taken into account. The availability of this information thus varies according to the place and the time: some urban centres are more favourable than others to this circulation. Services which demand both competence and information such as consultancies, stockbroking, financial services, advertising etc. tend to group together in these centres. Other services such as transport or security services depend on the localisation of industrial establishments and on the constraints on the circulation of goods. Services and notably business services are then going to be at the origin of specific urban dynamics (Noyelle and Stanback 1984).

Until the end of the 1960s the localisation policy of business services was simple. It was limited to following geographically the main consumer in order to facilitate the response to the original need which was developing strongly thanks to permanent contact. However, with the end of the 1960s and the change in economic context, orientations became more diverse.

First we can notice that in France, for example, under the effect of a certain spatial distribution of medium-sized industries and of a deconcentration of industrial activities, the volume and therefore the attraction of regional markets increased. The growth rate (Lazzeri 1985) in personnel in business service activities becomes clearly higher in the regions than in the Ile de France (6.75 per cent per year as compared to 3.3 per cent between 1968 and 1982). Research carried out among service suppliers (Laget 1984; Monnoyer and Philippe 1986) shows that a business service setting up in the provinces shows a localised aim of market penetration wherever the geographical location of the company's head office might be. These companies have therefore adapted their localisation upon demand from their clients and according to the need for swift and close relations. The supply of services has accordingly entered into the beginning of a spatial deconcentration, at least in France. It is also to be noted that certain foreign research centred on the impact and the localisation of head offices (Coffey and Polese 1983) is beginning to tackle the question of the sale of services outside the supplier's local region (Coffey and Polese 1986).

Contact needs and structure in the services sector

The contact demand between service suppliers and consumers has repercussions on the nature of the services offered as well as on the structure of the service sector. Availability, contact and the need for face-to-face meetings with consumers have increased the cost of services. It is useless to hope for gains in productivity linked to production or for the appearance of some sort of experience curve similar to that in the industrial sector. The only synergy that large service companies can display concerns their capacity to deal with problems arising from the multiplicity and diversity of their experiences.

An economic environment which puts a value on the unique aspect of a service and the relationship need between the supplier and the consumer can be found in what Michael Porter (1980) calls a 'dispersed sectoral structure'. Such structures are characterised by the existence of economic factors which slow down the concentration, thereby preventing the founding of large companies. In the case of service activities these factors are many:

— the modest investments to initiate the activity causes an increase in the number of actors on the market;
— the absence of scale economies due to the non-reproductibility of the products makes an increase in market share pointless;
— the high cost of transport between the producer and the buyer penalises distance and therefore any efforts at wide-ranging market penetration;
— the high level of creativity needed for the conception of certain services implies calling upon creative personnel who are not easily integrated into large units. Besides, the diversity of needs implies a considerable differentiation of the service and, according to the argument that there is real personalisation involved, value is imbued in what is produced.

For the service company such a structure is a real handicap and a barrier to development. Its local influence is limited to a certain geographical dimension compatible with the need for local contacts. Its productivity is restrained by the cost constraints represented by the impossibility of reproducing the service. Its market is restricted by the real impossibility of acting on prices or on the buyer's choice.

In such sectors the development of service companies requires that this dispersion be eliminated or dealt with. Companies will choose the first strategy if it proves to be possible to get round one of the fundamental obstacles to concentration. They will choose the second strategy if it proves to be possible to be more successful than its rivals while still only cornering a modest share of the market. Each of these two paths might be the realisation of a choice made by a business or the exploitation of an evolution in the sector. It can happen though, as Michael Porter (1990) has noted, that a sector remains dispersed even though the economic environment would have allowed its structural modification, simply because no enterprise could exploit, or knew how to exploit, the potential for evolution.

Daniels (1985) underlines the fact that in order to facilitate analysis, geographers and economists have all too often combined external business services with activities in offices and in head offices. The reality of the service sector and of business services in particular is more complex. In addition those large organisations that have a head office and decentralised branches, there is a host of small firms whose localisation may depend on that of large organisations but having their own growth patterns. Taylor and Thrift (1984) have drawn up a typology of these businesses and distinguish among the following:

— the 'dawdlers' who survive often because they have a 'niche' in the market;
— intermediate firms which manage their relationships with large firms either by a loyal opposition (extended specialisation of a restricted number of products) or by satellite growth (franchise, subcontracting);
— dynamic companies which have strong but fragile growth.

There are connecting paths between these categories but very few small business services experience rapid growth patterns because of their own organisational limits and their dependence on large organisations. It is obligatory for those which do succeed in achieving significant growth to handle their geographical location, for business services must be set up in the 'right place' in order to satisfy their customers.

Technological change: a factor in the renewal of strategies for the development and the spatial decompartmentalisation of producer services

Growth and spatial dynamics are closely linked. Until quite recently the dynamics of localisation were influenced more by factors that were external to firms (increase in revenue, legislation) than by internal factors (organisation, technological developments). The information explosion and then the development of communication technologies has modified this situation and allowed an evolution in the structure of the service sector.

The insertion of data processing and information technologies into business services

Computer-based analysis in fact lies in the definition of basic tasks whose handling consists in so many sub-programs independent from one another, but the whole of which allows the handling of several distinct global problems (at least in certain languages). The use of such an analysis during the conception phase of services encourages a consideration of the service – not as an entity but broken down into distinct phases where production and sale may be handled separately. Computer-based analysis also leads to the drawing up of processing 'models' which integrate the variables affecting the problem under examination in the form of unknowns whose value is not fixed. The use of such an analytical method in the conception phase of services means that we can anticipate their adaptation for dealing with demands that are similar in the needs required but differ with respect to the value of the variables that they bring into play. If the service keeps its character flexible according to the clients' needs, it is no longer a 'unique product' which is non-renewable but like immaterial non-decomposable goods it becomes reproducible, identical. This new possibility could lead to the concept of a standard service or standardised elements of a service which could therefore benefit from the reduction in costs which are brought about by economies of scale during serial production. Turning towards a standardisation of services and their multiple reproduction displaces the problem of the personalisation of a service and valorises the search for an increase in market share. It therefore causes several factors acting on the dispersion of the sector to disappear.

As for the development of communication techniques, this modifies the perception of distances since it accelerates the transport of information (teleinformatics, electronic mail), allows analysis and processing at a distance (teleprocessing) and facilitates the collaboration of several people at a distance (teleconference). If the service producer masters these techniques sufficiently, he can modify the forms of his servuction by adapting it to the opportunities offered by these technologies and thereby attenuate the necessity for proximity. This transformation depends on the nature of the information in order to process working information (day-to-day management) or development information. During the transaction the communication can be carried out either by a telephone contact, by telex, by teleinformatics or may even require the two parties meeting. From this point the service producer's efficiency is shown by his capacity to himself adopt and then to get adopted that means of communication which, to the equal satisfaction of both parties, preserves his independence as regards the geographical localisation of his client.

In manufacturing industry it is possible to set up production processes that are entirely new without affecting the nature of the goods produced. In services, technological innovation has consequences for the very nature of the service. Daniel Bell (1973) points out that, unlike industry which works with goods, services involve people exchanging information (activities of research, consultancy, control) and/or energy (facilitating services). We must take into account the particularities of the function of service production and the structure of firms, which have already been mentioned. The client's participation in the act of production (Langeard *et al.* 1981) might be through exercising a function of specification (analysis), co-production (research), marketing (word of mouth) or quality control of the service given. The client can participate physically (self-service) or intellectually. The firm must therefore adapt the method of communication to the form of the client's participation (intensity, intervention phases).

The other feature consists of the existence of stages in the production of services. The service must be conceived, produced and sold. In the same way, the firm which carries out this production must be run like any industry: its administration can take the form of a 'head office' in the case of enterprises which are broken down into divisions. By their inclusion in the servuction process, information technologies will provoke a certain decomposition/objectivisation of all the elements that make up a service. They will have different impacts, depending on whether their action concerns the facilitating phase, the production or the conception of a service or whether they are used for the administration of the company. All these elements bestow a particular plasticity (Mills *et al.* 1983) on the organisation of business services which is the basis of their strategic orientations.

Strategic orientations and their consequences for the spatial dynamics of firms

A first orientation consists in giving preference to the concept of a 'standard service', conceived in theory by the supplier according to his knowledge of the market and of what is needed. Such a decision corresponds to what marketing people call a 'push'. This is the opposite of a second orientation consisting in presenting oneself as capable of replying in an individualised manner to a demand conceived by a client, known in marketing as a 'pull'.

This two-sided presentation might appear to be simplifying a reality which is as complex and varied as that of service activities. However, the standardisation process can be explained by the use of specific methods distinct from those needed by the elaboration of the offer to a demand during a personalised servuction. It must be thought out in terms of 'standard' or universality right from the conception phase, for if this is not done the eventual production detour risks being burdensome. On a deeper level, the juxtaposition of two approaches within the same firm proves to be difficult for they do not require the same human qualities from the conceivers and correspond to different 'jobs'. Offering a standardised service and facing up to an automatic process changes the client's habits and leaves him fearing a certain reduction in the quality of the service provided as in servuction. The adoption of cost-reducing technology should not be done to the detriment of the quality of the service and the servuction such as the user perceives them. Not respecting this rule risks bringing about rejection, which goes directly against the goals of increasing the market. The evolution of services towards standardisation therefore supposes on the part of the producer, extensive knowledge of the clients' needs and of the role played by the service requested in the organisation of the client firm.

Can standardisation affect a service in its entirety – its conception, its production and its sale? Through our case studies (Monnoyer and Philippe 1986) we have been able to distinguish two main strategic orientations: in the first, the concept of a service and its sale have been rethought and have become activities with free geographical localisation (a software production company; banking automats); in the second, only the sale is decentralised (service franchise, maintenance by telesurveillance).

If standardisation is able to bring about progress in productivity and market expansion such a tactic is hardly conceivable where the service is a response to an original problem that assumes consultation between service provider and buyer. In that case, in order to ensure its development and to free itself from the constraints which the dispersal of demand imposes, the firm must valorise its knowledge of the local market and the needs of its clientele, all the time seeking to benefit from technological progress which reduces distance as much for the transport of personnel as for that of information. We have been able to distinguish two possible strategies for firms: an in-depth penetration of the local market through offering diversified services (consultancy companies) and overcoming the cost of distance by the quality of the service (the case of a translating service or an advertising agency).

Each strategic orientation is determined by the firm's structures and by the nature of its activities. They all demand an explicit desire for implementation, because the human factor in services – determination, efficiency and talent – are always more important than the performance of machines and the procedures that they use.

Conclusions: the repercussions of strategic choices on localisation

The different strategic orientations which open up to service activities can exert contradictory influences:

— as a result of the distribution of information technologies, the decentralised implantation of firms seems possible and susceptible to open regional markets. Once the investments linked to such a choice have been made, it can bring about external savings linked to a localisation outside the great urban centres.

— However, the importance of the demand from large firms and central administrations ensures an active market for companies settled in large cities, which does not exclude the possibility of a penetration of local markets thanks to the use of long-distance selling strategies.

The dominance of one orientation over the other will deeply affect the development of small business services localised in the provinces. We have noted the importance of the demands which the implementation of these strategies include. Not only do the level of the personnel's qualifications and their aptitude towards innovation condition the success of the conception of standardisation strategy phases, but also its capacity to dominate new technologies is revealed to be indispensable to the acceptance of and to the success of long-distance selling strategies. However, if the use of telecommunications is a profitable investment, the immediate cost holds back some small firms. Thus, the choice of regional localisation for small and medium-sized businesses seems to be subject to three conditions:

— access by regional firms to new information technologies;
— the emergence of local demand for business services;
— the existence of a potential adaptable workforce.

If these conditions are not met, large business services will, on the contrary, find it easier to reinforce their multiregional organisation and to consolidate their competitive position. Examination of localisation dynamics shows that for the moment few movements have any effect on the head offices of large firms in France.

References

Barcet, A., Bonamy, J. and Mayere A. (1983) *Economie des services aux entreprises. Approche empirique et théorique*, Lyons, Economie et Humanisme.

Bell, D. (1973) *The Coming of Post-industrial Society*, New York, Basic Books.

Coffey, J.W. and Polese, M. (1983) Towards a theory of the inter-urban location of head office functions. Paper presented at European Congress of the Regional Science Association, Poitiers. August.

Coffey, J.W. and Polese, M. (1986) *Trade and localisation of producer services: a Canadian perspective*. Colloque on services and economic development; towards a new classification of service activities, University of Geneva, 6–7 May.

Daniels, P.W. (1985) *Service Industries: A Geographical Appraisal*. London and New York, Methuen.

Eiglier, P. and Langeard, E. (1987) *Elements pour une théorie des services: applications à l'entreprise*. WP n° 142, Aix en Provence, IAE.

Eiglier, P., Langeard, E. (1979), *Servuction*, London, McGraw.

Flipo, J.P. (1984) *Le management des entreprises de services*. Paris, Editions d'organisation.

Laget, M. (1984) 'Politique industrielle et service aux industries dans le système économique régional in *Régions et Politique industrielle*, Paris, Colloque ADEFI-GRECO, Editions Economica.

Langeard, E., Bateson, J.E.G., Lovelock, C. and Eiglier, P. (1981) *Service Marketing: New Insights from Consumers and Managers*, Boston, Marketing Science Institute.

Lazzeri, Y. (1985) *L'interaction entre les prestataires de services et les PMI*, Vol. 2, Aix en Provence, CER.

Mills, K.P., Hall, L.J., Leifrecker, K.J. and Margulies, N. (1983) 'Flexiform: a model for professional service organisation', *Academy of Management Review*, 8, 1, pp. 118–31.

Monnoyer, M.-C., Philippe, J. (1986) *Modernisation des activités de services et technologies de l'information*, Rapport au commissariat général au Plan 21986, Aix en Provence, CER.

Noyelle, T., Stanback, H.T. (1984) *The Economic Transformation of American Cities*, Totowa, NJ, Rowman and Allanheld.

Polese, M. (1983) 'Le commerce interrégional des services: le rôle des relations intra-firme et des facteurs organisationnels, *Revue d'analyse économique*, 59, 4, pp. 713–28.

Porter, M.E. (1980) *Competitive Strategy*, New York, Free Press.

Pred, A.R. (1977) *City Systems in Advanced Economies*, London, Hutchinson.

Taylor, M. and Thrift, N. (1984) 'Business organisation, segmentation and location', *Regional Studies*, 17, 6, pp. 445–65.

Valeyre, A. (1985) La dynamique spatiale des emplois de services liés à la production industrielle, *Revue d'économie régionale et urbaine*, 4, pp. 703–25.

Valla, J.P. (1982) Elements d'une approche marketing du concept de filière, *Revue d'économie industrielle*, 21, pp. 76–92.

Veys, P. (1981) *Contribution à l'étude des systèmes de servuction*, Ph.D thesis, Aix en Provence, IAE.

9 The functional and spatial division of labour in information technology consultancy firms in Western Europe

*Frank Moulaert, Flavia Martinelli and Faridah Djellal**

L 86   West Euro

R 12

Introduction

High-technology consultancy in general, and information technology consultancy (ITC) in particular, are considered as professional services which play a determining role in the restructuring of contemporary economic activities. There is a need for specialised knowledge about high-technology systems and the way they are organised and should be applied in firms. This explains among other factors why these services have witnessed such high growth figures. For the time being, let us define high-technology consultancy as the ensemble of customised intellectual activities preparing and accompanying the installation, the functioning or the restructuring of high-technology systems in user organisations (Moulaert, Chikhaoui and Djellal 1991).

Note that this definition is process orientated: it looks at how the production system and organisational structure of firms are conceived and developed. In order to avoid any misunderstanding, let us make it clear from the beginning that the purpose of this chapter is not to explain in detail the increasing role of professional services and advanced consultancy in contemporary economic systems. Nor is it our object to explain the rise of free-standing high-technology consultants or to provide a systemic statistical approach to this very important development phenomenon in contemporary economies. Instead, we shall use a limited sample of fifteen information-technology consultancy firms located in Western Europe, with which we have had in-depth interviews, to examine how today's information-technology consultancy

* We wish to thank NOTA (Dutch Parliament's Office of Technology Assessment) and CNRS-PIRTTEM who made this research possible.

business functions, what kind of services these firms offer and how they interact with their clients; how their production and distribution organisations are structured and how they are imbedded in the network of contemporary economic rebuilding (Moulaert *et al.* 1990).

Following the general definition of high-technology consultancy, information technology consultancy (ITC) can be defined as the customised intellectual activities preparing and accompanying the installation, functioning or/and implementation of IT systems as they should serve the informational needs of client organisations, or more specifically, business organisations. In this definition, there is a technological as well as an organisational dimension. In fact, an information system stocks, transmits and processes information. To operate, it uses hardware, systems, communication and application software as well as orgware. The later assures the correspondence between the information system and the organisation of the business functions to which it belongs. In this way, IT is an integral part of the system of information and communication pervading virtually all functions within the business organisation.

Therefore, to understand how IT is used, we ought to understand how information systems work and what their strategic and operational meaning is to the firm. So, when we talk about ITC, we are simultaneously referring to IT assessment and organizational assessment. That means that IT consultants should assist the clients not only with respect to the technological dimension of the development and the improvement of their information systems, but should also provide them with the essential know-how for organising their business and their information systems so that the IT – computing and communication technology – is used in an optimal way (Dussauge and Ramantsoe 1987).

The organisational dimension of IT consultancy is a powerful discriminant in consultancy business, IT consultants differ according to their view of technological and organisational dynamics. There exist very different views on technological and organisational dynamics, all to be found in consultancy practice, industrial economics literature and theories of organisation (Dosi *et al.* 1988).

In summary, we can say that there is a fundamental difference between the functionalist view and the structural-realist view on ITC. According to the second view, organisational dynamics are much more than functional categorising and rational behaviour in view of well-defined objectives: irrationality, interpersonal and interorganisational politics, enterprise culture all interact with the functional trajectories. Consultants, although not all to the same extent, are aware of this reality ('enterprises are human', one leading American IT consultant based in Belgium told us) and try to deal with it in their methodology (Moulaert *et al.* 1990).

In sum, we can say that IT consultancy differs from the more general notion of high-technology consultancy by its stronger and more global relation to the organisation of the client firm. As a consequence, it is methodologically unacceptable to study IT consultancy as a production process in the conventional sense of the term, that is as a transformation process whose links with the market are limited to input and output bounds without interaction between producers and clients during the process itself (Bonamy *et al.* 1989; Eiglier and Langeard 1987; Moulaert 1989). And since ITC includes the analysis of important parts of the client organisations, it can only be delivered in close interaction with the agents in these organisations. Therefore, ITC as an economic activity must be studied as a *production interaction process*, not merely as a production process.

Who are the IT consultants?

The consultancy organisations in our sample are free-standing consultants, technically independent private consultancy organisations – and not sections or departments of other enterprises – with a completely different activity, satisfying only the internal consultancy needs of these enterprises.

IT consultancy firms can have very different sectoral origins. In Europe, a very important sectoral origin is software and systems houses. Examples are Cap Gemini Sogeti (systems house) and Logica (software house) which over the last few years have developed important IT consultancy activities. Through acquisitions, through the development of specialised departments, they have profiled themselves as consultants, that is as providers of strategic and functional analysis of information systems.

Another very important sectoral origin or sectoral trajectory is that of accountants. This is the trajectory that finds its origin in the Anglo-Saxon countries and to a certain extent in the Netherlands. These accountants, who often consist of world-wide partnerships, have developed important IT consultancy and service activities. Perhaps the best example is Arthur Andersen with half of its activities in IT services and consultancy.

A third sectoral origin is the computer and communication hardware producers such as IBM, ATT and Bull which over recent years have developed their service activities, first of all in the software domain but more recently in the field of systems integration, a very important part of ITC work (as we will see in a later section). IBM, for example, says that systems integration is its fastest-growing market. Because of systems integration and IT services, within the next few years IBM will become primarily a service provider (with more than 50 per cent of its turnover in services).

A further sectoral origin is production and work organisation consultants such as Berenschot in the Netherlands and Bossard Consulting Group (affiliated with CGS). At one time, consultants of this type were called 'Taylorists' because they were the specialists who introduced the Taylorist division of labour in manufacturing. Recently, because of different market factors, they have had to diversify to, or specialise in, IT consultancy.

Of course, there are also what we could call 'pure IT consultants': consultants who developed their market on the basis of IT consultancy only. Most of these 'purists' are small and act in partnership with other firms of the types just mentioned. To make the overview of sectoral trajectories complete, we should not forget that a number of other professional service suppliers in marketing, in strategic management, in advertising etc. have developed ITC activities. So, as an intermediate conclusion, IT consultancy can be considered as an emerging sector: the activity is growing fast and today has reached about 0.5 to 1.5 per cent of GNP, depending on the country. Confusingly, the activity is covered by different sector labels. And the statistical practice is still that when one talks about IT consultants, either one forgets half of the world by looking only at those IT consultants which can be identified in statistical data on software services and engineering or one has to collect very partial data belonging to diverse sectoral settings.

For the remainder of the analysis, when talking about ITC consultants, we shall mean independent consultancy firms which have a certain consultancy style, deliver certain consultancy products but come from different sectoral origins.

The production–interaction model

In the first section of this chapter it has been argued that it would be analytically unacceptable to analyse the consultancy activities from a production or a production process point of view only. IT consultancy affects and involves the client organisation to such a large extent that the client co-defines and quite often co-produces the consultancy products. In any case, we must consider the consultancy process not merely as a process of production but a process of *production* which is delivered in *interaction* with a client: a production–interaction process.

In fact, referring to the more general literature on professional services and interaction with clients (Bonamy *et al.* 1989; Martinelli and Moulaert 1991; Ermes 1988; Monnoyer and Philippe 1991), one can argue that consultancy services are among the professional services which involve the client organisations the most and for which in any case we should as much analyse the interaction between producer and client as we should analyse the supply and the production behaviour or the demand and consumption behaviour. What does this mean? What are the consequences of this approach for the analytical terminology?

For the terminology, it means that it is very hard to talk in terms of production and consumption separately. In fact, within this interactive setting, even a definition of a market becomes very difficult. Still the following scheme can help us to explain what production for the market means, what consumption in a market means, what co-production and what co-consumption mean. The squares in Figure 9.1 represent three types of economic behaviour: production, consumption and market exchange.

The following cases are then possible for producer and user:

— case 1: auto-production; auto-consumption;
— case 2: co-production, co-consumption by original producer and original user;
— case 3: co-consumption by producer;
— case 4: co-production by user.

Let us look at a few examples. In co-production the client becomes a co-producer with the consultant. For example, the consultant can do a certain kind of strategic analysis of the business functions of the client organisation. A specialist consultancy team can teach the client how to analyse the organisation of the different business functions. In a next step, the client will do the analysis himself using the methodology which was introduced by the consultant. This is a style of consultancy one finds in important international consultancy organisations. In any case, we have a situation where at least the analytical stage of the consultancy activity is undertaken in co-production. The consultant and the client *together* do the analysis.

At the same time, there can be a situation of co-consumption. For example, the consultant can develop a data-base system for a very important client who has a long-term experience in certain markets. And, at the end, because of its suitability for the multiple applications of the client, the data-base system turns out to be useful for the management of the information in the consultant's own business. In this case, the consultant becomes a user of the product which he has developed together with the client: we have a situation of co-consumption. This situation will also be a situation of co-production if the client is involved in the production of the system as well. The next step then, which establishes the link with the market, is when the data-base system is offered, for example in a joint venture by the client and the consultant, to other clients in the market. In any case, it is clear that these forms of interaction correspond to reality and adopt various institutionalised forms such as joint ventures, marketing agreements or shared-use agreements.

Stages in the production–interaction model

In this section, we look in some detail at the different stages in the production–interaction model (see Figure 9.2).

The first stage in the production–interaction process is the *initialisation* stage when the consultant is invited to do the job. There are different ways for a consultant to come to the consultancy job itself. He might enter the client firm through a feasibility study commissioned by the client or through a training program offered to electronic data process-

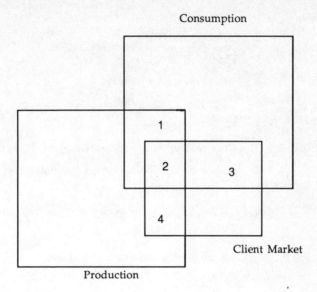

1- Auto-production
   Auto-consumption

2-Co-production
   Co-consumption

3-Co-consumption

4- Co-production

Figure 9.1 Production–consumption interaction in ITC

ing (EDP) staff. Sometimes supply of other types of services serves as an introduction to an ITC job.

The second stage is *strategic analysis*. Strategic analysis is the analysis of the business system, that is the business organisation and its different functions, including the information function. This, of course, is done from an information system point of view: the consultant will in the first place look at how the information system in different business functions works, how the information flows between the functions are organised and coordinated and if the modes of communication and coordination really correspond to the information needs of the business organisation.

The third stage or *functional analysis* is focused on different functions: marketing, production, distribution, R & D. Functional analysis looks in detail at how the information system works or should be developed or improved for different functions of the business organisation.

1 - Initialization

2 - Strategic analysis

3 - Functional analysis

4 - Macro-and micro-design

5 - Selection and/or production of software

6 - Selection of hardware

7 - Construction and implementation of IT system

8 - Follow-up (including quality control)

Source : Moulaert et al. 1990.

Figure 9.2 Stages in the production–interaction model
Source: Moulaert *et al.* 1990

Therefore, it also evaluates the distribution of functions over functional units.

The fourth stage, the *design* stage, pulls together the conclusions of strategic and functional analysis, and leads to a picture of what the information system should look like. Depending on the style and the tradition of the consultancy firm, this pursuit of informational optimality may also involve redesigning the business organisation itself. This would be the case when the existing structure does not allow effective data processing and transmission in view of the different business objectives. In any case, the design stage involves the modelling of information systems including its different functions, the location of the different nodes in the information network and the general structure of its data model. A distinction must further be made between macro- and micro-design, the latter detailing the information functions and units into programable variables and relations.

The fifth stage is the *production and/or selection of software*. This selection is of course fundamentally affected by the operating system and communication environment and the designed information functions and applications. Therefore, there is quite a strong interaction between the fourth and fifth stage.

Of course, the fact that we reason from a business organisation point of view should not keep us from stressing the importance of the hardware. *Selection of hardware* is a very important issue: do we need very flexible equipment? Do we need a centralised system? Do we need a decentralised system with autonomous workstations? These are questions whose answers are strongly determined by the design of the information functions.

Construction brings all the previous elements together: the organisational diagram of information functions, macro- and micro-design, software, hardware. And the *implementation* introduces the user to 'le mode d'usage', allows him to test the system and let him decide if the specificiations defined in the initialisation stage have been respected. This, of course, is a natural approach to *quality control* which in Figure 9.2 is called a stage, but which in reality should be interpreted as a transversal function: there should be quality control from stage to stage, and it should guarantee that specifications for the end product of each stage are respected. Other transversal functions are training and maintenance of the information system.

Of course, this schematic representation of stages in a consultancy process of production and interaction should be considered as a smallest common denominator. It is an exhaustive reconstruction of stages and we should note that in reality many IT consultants are not involved in all of them. For the 'real' consultants, the stress will be on strategic analysis, functional analysis and macro-design. These consultants will then pass on the micro-design, the actual programing and the implementation of the system to systems and software houses. In many situations, those systems and software houses would belong to the same financial group, larger firm (partnership) or control sphere as the consultant.

It should be stressed that the heart of the consultancy profession consists of strategic and functional analysis. These are crucial in defining the competitive edge of the consultancy firm. This means that the quality of and the advancement in methodology for strategic and functional analysis are main factors defining the competitive strength of the consultancy firms. Therefore, R & D on methodology and new products is very important to preserve and reinforce the competitive position; and training is essential to communicate the newly developed methodological tools to the different types of professionals in the consultancy teams as well as to the clients who will be involved in the production–interaction process with the consultants (Moulaert, Martinelli and Djellal 1990; Martinelli and Moulaert 1991).

Interaction at different stages

This section seeks to build a bridge between the way information technology consultancy is delivered to clients and the way consultancy organisations locate in economic space.

First, we have to look at the potential consequences for the locational behaviour of consultants which stem from the interaction between consultants and clients at different stages in the production chains. Which are the factors affecting this interaction?

Counterparts in consultancy and client organisation

It is important to understand who are the counterparts in the consultancy and client organisations who are involved in the different stages of the consultancy job. For example: counterparts in the consultancy and client organisations can be high-level managers at the level of the corporate management, or at the level of the management of the EDP department on the client side and a senior partner on the consultancy side. Interaction may also occur between specialised interfaces within the client organisation and different professional teams belonging to the consultancy firm.

Stages in the production–interaction chain

A very important factor is the stage in the consultancy process and its potential consequences for the degree of involvement between consultant and client. There is an important difference in the degree of involvement at for example the stage of strategic analysis, the stage of systems development or construction. The strategic or even functional analysis stage requires a large volume of backward and forward movement between client and consultant. At the stage of construction, in contrast, a good deal of the software can be developed in-house by the consultancy organisation, a substantial part of the orgware can be designed at the consultancy firm and so on. It is only at the final stage, the stage of the implementation of the system, that the consultancy professionals must be present at different locations of the client organisation. Therefore, the stages in which the consultancy firms are specialised can be important determinants of their locational behaviour.

The modes of involvement

If the consultant is used for a relationship of jobbing, teams and professionals are locationally less dependent. If, on the other hand, the main collaborative style is a sparring relationship, spatial proximity can be important, and the location of certain functions or units in the consultancy firm could be much more constrained by the location of the different agents in the client organisations.

Similar observations could be made for full externalisation, that is when the whole consultancy process ranging from strategic analysis down to implementation is handed over to the consultancy organisation (Tordoir and Gadrey 1988). In that case, the consultancy firms can use different locational strategies according to the stages in which they are involved. In general, the stage and product specialisation of the consultancy organisation will have some impact on its dominant mode involvement.

The sectoral origin and the professional style of the consultancy firm

There are different possibilities for classifying consultancy styles. One is to confront bottom-up with top-down approaches. If you have a bottom-up consultancy style, a self-administrative style of consultancy, the client is encouraged to do as much as possible of the job himself. The client organisation or parts thereof are involved in the whole process. For this very 'democratic' model of consultancy, it is clear that you will have an ongoing interaction between consultant and client, throughout the whole chain. This will certainly imply 'proximity' between agents in both organisations.

If, in contrast, you have a top-down, somewhat paternalistic consultancy style, in a somewhat exaggerated way, one could say that the consultant steps in with his suitcase full of instruments saying: 'Well, tell me what your problems and wishes are, let us write them down, let us have a short meeting about different possibilities, produce a preliminary report and see if you agree with the specifications. If you agree, I will do my work, I will come back when needed and when we will have results, we will discuss and implement them.' In this situation, the specialists dictate the solutions to the client. Much less involvement is required and proximity between parties plays a smaller part.

All these factors affecting interaction have a potential impact on the locational behaviour of the consultancy firm and its different units. Of course, these factors will only effectively intervene with locational strategies to the extent that:

(1) the client organisations 'reach out of space': we should not talk about dislocation or deconcentration suppliers' space, when the client organisations themselves are concentrated in space. The specialisations of the consultancy firms act as an important qualifier to this statement: only those sections of the client organisation which interact with the consultancy firm are relevant for the degree of the concentration stage. A consultancy firm dealing in stages 1 through 3 talks to corporate or division headquarters only. The spatial concentration of markets is very high in this case.
(2) the frequency and the scale of involvement is high. When talking about small jobs, or jobs which require only occasional interaction between consultancy firm and client, it does not make sense to develop great theories about spatial mobility and location. Still, stage and style of consultancy are important qualifiers in this respect.

When distances between agents involved are small, transportation combined with telecommunication can solve many of the contact problems; and (re) location becomes superfluous.

Functional and spatial division of labour in IT consultancy business

Internal professional specialisation and cooperation

In the previous sections, we have used the production–interaction model to identify the different stages and products supplied by IT consultants and to make preliminary observations on how different degrees of involvement and various consultancy styles can affect the locational behaviour of consultancy firms.

The different stages in the production–interaction process give us an idea of how a consultancy firm can be divided into functional units providing different consultancy products. This corresponds to a division of labour from a market perspective. Such a division, however, neglects the internal functions of the consultancy firm, that is those functions assuring its administration, organisation and operation.

In this section, we look at a combined market and internal function-orientated division of labour within IT firms. Several approaches to such a division exist. What is presented here is a smallest common denominator of the division of labour in IT consultancy in which most IT consultancy firms will recognise themselves. Figure 9.3 combines a market and an internal function approach to the division of labour:

Functions with market destination / Internal Functions	Consultancy/ analysis/design (stages 1-4)	Systems development (stages 4-7)	Miscellaneous IT Services
General administration			
Research & Development			
Methodology and Technology			
Internal training			
Marketing			

Figure 9.3 Functional division of labour in IT firms

Filling out this figure on an enterprise basis is an empirical task: the organisation and combination of functions in functional units, agencies, laboratories and consultancy departments varies among firms (Moulaert and Djellal 1990). But in a knowledge-intensive, human-capital-based professional business like ITC, a realistic picture of the division of labour must also have a professional dimension. This professional dimension is usually explicitly present in the organisational diagram of the firms. An example is given in Figure 9.4.

In practice, many combinations of functional units and professional teams are possible. One can have, for example, R & D and training together in one unit, or combine strategic and functional analysis in one group and design and software development in another. In the different types of firms, the regrouping into functional and professional teams is done according to market focus, sectoral specialisation of the clients, as well as methodological approach and consultancy style and tradition. All these are affected by the sectoral trajectories from which the consultancy firms have evolved.

In any case, professional specialisation is strong. We notice strong professional specialisation between functional units and teams. Units and teams are often organised by client sector, client business functions as well as methodological and technological specialisation. Yet, consultancy business shows a remarkably high professional flexibility.The function of teams can be switched between large clients and projects. Know-how is transversally combined; jobs are redefined and professional expertise is generated to function and to correspond with changing markets and research needs.

However, professional specialisation and market flexibility do not necessarily mean a mushrooming of agencies linked to client sectors or regions. The use of space is strongly dependent on the sector origin and the methodological approach of the consultancy firm, the size and organisational structure of the clients and the degree of spatial concentration of the national and regional markets served by the consultants.

The division of labour in IT consultancy is certainly affected by the size and organisational structure of the consultancy firm itself, but it also depends on the characteristics of the IT consultancy market: its size, its sectoral specialisation (client point of view) and product diversification (supplier point of view). Professional specialisation and interdisciplinary synergies are very important assets in the IT consultancy business. To cover the whole chain of production stages as well as client sectors, interchange of specialised expertise is inevitable. This can occur either through cooperation with other consultants or specialised service firms or within the larger consultancy organisation itself. The size, the legal form and the functional articulation of the consultancy firm are then determining factors of the modes by which interdisciplinary cooperation is accomplished. Moreover, the type of client market influences the functional and spatial organisation of the consultant.

A typology of consultancy firms

Taking into consideration all these different criteria, for the purpose of this chapter we can identify a somewhat eclectic typology of consultancy

- Project specialists

- Technologists

- Methodologists

- Programmers and systems analysts

- Management and strategy consultants

- Marketing specialists , etc ...

Figure 9.4 ITC – a professional division of labour

firms: (i) the international consultants, corporations or partnerships; (ii) the large national consultants; (iii) small national consultants; (iv) hardware producers.

INTERNATIONAL CONSULTANTS

International consultants can be divided into corporations and partnerships. But, in the case, all of them work in network configurations with multifunctional units and interprofessional teams.

Multinational partnerships have a very strong 'market-orientated' spatial structure: the functional division of labour is reproduced at the national and supra-regional level. But R & D on products and methodology as well as the organisation of the intra-firm information and communication systems are kept at the international level. The best known multinational ITC partnerships are of Anglo-Saxon or Dutch origin and have strong backgrounds in accountancy and organisation consultancy (for example, Arthur Andersen, Ernst Young, KPMG).

The multinational corporations usually have a systems house origin. Here we think in the first place of the large French systems houses like Cap Gemini Sogeti and the Sema Group which have developed 'combined functional and market orientated divisions of labour'. Through a policy of acquisition and implantation, these firms have managed to combine national or even international problem solution and sector expertise in regional markets:

We are organised in agencies (with 50–60 staff members each). Each agency serves a given territory. This territory is defined according to two or three dimensions. The first two concern the region and the type of clientele. Sometimes, a third dimension is added, corresponding to the type of expertise which is required. Ideally, if our scale would permit, we would organise our business according to four or five dimensions. As we grow, we will specialise more.

When a project can be handled with skills available at the agency, then the agency director will contractualise the project and will designate the project leader and the team, which will differ according to the skills needed. In case necessary skills are not available with the agency, the agency can rely on skills coming from other agencies, headquarters, R & D facilities, either in or outside France. We have procedures which allow the management of national and international projects assured by several agencies [largest European systems house].

This quotation should not give the impression that this firm has a spatially decentralised functional division of labour for all stages in the production chain and for all support functions. In fact, the agencies are mainly involved in design construction and implementation. They do functional analysis, but, as in the above French case for example, they often fall back on Paris offices which are specialised in strategic and functional analysis. Training is centralised in Paris, and R & D in Grenoble, Toulouse and Paris. Headquarter functions are divided among Paris, Lyons and Grenoble.

It should be noticed, however, that the spatial structure of national economies affects the spatial organisation of firms. Arthur Andersen, for example, which in general has a tendency to concentrate its activities at the supra-regional level, has a more decentralised structure in Italy because the Italian economy is, spatially speaking, less centralised than the French. So, if we compare the Arthur Andersen division of labour in France with its division of labour in Italy, the differences are explained by the differences in spatial structure of the national economies (Moulaert *et al.* 1990).

THE LARGE NATIONAL CONSULTANTS

Here we have very different sectoral origins. We have the technical engineering consultants, or the larger systems houses which were not really successful or ambitious in the international market; or we have organisation consultants who have developed significant specialised consultancy potential and activities. The spatial containment of their operations is certainly a potentially negative factor for development. But the extent to which these consultants manage to keep and develop their market 'niches' must not be underestimated as a growth factor, or even as a leverage for international market penetration. Like international consultants with a systems origin, the spatial structure of national consultancy firms whose main activities are in systems development will be more decentralised than those firms specialising in analysis and design.

SMALL, NATIONAL/REGIONAL CONSULTANTS

Many of these smaller firms originate from other service firms. A good example is that of the banks, which have developed internal data processing with specialised software to support their activities. For the same purpose, they went into consultancy; at the end, they felt strong enough to succeed in the external market. In this way, an internal EDP department transforms into an external information technology service and consultancy supplier.

Many of these ITC spinoffs do not reach far beyond regional boundaries. Most of them are active in their original, limited geographical bases and are faced with severe competition from larger consultancy firms. For those small firms, only two market strategies, preferably combined, are possible: (1) to develop a really strong market niche; (2) to join larger networks with flexible institutional settings. This would provide smaller consultancy firms with an access to large international markets.

HARDWARE PRODUCERS

The role of hardware producers in the IT consultancy and service market is considerable. As such the French Ministry of Industry found that in 1985, 24 per cent of IT engineering ('Etudes Informatiques') was supplied by electronics hardware producers (SESSI 1986). Still, hardware producers realise that they lack some of the competence to deal with the organisational aspects of what they prefer to call IT 'systems integration' – in our terminology, IT consultancy excluding strategic analysis but including construction of the IT system. The approach of hardware producers is overly centred around the integration and development of technical environments and does not devote sufficient attention to the organisational aspects of the consultancy job. There is a growing awareness of this problem. IBM and Bull (France), for example, have developed their own, be it limited, know-how with respect to strategic analysis of client business functions. But the main tendency is to seek different forms of cooperation (alliances, subcontracting – mostly on a temporary or project basis) with consultants and systems houses for strategic analysis as well as for organisational design and construction. Cooperation with systems houses (and their consultancy departments) seems to go more smoothly than with organisation and technology consultants. In fact, there is severe competition between hardware producers and large, multidisciplinary consultants for the systems integration market. In general, the functional division of labour of hardware producers involved in systems integration consists of regionally decentralised agencies for standardised design and construction and a limited number of systems integration offices for complex projects involving functional (sometimes also strategic) analysis and customised design.

Conclusion

ITC is a specialised and crucial area of the broader domain of high-technology consultancy. Its specificity lies partly in the characteristics of IT itself, and partly in its strong organisational content. Information systems have become the spine of organisations and ITC thus has a major role in the current transition to a flexible mode of production. These aspects also explain the quite rapid growth of the ITC sector and its evolution along several still converging trajectories (Moulaert *et al.* 1990).

We have also stressed that the production process of ITC must be seen as a complex interaction process between supplier and client. The features of this interaction are therefore crucial for understanding the organisational and locational dynamics of the sector. This is particularly true on the supply side. We have shown that the emphasis given by IT consultants to certain stages of the production–interaction chain (strategic and functional analysis as well as macro-design versus micro-design and construction), which is in turn influenced by sectoral origins, strongly affects the type of relationship established with the client and the corporate organisation. On the demand side, interaction is influenced by the organisational structure of the client firm, its business culture, its experience in managing professional services. Still, the different forms adopted by interaction (sparring, jobbing, designating) are mainly determined by the methodological traditions of the consultant and the stage at stake in the production–interaction chain.

Since ITC is still growing and qualitatively evolving, its functional and spatial division of labour is typically that of a developing sector: it is diversified according to its different sectors of origin, product markets, methodological traditions and institutional environments. Despite this diversity, some general observations can be made. First, there is a growing financial concentration in the sector. This follows the integration of ITC with other advanced producer services markets. Smaller consultants, who want successfully to meet the competition of the larger groups, are forced to hyperspecialise and, in order to increase the ambit of their market, to form networks with colleagues in other regional or national markets.

As to the spatial division of labour of large consultants, we observe a strong clustering of a limited number of units providing only strategic and functional analysis, methodological and technological support, R & D as well as training. However, international consultants with an engineering and organisation background, as well as an accountancy background, have a stronger tendency to cluster their operations spatially than international systems houses and hardware producers who typically serve their markets through a more spatially decentralised network of agencies. Still, the spatial structure of the market qualifies this general conclusion. In national economies with a more decentralised spatial structure (Italy, in contrast to France or the Netherlands, for example), the former type of IT consultant also adopts a stronger, specialised regional location strategy. To the extent that systems houses and hardware producers manage to conquer a larger part of the strategic and functional analysis markets, technology and organisation consultants will be forced to do construction of IT systems and provide related services. In the future, this could mean a stronger presence in second-tier economic regions.

134   F. Moulaert, F. Martinelli and F. Djellal

References

Arthur Young Conseil (1987) *Stratégie d'Entreprise et Planification du Système d'Information*, Paris, Arthur Young Conseil.
Bade, F. (1982) 'Localisation industrielle, division fonctionnelle du travail et développement régional', *Revue d'Economie Urbaine et Régionale*, **4**.
Barcet, A., Bonamy, J. and Mayere, A. (1989) details in Moulaert (1989) in the bibliography.
Chikhaoui, Y. (1988) *La croissance des conseils d'ingénierie en haute technologie en France et leur concentration spatiale: réflexions théoriques et analyse statistique*, Master's dissertation, UFR de Sciences Economiques et Sociales de Lille, October.
Dosi, G., Freeman, C., Nelson, R., Silverberg, G and Soete, L. (1988) *Technical Change and Economic Theory*, London, Pinter.
Dussauge, P. and Ramantsoe, J. (1987) *Technologie et stratégies d'entreprise*, Paris, McGraw Hill.
Eiglier, P. and Langeard, E. (1987) *Servuction, le marketing des services*, Paris, McGraw Hill.
ERMES (1988) *La demande de services complexes des firmes multinationales et l'offre correspondante, Lille*, Paris, UFR de Sciences Economiques et Sociales de Lille I, Research report for Le Commissariat Général du Plan, July.
Gadrey, J. (1988) 'Stratégie et structure des grandes entreprises et modes de recours aux services complexes' in Ermes, 1988.
Hymer, S. (1972) 'The multinational corporation and the law of uneven development' in J.N. Bhagwati (ed.), *Economics and World Order*, London, Macmillan.
Martinelli, F. (1986) *Producer services in a dependent economy: their role and potential for economic development*, Ph.D. Dissertation, Berkeley, University of California.
— (1989a) 'Services aux producteurs et développement régional' in F. Moulaert (ed.), 1989.
— (1989b) 'Struttura industriale e servizi alla produzione: un interpretazione degli squilibri regionali in Italia', *Politica Economica*, **1**, 1991, Chapter 6 in this book.
— and Moulaert, F. (1991) *Information Technology Consultancy and the Technology Diffusion Process*, working paper, Lille, CNRS/IFRESI.
Monnoyer, M.-C. and Philippe, N (1991) Chapter 8 in this book.
Moulaert, F. (ed.) (1989) *La production des services et sa géographie*, special volume of *Cahiers Lillois d'Economie et de Sociologie*.
— Chikhaoui, Y. and Djellal, F. (1988) Les conseils en ingénierie informatique et de (télé)communications, in Ermes, 1988.
— (1991) 'Locational Behavior of French High Tech Consultancy Firms', *International Journal of Urban and Regional Research*, **15**, 1.
— Martinelli, F. and Djellal, F. (1990) *The Role of Information Technology Consultancy in the Transfer of Information Technology to Production and Service Organizations*, The Hague, NOTA.
— and Djellal, F. (1990) *Les conseils en technologie de l'information: des économies d'agglomération en réseau*, paper presented at the Conference on 'Metropoles in Disequilibrium', Lyons.
Tordoir, P. and Gadrey, J. (1988) 'Buying the overheads: effective management, of professional services in a changing corporate environment, paper presented to the 8th Annual Strategic Management Science Conference, Amsterdam.
SESSI, Ministry of Industry (1986–8) *Ingénierie, etudes et conseils*, Paris, Enquête Annuelle de Branche.

10 Producer services and the development of the space economy

P.W. Daniels L80 L89

R12

Introduction

Uncertainty and suspicion about the consequences for advanced economies for the decline in industrial employment and the increased proportion of jobs in the service sector is still prevalent. For example, the
creation of tangible goods creates wealth but services are 'parasitic' and
therefore responsible for reducing national wealth (see for example,
Bacon and Eltis 1976). Another view is that the rise of services is partly
an illusion; externalisation of demand by manufacturing firms for services formerly produced in-house 'creates' service employment which
really only represents a transfer from the secondary sector (Gershuny
and Miles 1983).

Whatever the correct interpretation there is also a close association
between services and manufacturing (as well as other services) since the
goods produced by the latter, for example, would have little value
unless they are designed to meet the needs of the market, transported to
that market, advertised, sold and subsequently serviced or upgraded as
appropriate. Advanced telecommunications and information technology has allowed services to offer a diversified and often highly
specialised range of inputs to markets which are themselves becoming
more demanding as manufacturers and other services endeavour to
make or package more sophisticated and useful goods/services. Most
notable in this context are producer (or intermediate) services which
have recently emerged as a fruitful area for research on their development, organisation, location behaviour and contribution to spatial differentiation in economic development and within cities and regions.

Some of the preliminary results of a recently completed project[1] on the
growth and location of large professional producer service firms in the
United Kingdom will be outlined in this chapter. This is followed by a
short summary of some of the empirical findings of a study of the supply
and demand for producer services at a local level in Merseyside (Daniels
1986c). The chapter concludes with a short overview of some of the
outstanding research questions arising from the relationship between
the development of producer services and the evolution of the space
economy.

Studies of service development continue to be retarded by inconsistencies in the definitions and classifications used. The debate about whether their recent emergence is symbolic of a post-industrial or a de-industrialised phase in advanced economies also persists (Dyckman 1986; Gershuny and Miles 1983; Blackaby 1979; Browning and Singelmann 1975; Bell 1973; Marshall *et al.* 1988). In view of the heterogeneous character of the service sector the task is complex and inevitably difficult. Therefore, for the present it has been necessary to try to comprehend the role of services in urban and regional development through the growing number of useful but disparate studies aimed at particular questions or problems pertinent to each national context. Meanwhile, it is questionable whether the search for a universal service classifications will reap the benefits equivalent to the effort expended; the diversity, and more important, the dynamism of activities to which we attach the general label 'services' ensures that any classification is quickly outdated. Certainly, such work should take place in parallel with rather than as a pre-requisite for empirical studies of the economic and social effects of the transformation to service-based economies. Any emphasis given to empirical research should not of course be at the expense of developing more concise theories of tertiary development, but there seems a great deal still to achieve in this direction (Moulaert and Dyckman 1986).

Producer services are especially prone to problems of this kind; yet they are emerging as one of the key actors in perpetuating uneven development within space economies (Marshall *et al.* 1988; Daniels 1986a). Employment in these services has grown rapidly (Noyelle and Stanback 1984; Daniels and Thrift 1986) in response to the growing demand for manufacturing and other services for the advertising, marketing, management consultancy, financial services or computer-orientated assistance, for example, required as intermediate input from specialist suppliers. Such services are tradeable, both within organisations and on the open market, and they must therefore make location decisions which ensure that they can adequately supply both existing and potential clientele. It is clear from the research already completed (see for example Noyelle and Stanback 1984; Noyelle 1985; Daniels 1986b; Ley and Hutton 1987) that these decisions have tended to favour large and complex metropolitan economies at the expense of smaller, older and often peripheral cities with an industrial infrastructure dominated by artifacts of the Industrial Revolution. London, New York, Tokyo, Paris and Sydney are attracting new producer services or experiencing the expansion of existing services at a much higher rate than Liverpool, Detroit, Osaka, Lyons or Newcastle (New South Wales). This process is also enhancing the dualism which seems to characterise the space economies of states with highly centralised political and institutional structures such as Britain or France, where areas already relatively favoured by a slower decline in manufacturing employment are also tending to benefit from the influence of agglomeration on the location and growth of producer services. The growth of activities associated with the City of London such as the expansion of international banking (Daniels 1986b; Leyson *et al.* 1987c) also underwrites concentration of related producer services. Centralisation of ownership of service and manufacturing corporations further constrains the demand for producer services in provincial areas.

Concurrently, however, there are indications that improved telecommunications systems are permitting the more routine functions performed within producer-services firms to adopt less central locations, but the majority of these 'back office' operations remain in the same metropolitan area as the headquarters. As Moss and Dunau (1986) have shown there are, however, differences between sectors; insurance companies have dispersed more extensively from metropolitan areas such as New York or Chicago than securities firms or the banking industry. Other research by Marshall (1982, 1983), Polese (1982) and Beyers *et al.* (1986) has highlighted the weaker than expected dependence of producer services on linkages with manufacturing and the significant, and growing, contribution of producer services to the basic (export) economy of regions or cities.

Producer services and the space economy: some recent research

Professional producer services: accountancy

A study, recently completed, on the operations of the largest indigenous and foreign-owned producer service firms in the United Kingdom focuses on seven types of firm which are unambiguously orientated towards the corporate sector: merchant/investment banks; general practice activities of chartered surveyors; engineering consultancies and architectural design firms; accountancy firms; advertising agencies, management consultancies; business information companies; and corporate legal practices. Among a number of features examined are the organizational and spatial patterns of growth of these firms and the ways in which their evolving spatial structure has mediated the growth of employment and output through its influence on demand, marketing ability or general adaptability to changing market conditions. Accountancy services will be used as a case study example.

TRENDS IN THE DEVELOPMENT OF LARGE ACCOUNTANCY FIRMS

Large accountancy firms have played a prominent part in the rapid overall growth of accountancy since 1960 (Leyshon *et al.* 1987a). It is possible to identify a number of trends in the evolution of this sector, some of which are not mutually exclusive, and these can be summarised as follows:

(i)   **concentration**: primarily explicable in terms of merger activity by client firms leading to merger of accountancy firms.

(ii)   **internationalisation**: the trend towards concentration is partially a function of the move towards an international operating scale in the activities of the largest firms, some of which have also become 'dominants' in national economies. The largest international accountancy firms are the so-called 'Big Nine' (recently reduced to the 'Big Six', see Noyelle, Chapter 12): Arthur Anderson; Arthur Young; Coopers and Lybrand; Deloitte, Haskins and Sells; Ernst and Whinney; Klynveld Main Goerdler; Peat Marwick Mitchell; Price Waterhouse; and Touche Ross. The roots of six of these firms can be traced to the City of London, although in all cases the North American partners are now in the majority.

(iii) **diversification**: large accountancy firms reveal an increasing willingness to provide an ever-widening range of specialised services provided that they will earn fee income. The growth of management consultancy is particularly notable.

(iv)   **corporate finance**: large accounting firms are moving into areas of the corporate finance market previously exclusively covered by the merchant banks, providing advice on takeovers and mergers or preparing companies for the Unlisted Securities Market listings.

(v)   **tax**: provision of tax and related advisory services following the steady increase in fiscal legislation since the 1960s. These services provide a useful initial contact with clients which often lead to the provision of other services. It is also much more profitable than auditing.

(vi)   **litigation**: growing involvement in financial systems has exposed the large accountancy firms to negligence claims. All the companies take out indemnity insurance against such claims. A number of attempts at cross-border litigation has stimulated the large firms to re-assess their 'world firm' policy, a number preferring to enhance the regional autonomy of national practices within the world firm's monitoring of quality control.

(vii) **automation**: information technology has contributed to reduced service production costs, an improvement in the quality of service and a diversification of the services provided. Computing was used initially for internal purposes; more recently it has been extended to client services such as bookkeeping, management of accounts, calculation of accounts from incomplete records or advice on selection and implementation of computer systems. The latter offers the prospect of compatibility between client and accountant's computer systems, leading to more efficient audits and scope for developing new sources of fee income.

EXPANSION OF UNITED KINGDOM OFFICE NETWORKS

These trends in the organisation and range of services offered by large accountancy firms, together with a steady growth of employment and fee income, provide the context for an exploration of their location behaviour (Leyshon *et al.* 1987b). The number of offices in the United

Kingdom operated by the 20 largest accountancy firms between 1975 and 1985 increased by 63 per cent (302 to 492) with many of them more than doubling the number of offices forming part of their networks. The development of these networks (see Figure 10.1) suggests that colonisation of areas not formerly served has been an important part of location strategy. A total of 128 locations were served by some or all of the leading firms in 1975; by 1985 offices had been opened in 83 entirely new locations with only 23 locations recording a net loss of offices. Concentration indices (see Figure 10.1) show that London was the only city with offices representing all 20 firms, but by 1985 all the large, as well as some smaller, provincial cities recorded substantial increases in concentration (most notably Aberdeen, Norwich and Edinburgh) as the leading firms established offices there for the first time. At the regional scale there was a differential rate of growth in favour of the southeast (+39 offices), the southwest (+24), East Anglia (+23) and Scotland (+29). The increase in East Anglia represents an almost five-fold increase from the five offices located there in 1975. Thus, although there have been absolute increases in the number of offices of the top 20 accountants in the provincial regions, such as the northwest, Wales, the northern region and Yorkshire and Humberside, their share of the national total has actually decreased overall.

It is clear that certain localities within each region are preferred for new office openings, mainly in and around the large cities. At least four reasons may be advanced for this location behaviour. First, each of the major firms is trying to protect or even to enhance its share of a growing market. As competitors develop their office networks, those with less comprehensive coverage tend to follow; prior to 1950 some firms were entirely based in London and are therefore now trying to catch up. Second, related to protection of market share is a desire to identify and exploit locations with business development opportunities. As the analysis of development trends in accountancy practice has shown, the large firms are positively seeking new clients and creating markets for new services. Thus, the expansion of high-technology manufacturing in the Thames Valley and in the vicinity of Cambridge, or the expansion of the offshore oil production industry in Aberdeen has been associated with an increase in the number of major accountancy firms represented in these areas. A third explanation is provided by the pull exerted by small firms which are a potentially valuable source of fee income that will compensate for the falling volume of audit fees from large companies (Leyshon et al. 1987a). The threshold for establishing new offices has therefore fallen and makes it possible for the large firms to begin operations in places where they do not already have any major clients (The Accounting Bulletin 1983). An expansion of public-sector work is the fourth factor contributing to the changing geography of accountants' office networks, especially the increased representation in the major cities.

It has been more difficult to establish the impact of the expansion of office networks on employment distribution. More than 40,000 staff were employed by the leading 20 accountancy firms in 1986. It has,

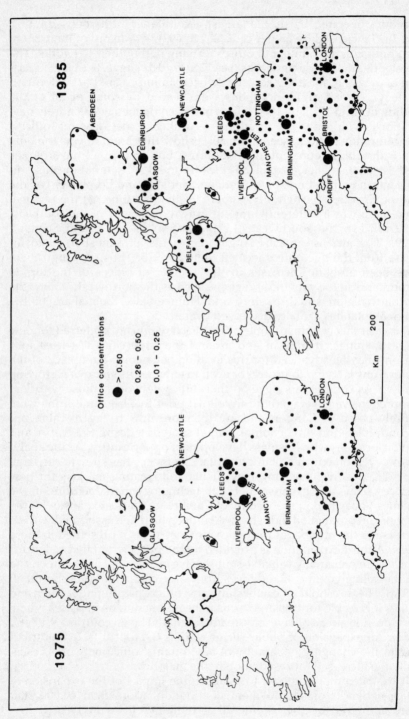

Figure 10.1 Offices operated by the top-20 accountancy firms in the UK

however, only been possible to obtain a regional disaggregation of employment for four of these firms in 1985. In these instances the southeast region was the location for more than 50 per cent of their total United Kingdom employees, with the majority located in London offices. When partners are separated from the overall figures it emerges that the bias towards the southeast is exaggerated further: 80 per cent of the partners were based there, with the majority again operating from offices in London. However, the limited evidence currently available suggests that the proportion of London-based partners remained constant between 1975 and 1985 so that the national spread of offices was accompanied by limited relative dispersal of partners.

OVERSEAS EXPANSION OF LARGE UNITED KINGDOM ACCOUNTANCY FIRMS

A significant expansion of international activities has accompanied the development of the domestic office networks of the major accounting firms. Their emergence as multinational or transnational service conglomerates (Clairmonte and Cavanagh 1984), employing more than 300,000 in 1986, has not in many instances, however, been a recent phenomenon. It has been a two-stage process: the first stage comprised an initial period of internationalisation (1890–9) during which accounting firms operating from the City of London followed the movement of British capital overseas. The second stage, covering a more contemporary period (1960 to present) has seen the formation of international partnerships as the basis for advancing multinational activities. The setting up of partnerships between British and American firms was a frequent event during the early part of this phase but, more recently, European partnerships have been formed, such as Klynveld Main Goerdler and Binder Djiker Otte. During this second stage, merger has been the preferred strategy for developing the overseas office networks of the leading British accountancy firms. This has not only increased overseas representation of participant firms but has also provided the infrastructure allowing systematic entry to previously unserved national markets. An example is provided by Coopers and Lybrand: four key firms within the group have responsibility for developing business in specific geographic areas such as the South Pacific region (Australia) and South America and the Far East (United States). Each key firm is required to identify areas where Coopers and Lybrand should be represented in their geographic area and to select a suitable local firm with which the international firm can enter into an association, merger or takeover. Alternatively, they may recommend that a new firm be created to serve a particular location. Hence, the international office network of Coopers and Lybrand increased from 35 offices (1,000 employees) in 1950 to 352 offices (22,500) employees in 1979. The international network of Deloitte, Haskins and Sells (see Figure 10.2) was created following the merger of the American practice of Haskins and Sells with the British accountants Deloitte, Plender, Griffiths and Co. in 1952.

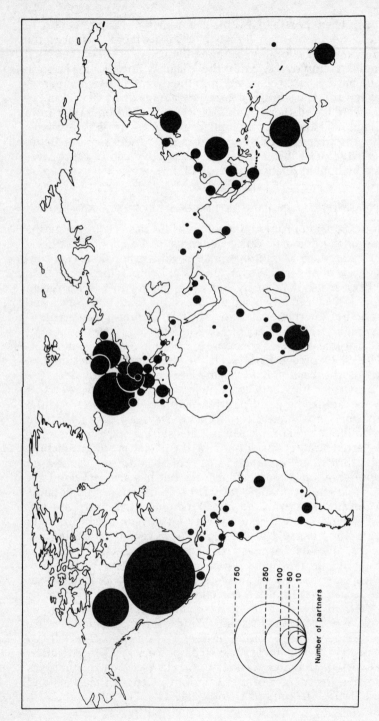

Figure 10.2 Deloitte, Haskins and Sells, international world distribution of offices and number of partners, 1986

Although mergers are the preferred strategy (Leyshon *et al.* 1987b), they are not always necessary or possible. National firms may in some cases be invited to join in a representative or correspondent capacity; integration in these circumstances is low compared with a full merger but this may take place later if, for example, an accounting group wants to consolidate its presence. In other cases mergers may not be practicable because suitable local firms do not exist; international firms may then be forced to set up entirely new offices which will eventually take control of their own operations in a way consistent with the profit centre mode of operation practised by the leading accountancy conglomerates (Leyshon *et al.* 1987a).

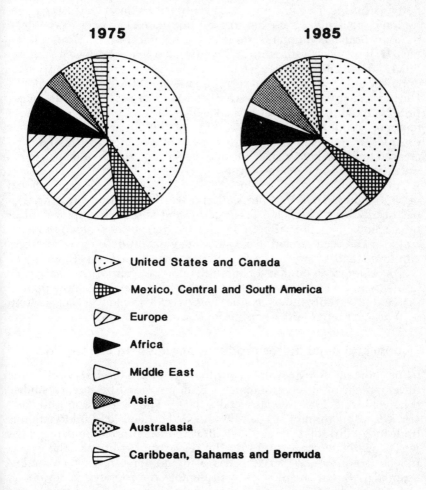

Figure 10.3 Worldwide distribution of offices of the top-20 accountancy firms in the United Kingdom

The total number of overseas offices operated by the leading 20 British accountancy firms more than doubled between 1975 and 1985 from 2,323 to 4,991. All eight regions shown in Figure 10.3 experienced an absolute increase in the number of offices with the United States, Canada and Europe as the key locations with more than two-thirds of the total in 1975 and 1985. However, Europe had more offices than North America following the opening of more than 1,000 establishments during the decade by the leading 20 British firms. Much of this growth (32 per cent) was concentrated in the Netherlands and the United Kingdom. The largest relative increases (290 per cent) took place in Asia and Australasia (138 per cent). Overall, the development of the overseas office network has been proportionally greater than the domestic office network during the same period. This not only reflects increasing penetration of new markets but also the late adoption of an overseas strategy by some British accountants; three of the 20 largest British firms did not have any overseas offices in 1975 and four others had fewer than ten offices. The 'follow-the-leader' syndrome typical of the expansion of domestic office networks also seems to operate at the international level. During recent years the large-scale international presence of the major British accounting groups was matched by a new generation of multinational accounting firms. Thus, nine of the 20 largest British firms operated 88 per cent of all the overseas offices in 1975; this had decreased to 71 per cent in 1985 despite the steady growth of international operations among the largest firms.

The consolidation of accountancy services into large international networks dominated by European and North American firms has not necessarily been paralleled by an equivalent spread of employment or transactional benefits. Although in relative terms the position of North America has been eroded, it remains pre-eminent in terms of numbers employed and share of fee income. Hence, between 1981 and 1985 North America accounted for more than 50 per cent of the chargeable hours (world-wide) logged by Peat Marwick Mitchel while more than 75 per cent of Arthur Andersen's net fees (world-wide) in 1985 came from American earnings; an increase from 69 per cent in 1981.

Supply and demand for producer services on Merseyside

Some more specific answers about the role of producer services in the development of space economies will be provided by locality studies (Marshall *et al.* 1988; see also Cooke 1986). The output from producer services in the form of specialised knowledge, skills and information is tradeable with other industries within the same urban area/region as well as with purchasers outside the region and overseas. The export function of producer services has also, until recently, been underestimated. But there remains considerable uncertainty, for example, about the significance of the spatial imbalance in the development of producer services (of the kind illustrated above for accountancy services) for peripheral localities with an outmoded industrial infrastructure and which have failed to attract the kinds of economic activities accompanying structural changes at the national level. One such area in the United Kingdom is Merseyside which has recently been the subject of an exploratory study of aspects of the supply and demand for producer services (Daniels 1986c; see also Hubbard and Nutter 1982).

Goddard (1978) has stressed that the availability at the local level of the kind of information and advice provided by producer services is vital to the future economic performance of lagging regions. Yet, apart from some information relating to the interdependence between manufacturing industries and business services (Marshall 1982, 1983), we remain poorly informed about the supply and demand for producer services. If Merseyside firms are to be able to retain their comparative advantage they will require knowledge of, and an easily accessible supply of, producer services. Unless these are available in the locality (within the urban area or sub-region) the cost of obtaining them – such as travel time to meetings, delays caused by the inability of the client and supplier to meet as often as required, or simply lack of knowledge – may be a sufficient deterrent to limit utilisation or, more seriously, to prevent use altogether. This may cause firms to grow more slowly or even to cease production because of their inability to compete with firms located in cities with readier access to a more comprehensive pool of producer services. Some of the results of the Merseyside study are very briefly outlined here; it must be stressed that the research has been designed initially to assess the practicalities of obtaining supply and demand information from service and manufacturing firms. The choice of Merseyside has been a matter of convenience but, given that more than 200 firms participated in a telephone survey and more than 50 firms responded to a longer postal questionnaire, there are some interesting findings that suggest it would be worthwhile implementing a more rigorous study of the supply and demand for producer services on Merseyside and contrasting localities.

In common with a number of other recent studies (Pederson 1985; Beyers et al. 1986; Ley and Hutton 1987; Bailly et al. 1987), the myth that producer service performance at locality level is dependent upon demand from manufacturing is again dispelled. Even in this study, in which the majority of establishments are small (less than 5 employees) the export function is clearly significant. Producer services in general are perceived as a useful input to the activities of Merseyside firms, but there is a distinction between ubiquitous and specialized demand: the former applies to insurance, banking or some aspect of accounting while the latter relates to producer services required infrequently (but often intensively) such as computer services, advertising, marketing or management consultancy. Large firms were more likely than small firms to use specialised services although many establishments had used the full range of services specified for the study on at least one occasion during the last two years (see Table 10.1).

Externalisation of demand for intermediate services, whether ubiquitous or specialised, has largely focused on local suppliers rather than

Table 10.1 Necessity for intermediate services for conduct of business, by size of establishment and sector

| | Size of establishment and sector | | | | | |
| | Services | | | Manufacturing | | |
Services	< 5	6–40	> 41	<5	6–40	>41
Accounting and bookkeeping	96*	97	100	96	100	100
Advertising	47	52	75	36	63	78
Computing	22	57	100	20	56	78
Insurance	85	97	100	96	97	100
Legal services	46	72	88	48	59	67
Marketing	33	55	50	40	41	78
Transport services	49	59	50	88	91	100
Management consultancy	13	25	13	4	13	22
Banking, credit etc.	96	99	100	100	100	100
Eng. and archit. services	28	35	25	56	66	89
Training	35	79	100	32	72	89
Research & development	13	27	25	20	50	78
Number of establishments in each size group	72	71	8	25	32	9

Source: Telephone survey, Nov–Dec 1985; Jan–Feb 1986

* Proportion of all establishments in size group indicating service necessary for conduct of business

leakage to other parts of the country. This runs counter to the expectations created by earlier studies; even establishments with head offices outside Merseyside, especially in London and the southeast, do not reveal a strong orientation towards those locations for producer service purchases. Service establishments show this attribute more strongly than manufacturing establishments. Suppliers in the southeast and London were, however, used by some firms for specialised services such as advertising and marketing. Leakage of expenditure on purchases outside Merseyside was not substantial although it proved difficult for establishments to disaggregate their accounts in a way that could provide absolute values for such flows.

Most Merseyside establishments spent 10–20 per cent of their total expenditure on all inputs on the purchase of producer services. As a proportion of total expenditure the sums involved were increasing, especially among manufacturing establishments. It is likely that, because of their functional attributes, service establishments are able to internalize some of their requirements, especially for some of the ubiquitous producer services. Manufacturing establishments are unlikely to be able to respond in this way. Hence, small single-site manufacturers were increasing expenditure on producer services such as advertising as their turnover grew or new products required promotion in new or larger markets. Producer services may indeed be a pre-requisite for the effective assembly of a good or service, but increased expenditures by users should be interpreted carefully since they may only arise from higher charges for specialised services. More detailed information is required on the types of producer services actually purchased and for what purposes as better measures of cost trends.

Proximity is less important for the choice of producer service suppliers than expected. Many establishments did not mention it at all, although for ubiquitous services such as banking it was certainly cited more frequently than for specialised services. Business inertia, that is dependence on suppliers 'always used', emerges as the main explanation for choice; in the absence of comparative evidence it is difficult to know whether this is a feature peculiar to Merseyside firms. Cost factors are not significant, perhaps because the narrow range of suppliers on Merseyside provide very limited opportunities to assess supply on the basis of this factor and so create downward pressure on prices. The alternative is to compare costs from suppliers outside Merseyside, but since this involves further expenditure of time and effort it is an exercise which the predominantly small firms in this study were not disposed to undertake. Since there is a great deal of inertia in choice of supplier, together with limited leakage of demand outside Merseyside, it is difficult for local producer service firms to develop unless they endeavour to enter markets outside the locality.

Thus, some 20 per cent of Merseyside establishments generating intermediate output export to other locations. Most are service-sector firms and they serve a much more extensive geographical area than manufacturing establishments; locations in the United Kingdom outside London and the southeast, together with some overseas locations, are particularly prominent. In general, however, there is a clearly developed distance decay component, also found by Pederson (1985) for Ejsberg, with demand from clients in Manchester and the northwest absorbing the largest share of the exported services. A growing reliance on exports is corroborated by the larger proportion of service establishments, irrespective of size, that indicated a declining demand for their output from other Merseyside firms. The decreases were linked to the reduction over a number of years in commercial and manufacturing activity on Merseyside, loss of confidence in the economy because of political uncertainties in the area (especially in Liverpool) and difficulties associated with Merseyside's image. Establishments faced with decreasing demand from Merseyside firms were not shedding labour; most had been trying to compensate for this decline by seeking clients outside the area. This is clearly desirable because the benefits will accrue in large part to the Merseyside economy but there is always a risk that firms making a successful adjustment will re-locate to be nearer their markets in other parts of the country.

Producer service dynamics and the space economy: further research

Existing research on producer services has largely concentrated on selected, and certainly, very limited, themes of the kind illustrated here. Marshall *et al.* (1988) identified a number of topics considered worthy of further investigation in the interests of a better understanding of the mechanisms that shape the location and dynamics of producer services in advanced economies. An initial hurdle continues to be the paucity of suitable official statistics; an improvement in the statistical data base is a fundamental requirement for research in most countries (the research currently taking place in Switzerland may well provide the way forward for more effective use of existing official statistics as well as providing new possibilities, see Bailly *et al.* 1986). In the absence of a major improvement in official statistics Marshall *et al.* (1988) suggest that future research should concentrate on primary date generation together with more intensive exploitation of the large volume of literature, including specialised archives, available from trade and professional associations, consultancy organisations or specialist publications on producer services.

Aspects of the demand and supply for producer services also require much more work. Issues such as the changing structure of demand for white- and blue-collar services, the decision-making process in respect of internal versus external consumption of producer services with reference to large/small firm differentials or private/public sector contrasts or the precise attributes (if any) of the strategic role of producer in the adoption, adaptation or innovation activities of services and manufacturing are just a few of the items that would enable a fuller appreciation of the changing demand environment. On the supply side relatively little is known about the effects of organisational change, the perception of client needs and how to respond to them, the ways in which suppliers adapt to changes in the sectoral or geographical characteristics of their markets or whether the availability of producer services does actually help the performance of client firms. Supply and demand questions can be usefully addressed either at the level of sector (individual producer service) studies or within the framework of localities; the latter is advocated by Marshall *et al.* (1988) as a priority for the detailed monitoring of changes in producer service activity and their economies.

Other priorities for research include: the nature of producer service employment (in particular the processes of employment change); the impacts of technological change on employment in producer services and on the demand for these services; the degree to which the structure of producer service organisations will reflect the adoption of information technology; and the effectiveness of policies for producer services' development in problem regions or cities finding it difficult to adjust to the post-industrial economy (Daniels 1987). It is also necessary to analyse the processes involved in the internationalisation of producer services since the locational outcomes undoubtedly have significant impacts on national scale space economies (Daniels and Thrift 1986;

Howells and Green 1986; Key 1985).

It is likely that there are significant local multipliers, in the form of demand for other producer services, direct employment or final consumption (for example the local housing market or retail services) that enhance the comparative advantage of core regions and major financial centres in particular (Friedmann and Wolff 1982; Leyshon *et al.* 1987c). Much remains to be researched with reference to the importance of the national and international offices created through the recent expansion of accountancy services; number of staff, partner status, patterns of work referral, degree of specialisation are indices that can be used to establish the status of individual offices in the organisational hierarchy and the implications for the spatial division of labour. It is also necessary to examine the linkages typical of large accountancy firms as a further mechanism for understanding their growth and location strategies.

Note

1. The project, on the location of large professional producer service firms in Britain, was funded by the Economic and Social Research Council (Grant No. D0023 2194). The research was conducted jointly with Professor N.J. Thrift, University of Bristol with Dr Andrew Leyshon, now at the University of Hull, as the project's Research Assistant.

References

Accounting Bulletin (1983) 'Accountants poised to dominate consulting market', November, pp. 6–10.

Bacon, R. and Eltis, W. (1976) *Britain's Economic Problem: Too Few Producers*, London, Macmillan.

Bailly, A.S. *et al.*, (1986) 'New "articulations" of the systems of production and role of services: a comparative international analysis', Lausanne, CEAT.

— Maillat, D. and Coffey, W.J. (1987) 'Service activities and regional development: some European examples, *Environment and Planning A*, **19**, pp. 653–68.

Bell, D. (1973) *The Coming of Post-Industrial Society*, London, Heinemann.

Beyers, W.B., Tofflemire, J.M., Stranahan, H.A. and Johnsen, E.G. (1986) *The Service Economy: Understanding the Growth of Producer Services in the Puget Sound Region*, Seattle.

Blackaby, F. (ed) (1979) *Deindustrialization*, London, Heinemann.

Browning, H.C. and Singelmann, J. (1975) *The Emergence of a Service Society*, Springfield, Va, National Technical Information Service.

Clairmonte, F. and Cavanagh, J. (1984) 'Transnational corporations and services: the final frontier', *Trade and Development*, **5**, pp. 215–73.

Cooke, P. (ed) (1986) *Global Restructuring, Local Response*, London, Economic and Social Research Council.

Daniels, P.W. (1986a) 'Producer services and the post-industrial space economy' in R. Martin and R. Rowthorn (eds) *Deindustrialization in Britain*, London, Cambridge University Press.

— (1986b) 'Foreign banks and metropolitan development: a comparison of London and New York, *Tijdschrift voor Economische en Sociale Geografie*, **77**.

— (1986c) *The Supply and Demand for Intermediate Services on Merseyside*, Department of Geography, University of Liverpool.

— (1987) 'Producer services research: a lengthening agenda', *Environment and Planning A*, **19**, pp. 569–71.

— Leyshon, A. and Thrift, N.J. (1986) 'Producer Services in an International Context' in *Uneven Development in the Service Economy: Understanding the Location and Role of Producer Services*, Institute of British Geographers Producer Services Working Party, University of Birmingham.

Dyckman, J.W. (1986) 'The program of research', in Coppieters *et al.*, *The Functions of Services and the Theoretical Approach to National and International Classifications*, Lille, Johns Hopkins European Centre for Regional Planning and Research, pp. 1–16.

Friedmann, J. and Wolff, G. (1982) 'World city formation: an agenda for action', *International Journal of Urban and Regional Research*, **3**, pp. 309–94.

Gershuny, J. and Miles, I. (1983) *The New Service Economy: The Transformation of Employment in Industrial Societies*, London, Pinter Publishers.

Goddard, J.B. (1978) 'The location of non-manufacturing occupations within manu-facturing industries' in F.E.I. Hamilton (ed), *Contemporary Industrialization: Spatial Analysis and Regional Development*, London, Longman.

Howells, J. and Green, A.E. (1986) 'Location, technology and industrial organization in U.K. services', *Progress in Planning*, **26**, pp. 83–184.

Hubbard, R.K.B. and Nutter, D.S. (1982) 'Service sector employment in Merseyside', *Geoforum*, **13**, pp. 209–35.

Key, T.S.T. (1985) 'Services in the U.K. economy', *Bank of England Quarterly Review*, **25**, pp. 404–14.

Ley, D. and Hutton T. (1987) 'Vancouver's corporate complex and producer service sector: linkages and divergence within a provincial staples economy', *Regional Studies*, **20**. 1987, **21**, 413–22.

Leyshon, A., Daniels, P.W., and Thrift, N.J. (1987a) *Large Accountancy Firms in the UK: Operational Adaptation and Spatial Development*, Working Papers on Producer Services, No. 2, University of Liverpool and St. David's University College, Lampeter.

— (1987b) *Internationalization of Professional Producer Services: The Case of Large Accountancy Firms*, Working Papers on Producer Services, No. 3, University of Liverpool and St. David's University College, Lampeter.

— (1987c) *The Urban and Regional Consequences of the Restructuring of World Financial Markets: The Case of the City of London*, Working Papers on Producer Services, No. 4, University of Bristol and University of Liverpool.

Marshall, J.N. (1982) 'Linkages between manufacturing industry and business ser-vices', *Environment and Planning A*, **14**, pp. 523–40.

— (1983) 'Business service activities in British provincial conurbations', *Environment and Planning A*, **15**, pp. 343–59.

Marshall, J.N., Wood, P., Daniels, P.W., McKinnon, A., Bachtler, J., Damesick, P., Thrift, N., Gillespie, A., Green, A., and Leyshon, A. (1988) *Services and Uneven Development*, Oxford, Oxford University Press.

Moss, M.L. and Dunau, A. (1986) *The Location of Back Offices: Emerging Trends and Development Patterns*, New York, New York University Sylvan Lawrence Research and Data Center.

Moulaert, F. and Dyckman, J. (1986) 'Towards a theoretical model of tertiary develop-ment', Paper presented at 26th European Congress of the Regional Science Association, Krakow, 26–29 August.

Noyelle, T.J. (1985) *New Technologies and Services: Impacts on Cities and Jobs*, College Park, University of Maryland Institute for Urban Studies.

Noyelle, T.J. and Stanback, T.M. (1984) *The Economic Transformation of American Cities*, Totowa NJ, Allanheld.

Pederson, P.O. (1985) *The Role of Esbjerg as a Business Service Centre*, FS No. 19, Brussels, FAST Programme.

Polese, M. (1982) 'Regional demand for business services and inter-regional service flows in a small Canadian region', *Papers of the Regional Science Association*, **50**, 151–63.

11 Branch plants and services underdevelopment in peripheral regions: the case of southern Italy[1]

Flavia Martinelli

R 12

R 32

L 80

Italy

R 58

Introduction

In Chapters 2 and 6 of this book the following argument was developed: (i) producer services are largely an outcome of the increased technical and social division of labour occurring within production, as a consequence of the growing size of modern corporations, the increasing internationalisation of linkages and competition and the development of new information technology; (ii) as such their development and location must be considered a prime function of demand, that is the extent and structure of the productive system constituting their market. In this respect, a relevant role in explaining the relative development of producer services in a region is played by the corporate characteristics of firms; (iii) the development and location of producer services influence in turn the performance of regions and reinforce an international division of labour in which peripheral regions are left with the least value-added activities.

In this chapter, as an illustration of the above mechanism and, more precisely of the negative impact of branch plants on the development of producer services in peripheral regions, empirical evidence on the case of the Mezzogiorno – the historically lagging southern region of Italy – is presented.

Industrial structure and producer services underdevelopment in the Mezzogiorno

Since the end of World War II the economic structure of the Mezzogiorno has experienced a profound transformation, partly as a consequence of four decades of government intervention and partly because of the accelerated process of integration within the national and international economy. Among the most visible structural changes one must record the quite rapid shift in the sectoral composition of the regional economy, from agriculture to manufacturing and services.

However, despite the above important changes, the lag *vis-à-vis* the rest of Italy has remained high. According to recent estimates (Svimez 1987), the per capita gross regional product of the Mezzogiorno in 1986 was still little over half that of north-central Italy (59.2 per cent), the official rate of unemployment double (16.6 per cent against 8.3 per cent) and the region remained a net importer of goods and services (17 per cent of the gross regional product). Despite its growth, manufacturing value added represented only 19 per cent of total regional value added, compared to 35 per cent in the rest of the country. Moreover, aggregate labour productivity remained substantially lower, especially in manufacturing (74 per cent of the north-central value).

Although the Mezzogiorno cannot be considered poor anymore, underdevelopment cannot be ruled out. It only has different features. The peculiar patterns of transformation of the last decades have indeed generated a still fragile and dependent productive structure, quite distinct from a model of self-sustained integration (Giannola 1982, 1987a; Vinci 1984; Martinelli 1985; Dunford 1986).

Two features of this new form of underdevelopment are particularly relevant here: (a) the dependent and dualistic character of the regional *manufacturing structure*; and (b) the underdevelopment of a crucial sector of contemporary economic development – *producer services*.

The Mezzogiorno's manufacturing structure

Although in the last decades the manufacturing industry of the Mezzogiorno has experienced important structural transformations and its employment has recorded – especially in the 1970s – a significant growth (Giannola 1987a), the overall weight of this sector in the regional economy remains low (19 per cent of total regional value added in 1986 compared to 35 per cent in the rest of the country; cf. Svimez 1987). As has been extensively demonstrated (Graziani 1977; Del Monte and Giannola 1978; Del Monte 1984; Martinelli 1985; Giannola 1987a), a determinant role in these changes was played by exogenous investments, that is the location in the region of branch establishments by large national (especially state-owned) and multinational corporations. These ventures formed the bulk of manufacturing investment in the south from the early 1960s to the mid-1970s and contributed to the formation of a nucleus of 'modern' sectors, previously absent. As is also well known, however, this type of investment, although creating new employment and sustaining regional income, generated only limited developmental effects in terms of local linkages. Moreover, competition from northern producers contributed to undermining the traditional local industry (Graziani 1977; Graziani and Pugliese 1979; Giannola 1982). The lack of programmes geared to strengthening the local business structure, coupled with the policy of incentives to exogenous investment, has eventually engendered in the region a strongly dependent and dualistic[2] manufacturing structure.

Table 11.1 Distribution of manufacturing employment in the Mezzogiorno by industry and ownership of establishments[1], 1980, (%)

Ownership Industries	State	Non-southern North	Foreign	Total	Southern	Total plants
Traditional	**12.52**	**19.60**	**6.49**	**38.61**	**61.39**	**100.00**
Food	10.86	14.51	10.50	35.87	64.13	100.00
Textile	25.51	35.72	6.24	67.47	32.53	100.00
Clothing	13.15	16.18	2.73	32.06	67.94	100.00
Footwear	0.82	9.66	–	10.48	89.52	100.00
Furniture	0.00	14.19	0.22	14.41	85.59	100.00
Printing and publishing	3.92	12.68	7.61	24.21	75.79	100.00
Leather	–	3.43	–	3.43	96.57	100.00
Stone, clay and glass products	8.94	23.97	7.50	40.40	59.60	100.00
Lumber processing	2.78	9.58	3.63	15.99	84.01	100.00
Metalworking	20.16	20.81	8.89	49.86	50.14	100.00
Modern	**36.70**	**33.59**	**13.42**	**83.71**	**16.29**	**100.00**
Pharmaceuticals	–	37.40	49.39	86.80	13.20	100.00
Ordnance	–	23.59	41.55	65.14	34.86	100.00
Machinery	12.75	38.24	4.27	55.26	44.74	100.00
Electromechanical equipment	10.72	59.07	9.31	79.10	20.90	100.00
Electronics	43.23	14.53	39.49	97.25	2.75	100.00
Transportation equipment	49.65	32.89	3.50	86.04	13.96	100.00
Precision instruments	8.11	19.63	34.26	62.00	38.00	100.00
Paper and cardboard	18.57	41.39	5.01	64.97	35.03	100.00
Rubber and plastics	5.34	45.49	14.50	65.33	34.67	100.00
Chemicals	30.94	43.37	12.53	86.85	13.15	100.00
Petroleum	9.81	61.17	15.84	86.83	13.17	100.00
Primary metalworking	77.85	10.56	4.21	92.62	7.38	100.00
Non-metallic minerals	72.25	16.70	2.51	91.47	8.53	100.00
Miscellaneous	56.41	7.67	19.81	83.89	16.11	100.00
Total manufacturing	**24.22**	**26.37**	**9.85**	**60.44**	**39.56**	**100.00**

[1] Only establishments of firms with 10 or more employees are considered

Source: IASM-CESAN Data Bank, Naples (Martinelli 1985)

A few figures, based on the IASM–CESAN Data Bank (Martinelli 1985), suffice to account for this aspect (see Table 11.1). Excluding micro-firms (with fewer than 10 employees), over half (60 per cent) of manufacturing employment in the Mezzogiorno at the end of 1980 worked in establishments controlled by non-southern firms. Moreover, important differences in size and productive specialisation between local and branch establishments appeared. The average size of indigenous plants was in fact only 28 employees and over 60 per cent of them had fewer than 50 employees, whereas the average size of non-southern plants was 245 employees and over 50 per cent of them had more than 1,000 employees. Furthermore, local plants operated prevailingly in 'traditional' sectors (food processing, clothing, leather and footwear, lumber and furniture, construction materials etc.), to many of which they contributed over 75 per cent of the region's sectoral employment. Non-southern establishments, in contrast, almost monopolised 'modern' sectors (machinery, transportation equipment, electronics, chemicals, petro-chemicals, pharmaceuticals, steel) (cf. also Cercola 1984).

The strong dualism in size and productive specialisation of the Mezzogiorno manufacturing base shows, on the one hand, the difficulties encountered by local capital in the accumulation and diversification process and on the other, the still limited intra- and inter-sectoral integration of exogenous and local operations. The development of certain modern industries was clearly contingent upon the economies of scale of exogenous industrial groups. But although a number of southern firms have eventually developed and/or grown as subcontractors of exogenous large plants (Giannola 1987b; Del Monte 1984, 1987), the sectoral division of labour between exogenous and local capital appears still too sharp and the aggregate employment created by southern plants in modern industries still too limited.

The underdevelopment of producer services

According to the population censuses, aggregate tertiary employment in the Mezzogiorno has significantly increased since the end of World War II, from 23 per cent of total regional employment in 1951 to 48 per cent in 1981 – a percentage only slightly lower than the national average (51 per cent). However, important differences still exist in its sectoral composition.

Looking first at the intra-sectoral distribution of service employment by regions[3] and following the taxonomy in Chapter 6, the largest share of regional service employment in the Mezzogiorno in 1981 is found in the social infrastructure service group (40 per cent). This percentage is much higher than in the rest of the country (29 per cent). Consumer services account instead for a roughly similar share in all regions (35–37 per cent), whereas the shares contributed by producer services (20 per cent in circulation services and 4 per cent in business services) are much lower in the South than in the rest of Italy.

However, the above figures are meaningless if they are not weighed against demand. Therefore, regional tertiarisation quotients were calculated, using for each service subsector the number of employees as the numerator (an indicator of supply) and different demand indicators as denominators: total regional population was considered in the case of social infrastructure services and consumer services; total regional employment and total regional value added (as proxies for the overall production base) in the case of producer services.

Only in the social infrastructure subsector (public administration, education, health, and other welfare services) did the southern tertiarisation quotient in 1981 prove close to one (0.99), meaning that regional employment in these services is barely adequate to the local demand, that is in line with the national average. In consumer services, the quotient proved instead significantly lower (0.80), showing a relative undersupply of such services *vis-à-vis* the national standard, certainly related to the lower regional per capita income.[4]

But it is in producer services that differences in regional endowments are most revealing of the gap between the Mezzogiorno and the rest of the country, as well as of the spatial concentration of services in north-central regions. Either when measured against total regional value added or total regional employment, the tertiarisation quotients in the Mezzogiorno proved, in fact, lower than in the rest of Italy. Considering the first type of denominator as a more accurate indicator of demand, the aggregate quotients for circulation and for business services were in the Mezzogiorno respectively 0.86 and 0.83.

However, within both subsectors, important differences can be observed among individual services (see Table 11.2). The highest southern quotients (in some cases even above one) are found in those services that are either more traditional (for example legal services) or subject to political rather than market decisions (for example public R & D, communications, and transportation). In contrast, southern quotients were quite low in all those services more directly affected by market forces: banking and finance (0.74), wholesale distribution and commercial intermediation (0.74), insurance (0.70) and particularly the most specialised and innovative activities such as private R & D (0.47), marketing (0.47), information technology services (0.43), organisational consulting (0.40), advertising and public relations (0.37), where the southern supply relative to its production basis is less than half the national average. Many producer services, but particularly the latter business services proved, in contrast, quite concentrated in northern Italy and in the metropolitan provinces of Rome, Milan and Turin.[5]

Also with regard to in-house service employment the Mezzogiorno showed a significant undertertiarisation. The regional in-house tertiarisation quotient – calculated considering the total of entrepreneurs, managers, technical and clerical employees over total industrial employment in 1981 – proved in fact equal to 0.74, whereas, once again, it was much higher in northern Italy and especially in the metropolitan provinces of Milan, Turin and Rome.[6]

Table 11.2 Tertiarisation quotients* for producer services, by regions, Italy, 1981

Service industries	NW	C-NE	NW-C-NE (denominator = employment) a	S	NW	C-NE	NW-C-NE (denominator = value added) b	S
Circulation services								
Banking and finance (81+831)	1.10	1.07	1.08	0.78	1.01	1.08	1.05	0.86
Insurance (82+832)	1.19	1.07	1.12	0.67	1.09	1.08	1.09	0.74
Real estate (833+834)	1.21	1.08	1.14	0.63	1.11	1.09	1.10	0.70
Transportation ((7−79)+844+845)	1.29	1.25	1.27	0.29	1.18	1.26	1.22	0.32
Communications (79)	1.01	1.08	1.05	0.86	0.93	1.09	1.02	0.95
Wholesale distr. and intermediaries (61+62+63)	0.87	1.03	0.96	1.10	0.80	1.04	0.93	1.21
Business services	1.22	1.06	1.13	0.67	1.11	1.06	1.09	0.74
Public R & D (9401)	0.44	1.58	1.09	0.77	0.40	1.60	1.05	0.85
Private R & D (9402)	1.71	0.84	1.22	0.42	1.57	0.85	1.18	0.47
Legal services (835)	0.96	1.00	0.98	1.05	0.88	1.00	0.95	1.15
Accounting and fiscal services (836)	1.28	1.00	1.12	0.68	1.18	1.01	1.08	0.75
Professional and technical services (837)	1.24	1.00	1.11	0.72	1.14	1.01	1.07	0.80
Advertising and public relations (838)	1.78	0.85	1.25	0.33	1.63	0.85	1.21	0.37
Marketing services (8391)	1.58	0.95	1.22	0.42	1.44	0.95	1.18	0.47
Management and organisation consultants (8392)	1.61	0.97	1.24	0.36	1.47	0.97	1.20	0.40
Electronic data processing (8393)	1.39	1.12	1.23	0.39	1.27	1.12	1.19	0.43
Paper-processing services (8395)	1.10	1.10	1.10	0.74	1.01	1.10	1.06	0.81
Typing and photocopying services (8396)	1.17	1.12	1.14	0.63	1.07	1.13	1.10	0.69
Membership organisations (963+964+965+967)	0.78	1.28	1.06	0.83	0.72	1.29	1.03	0.92
Rental of production equipment (84−(844+845+846+847))	1.34	1.09	1.20	0.49	1.22	1.09	1.15	0.54
Other business services (9394+8397+8398+8399)	1.01	0.93	0.96	1.10	0.92	0.94	0.93	1.21

* The tertiarisation quotients are calculated as follows:

$$a = \frac{\text{Employment in service } i \text{ in region } j \,/\, \text{Total employment in region } j}{\text{Employment in service } i \text{ in the nation} \,/\, \text{Total employment in the nation}}$$

$$b = \frac{\text{Employment in service } i \text{ in region } j \,/\, \text{Total value added in region } j}{\text{Employment in service } i \text{ in the nation} \,/\, \text{Total value added in the nation}}$$

(Numbers in parentheses indicate the ISTAT industrial classification codes)

Source: Istat, 6° Censimento dell'industria, del commercio, dei servizi e dell'artigianato, 1981; Dati sulle caratteristiche strutturali delle imprese e delle unita' locali, Fascicoli regionali, Rome, 1985; Istat, Annuario di contabilita' nazionale, **14**, Rome, 1986

In conclusion, the growth of the tertiary sector in the Mezzogiorno has occurred mostly in the public or publicly controlled service industries, whereas the supply of producer services more directly related to market forces, both internal and external, is significantly underdeveloped in relation to the regional productive basis. The above data confirm, thus, also in the case of Italy, the trend to interregional and intraregional concentration of producer services.

The thesis

The above two features of the current southern economic structure – industrial dualism and service underdevelopment – are necessarily related. As postulated earlier, the underdevelopment of producer services in the Mezzogiorno must be explained as a function of the low aggregate level of regional demand. This, in turn, is a consequence of the limited overall development of manufacturing in the region and – most importantly – of its particular corporate structure. The dualism and dependent structure of southern manufacturing is a structural constraint on the demand side to the development of a local supply of services, both internal and external. The quantitative 'Stigler effect' is reinforced by a 'structural' effect of a more qualitative nature.

In fact, branch plants, which are likely to express a wider and more complex service demand than local firms divert a large part of this demand out of the region, within or outside the multilocational corporate structure. At the same time, local industry is not sufficiently strong and articulated to represent a significant demand pole and to stimulate a market response autonomously. Organisational know-how and scale limitations prevent an advanced division and specialisation of labour within or across these firms.

A cumulative process of negative interaction unfolds – the classical 'vicious circle' of regional disequilibrium theory, although with different facets. The low regional demand fails to activate a market response in terms of local supply. The latter, in turn, depresses the regional propensity to use local services, especially in small firms which are more dependent on this form of procurement.

The demand bottleneck: an empirical assessment

The above thesis has been empirically tested through a direct survey of a representative sample of 100 manufacturing establishments operating in the Mezzogiorno. Their service demand and relative modes of procurement along with a number of structural characteristics were investigated. In particular, the analysis highlighted differences in service behaviour between exogenous and local establishments. An attempt was also made to estimate the influence of several structural factors such as ownership, the size of operations, the type of products and processes, market outlets, etc. on service demand.

Methodology

The survey was carried out at the end of 1984 for 100 manufacturing plants operating in the two most industrialised regions of the Mezzogiorno, Campania and Puglia. It was limited to one particular manufacturing subsector, the electro-mechanical equipment complex, composed of four major industries: electrical equipment, machinery, transportation equipment and electronics. This is a relatively new sector in the region's economy. The sector is dominated by the exogenous investments of the early 1970s, although a number of local establishments have also developed.

The sample corresponds on the whole to 42 per cent of the population of establishments with 20 or more employees operating in the sector in both regions at the end of 1984. It was randomly drawn on the basis of the IASM-CESAN data and stratified according to four key variables: ownership, size, industry and region.[7] The questionnaire submitted (in person) to entrepreneurs or managers of establishments was structured in two parts. In the first part, a number of 'structural' characteristics of operations were investigated; the second part focused specifically on the extent, nature and characteristics of service demand by the establishments.

The structural characteristics of the sector in the Mezzogiorno

As already mentioned, the electro-mechanical equipment sub-sector is relatively new to the region and dominated by branch plants. According to census data, employment in the sub-sector has in fact almost doubled between 1971 and 1981 (from 98,000 employees to 173,000). Moreover, according to IASM-CESAN data, and excluding firms with fewer than ten employees, 85 per cent of sectoral employment at the end of 1984 worked in establishments, of non-southern ownership.

The structural dualism with regard to both size of operations and type of products/processes which characterises the whole of manufacturing in the Mezzogiorno emerges in this sub-sector as well. At the end of 1984, the average size of non-southern electro-mechanical establishments in the region amounted in fact to 481 employees, against only 34 for southern establishment. Furthermore, a clear 'division of labour' concerning productive specialisation appeared. Southern plants are, in fact, more specialised in production 'to order', often customised and in the manufacture of parts. Non-southern branch plants mostly operate in mass production.[8] (see Table 11.3). Other relevant differences concern the level of automation[9] and the value added per employee, southern plants recording lower average values than their non-southern counterparts.

With regard to backward and forward linkages (see Table 11.3), southern plants sell, on average, a greater share of their output to the regional market, whereas exogenous branch plants have, as expected,

Table 11.3 Mean values of main structural variables for southern and non-southern establishments: production and market characteristics (expressed as % of establishment sales)

Variables	Southern	Non-southern	K-W[1] test
Type of product:			
Finished product	45.8	51.4	
Semifinished/component	36.6	44.4	
Transformation/repair	17.6	4.1	+
Operation technology:			
Mass/flow production	11.4	47.5	*
Small batches	47.1	31.8	
Unit/jobbing	41.5	20.7	+
Production mode:			
For stock	7.2	19.8	
Standard order	32.0	37.2	
Custom order	60.5	43.1	
Destination:			
Consumer market	1.9	11.2	
Intermediate goods	39.5	51.6	
Capital goods	58.6	37.2	+
Automation level (0–4)	0.8	1.4	+
Sales/employee (mil. Lira)	62.0	86.7	*
Input sources:			
Purchased in the Mezzogiorno	33.4	21.6	o
Output markets:			
Sales in the Mezzogiorno	66.4	33.8	*
Sales in NC Italy	28.7	47.0	o
Sales export	5.0	19.1	o

[1] Kruskal-Wallis test significance level: * = .001; o = .01; + = .05

Source: Author's survey of 100 electro-mechanical establishments located in the Mezzogiorno, 1984

prevailingly extra-regional markets. Also in the case of intermediate goods, southern plants prove significantly more orientated to regional purchases (an average of 33 per cent of the value of total material inputs, as against 22 per cent of non-southern plants). Even if in these 'modern' industries, the majority of inputs inevitably comes from more industrialised regions, one of the general assumptions of branch plants literature, – a lower propensity of exogenous plants to establish material transactions within the local economy – is confirmed.

On the other hand (see the same table), and quite interestingly, it turns out that almost half of the establishments in the southern sample (44 per cent) work for at least 40 per cent of their annual sales as subcontractors of large exogenous plants and/or public service corporations (the public railroad, telephone and electricity companies). This finding supports the thesis that the last wave of exogenous investments in the Mezzogiorno (in 'modern' rather than 'heavy' industries) has indeed spurred some backward linkages and contributed to the formation of local suppliers (Giannola 1986; Del Monte 1984). However, in aggregate terms the employment generated is still quite low. More importantly, a significant share of the above subcontractors are branch plants themselves (30 per cent of the non-southern sample). This means that many of the material transactions occurring in the Mezzogiorno are actually 'internal' to the branch plant system and often, as it emerged from interviews, to the same industrial group (see also Amin 1982).

In sum, although the embryo of an endogenous electro-mechanical equipment sector has formed in the Mezzogiorno, it does not compete directly with exogenous operations, but exploits niche markets and/or provides specific inputs to the latter.

The demand for services

A first aim of the survey was to assess the extent and diversification of service demand in the sample and to investigate behavioural differences. On the basis of a list of 75 producer services, grouped in 12 'functional' service areas (see Table 11.4), entrepreneurs and managers were asked: (a) which services had been 'activated', that is used, even occasionally, during the last year of operation; (b) whether the service was supplied in-house, secured from the parent organisation or from a free-standing, specialised supplier (in the case of multiple procurement modes, the dominant one was considered); (c) in the case of services external to the establishment, the location of suppliers.

Given the difficulties involved in measuring or estimating the volume or value of services used, a gross quantitative indicator was first chosen: the number of services activated by establishments. On the basis of the service list provided to respondents, which represented a conventional 'maximum' of usable services, the percentage of services actually activated, in total and for each 'functional service area', was calculated. Although with some limits (for example differences in quantity and quality, within the same service were not considered), this simplified indicator has provided a synthetic measure of the extent and diversification of service demand in the plants investigated which has, in turn, allowed comparisons.

As shown in Table 11.5, where the average percentage of services used in total and within each functional service area by the southern and non-southern subsamples is compared,[10] local plants show in general a significantly lower propensity to activate services than their exogenous counterparts (52 per cent against 70 per cent of all services listed, with a southern/non-southern ratio of 0.74. The above aggregate difference is not too striking, probably owing to the peripheral nature of branch plants themselves. But more significant discrepancies emerge when individual service areas are considered. In the same table one can see that in the more basic functional areas (management, finance, legal and fiscal services, production, and maintenance), both ownership groups

Table 11.4 List of services considered in the survey, by consolidated service area

Management
  Strategic planning
  Organisation planning
  Operations planning
  Business administration
  Business control
  Profitability analysis
Financial services
  Financial planning
  Financial analysis
  Evaluation/research of financial
    resources
  Auditing
  Leasing
  Factoring
Accounting and legal services
  General accounting
  Cash flow control
  Fiscal consulting
  Legal services
Special secretarial services
  Specialised paper work and
    procedures
  Translation
  Interpreter services
  Conference services
  Fairs information and organisation
  Public relations
Telecommunications
  Telex
  Telecopier
  On-line intra-corporate network
  Information network
  Telecommunication network
Electronic data processing
  Accounting
  Invoice processing
  Payroll processing
  Inventory control
  Procurements
  Sales
  Word processing
  Data bank/archive
  Technical computing and design
  Graphics
  Production control

New technology services
  Hardware and system choice
  Software development
  Automation
Research & development
  Basic research
  Applied research and development
  New technology research
  Technology development
  Licence and patent research/
    acquisition
  Study centre
Design
  Product design
  Technical design
  Product engineering
  Process engineering
  Technical feasibility analysis
Production
  Operations design
  Production planning
  Scheduling and methods
  Layout
  Cost analysis
  Quality control
  Laboratory tests
  Inputs procurement
  Output inventory
Maintenance
  Of office equipment
  Of production equipment
  Of computer equipment
Marketing
  Sales planning
  Sales analysis
  Sales policy
  Marketing research
  Market analysis
  Advertising
  Promotional activities
  Fairs participation
  Intermediation services
  Import/export services
  Sales counter

Table 11.5 Mean percentage of services activated in each area (% 'area coverage') by southern and non-southern establishments

Service areas	Mean per cent of services activated			
	Southern	Non-southern	K-W[1] test	S/NS ratio
Accounting & Legal	9.25	98.5	+	0.94
Maintenance	89.0	95.0		0.94
Production	80.7	89.6	*	0.90
New technology services	58.0	71.0		0.82
Management	77.5	96.0	*	0.81
Finance	57.3	70.7	*	0.81
Design	58.2	76.6	*	0.76
Marketing	43.3	66.1	*	0.66
Electronic data processing	36.1	56.5	*	0.64
Special secretarial services	26.5	50.7	*	0.52
Telecommunications	16.6	36.6	*	0.45
R & D	23.5	56.5	*	0.42
All services	51.6	69.8	*	0.74
No. of establishments	46	54		

[1] Kruskal-Wallis test significance level:
* = .001; o = .01; + = .05
'Mean percent services' represent the average of the percentage of services activated by establishments out of total services listed in each area, across all plants in each ownership group.
Source: Author's survey of 100 electro-mechanical establishments located in the Mezzogiorno, 1984

on average use the majority of listed services and southern/non-southern ratios remain above 0.80 and are not statistically significant. In contrast, in the functional areas with a more strategic or innovative content (R & D, marketing, special secretarial services, telecommunications and electronic data processing), both groups activate on average a lower percentage of services, but southern/non southern differentials prove significantly greater (with ratios ranging from a maximum of 0.42 in the R & D area to 0.66 in the marketing area). It is also important to mention that in some of the latter areas many of the southern establishments interviewed have not yet activated any type of service.[11] An intermediate position is held by the design and new technology areas, where both ownership groups use on average a low percentage of services, and differentials are less important. It is also worth mentioning that in most functional areas (with the notable exception of management, design and production), the southern subsample shows quite high coefficients of variation, whereas the non-southern group has more stable distributions.

Further information on the type of services used by southern and non-southern establishments was derived from an analysis of contingency tables for each of the services considered. Not only do southern establishments use on average 'fewer' services than their non-southern counterparts, the services they activate also have a more 'elementary' nature. The highest differences in use are, in fact, found in all planning activities and in those services with a higher strategic or innovative content such as new technology research, engineering, marketing research, import–export services, telecommunication networking, etc. It is also interesting to note that in the electronic data-processing area southern establishments have activated mostly traditional management functions (accounting, invoice processing, word processing), whereas purchases, inventories and sales management, as well as graphic applications or production control are extremely limited.

The determinants of demand

The above analysis confirms the initial hypothesis of significant differences in service demand between local and exogenous establishments. However, beyond this major explanatory factor, it was deemed important to investigate the influence on service demand of other structural variables, that is the characteristics of production and markets.

A first assessment in this direction was made again with the method of comparing means across different categories. In this case the analysis was limited to seven of the 12 functional service areas – those more strategic or innovative in content and those with greater southern/non-southern differentials – grouped in three 'macro' areas: (1) new information technology (telecommunications, electronic data processing, new technology); (2) conception of products and processes (design and R & D); (3) sales promotion (marketing and special secretarial services). Interesting results emerged with regard to the size of plants and the type of markets.

With regard to size, figures reported in Table 11.6 suggest that the scale of operation does have an influence on the demand for strategic services, as differences in average demand for the three size classes considered prove significant in each macro area: the demand increases with the number of employees. Within each size class, the influence of ownership is confirmed: size being equal, southern plants show a lower propensity to activate strategic services than their non-southern counterparts. It appears, thus, that size reinforces ownership in explaining differences in service demand: the scale of operations does influence the technical division of labour, hence the demand for services and the prevailingly small size of southern plants does account for their lower aggregate demand. But size being equal, ownership still makes a difference: non-southern establishments can, in fact, rely on larger 'corporate' scale economies.

With regard to the type of market, the comparison was made between: (a) establishments with a diversified output market (that is with

Table 11.6 Mean percentage of services activated in the areas of new information technology, design and R & D, marketing and special secretarial skills, by ownership and employment size class

Size class and service area	Southern	Non-southern	K-W[1] test	All plants
Small (20–99)				
NIT	33.6	41.5		36.1
DRD	38.6	51.3		42.6
MKSS	36.3	51.9	+	41.2
No. of companies	37	17		54
Medium (100–499)				
NIT	45.4	54.0		51.5
DRD	37.5	66.4	o	58.1
MKSS	50.0	64.4		60.3
No. of companies	8	20		28
Large (>500)				
NIT	63.2	74.6		74.0
DRD	81.8	79.1		79.3
MKSS	94.1	77.2		78.1
No. of companies	1	17		18
K-W test				
NIT		*		*
DRD		o		*
MKSS		+		*

[1] Kruskal-Wallis test significance level:
* = .001; o = .01; + = .05
(tests do not include the one large southern company)

Source: Author's survey of 100 electro-mechanical establishments operating in the Mezzogiorno, 1984

less than 40 per cent of total sales sold to one single client); (b) subcontractors (ie establishments selling 40 per cent or more of their total production to one customer; (c) dependent branch plants (ie shipping more than 80 per cent of their production to the parent firm). As shown in Table 11.7, the type of market does influence the demand for services, but the relationship is statistically significant for the southern subsample only. Southern subcontractors activate, on average, the lowest number of strategic services, particularly in the conception and sales promotion macro areas. Since these establishments are supposedly an outcome of the local linkages established by branch plants and of the 'privileged' state procurement policy, such results have rather negative implications: subcontracting relationships in the Mezzogiorno do not contribute to the organisational development of local production. In contrast, southern establishments with a diversified and less dependent market, more exposed to competitive pressures, show a higher aggregate propensity to activate strategic and innovative services. As for non-southern plants,

Table 11.7 Mean percentage of services activated in the areas of new information technology, design and R & D, marketing and special secretarial skills, by ownership and market typology

Market typology and service area	Southern	Non-southern	K-W[1] test	All plants
Diversified				
NIT	40.4	54.6	+	48.1
DRD	44.0	66.1	o	55.9
MKSS	49.4	67.1	o	58.9
No. of companies	25	29		54
Subcontracting				
NIT	30.5	54.0	o	40.9
DRD	31.4	60.2	o	44.2
MKSS	25.9	57.0	o	39.7
No. of companies	20	16		36
Dependent				
NIT	47.4	67.3		65.3
DRD	81.8	73.7		74.6
MKSS	82.4	69.3		70.6
No. of companies	1	9		10
K-W test				
NIT				+
DRD	+			o
MKSS	o			o

[1] Kruskal-Wallis test significance level:
* = .001; o = .01; + = .05
(tests do not include the one dependent southern company)

Source: Author's survey of 100 electro-mechanical establishments operating in the Mezzogiorno, 1984

the type of market does not seem to affect their demand for services. Once again the ownership effect proves dominant: within each category of market, non-southern plants show a significantly higher aggregate propensity to use services.

An estimate of the influence of structural characteristics on service demand

An attempt to estimate the relative influence of the various structural variables was also made using multiple regression analysis (see Martinelli 1986). A number of indicators of production and market organization (the independent variables) were constructed and their influence on the number (percentage) of services activated in each of the three strategic service macro areas (the dependent variable) was estimated. Given the limits attached to the use of such a technique for cross-section samples, this exercise was conducted essentially to assess roughly the importance of causal relationships rather than achieve precise estimates.

On the premises of the initial working hypotheses, it was expected that the level of service demand in all three macro areas would be positively influenced by the level of market diversification and extra-regional exports, by the degree of automation, and by plant size. Furthermore, it was expected that the level of production 'for stock' would positively affect the demand for sales promotion services, whereas production more orientated to 'jobbing' would positively influence conception services.

A first group of regressions was carried out for the whole sample, including ownership (as a dummy) among the independent variables. Regressions confirmed the predominant role of ownership in explaining the level of demand. Moreover, the presence of the ownership variable created estimation problems because of the high correlation with other independent variables (in particular with size, extra-regional sales and automation). The analysis was thus carried out on the southern and non-southern subsamples separately. The description and notation of variables are reported in Table 11.8. In what follows only the main insights provided by the analysis will be summarised.

First of all,it must be noted that, although the overall adjusted R^2 values proved generally low (between 0.28 and 0.44), estimated coefficients were all significantly different from zero. This means that, although relevant, the variables considered did not explain the whole of the observed variance and further factors need to be assessed. Second, the analysis shows that the structural factors affecting the demand for services are substantially different within the two ownership groups.

In the southern subsample, service demand in all three macro areas is primarily a function of the level of sales per employee and of the level of extra-regional sales. This suggests that, beyond more structural characteristics of operation, such as size, products, or processes, it is 'performance' variables – such as a value of inputs in the production process and a market penetration capacity – which mainly explain the organisational development, and the greater use of strategic and/or innovative services in souther firms. In the new technology macro area, the effect of the two above factors is reinforced by the level of automation.

In the non-southern subsample the major determinants of service demand with regard to the new technology area are size and level of automation, whereas in the area of sales promotion the level of production 'for stock' replaces size. In the area of conception, the regression did not yield coefficients significantly different from zero. Such results suggest that the higher levels of demand for strategic services come from the most 'modern' branch plants, that is those with advanced technology, coupled with a large plant size or with standardised production. The latter, in fact, necessarily implies a structured sales promotion functional area.

In sum, in this analysis of the determinants of demand, ownership emerges as the strongest factor influencing the level of service demand.

Table 11.8 Notation and description of variables used in the multiple regression analysis

---

Dependent variables

% NIT	= % of services used in the area of New Information Technology (telecommunications, electronic data processing and new technology)
% DRD	= % of services used in the area of Conception of Products and Processes (design and R & D services)
% MKSS	= % of services used in the area of Sales Promotion (marketing and special secretarial services)

Independent variables

% JOBB	= % of jobbing production out of total sales (as opposed to mass or batch production)
% STOCK	= % of production for stock out of total sales (as opposed to production to order)
% AUTOM	= % level of automation (measured on an ordinal scale 0–4)
% EXPORT	= % of exports out of total sales
% EXREG	= % of extraregional sales
% 5 CUST	= % of sales to first five customers (an indicator of sales concentration)
TOTEMPL	= total establishment employment
SALES/E	= sales per employee
REGION	= the region of location (dummy variable for Campania = 0 and Puglia = 1)

Belonging to an articulate corporate organisation – as by definition that of branch plants – proves a major explanatory factor for the greater and more diversified demand, especially in the more strategic and innovative areas. Within the non-southern group, substantial stability of behaviour is observed. The demand for more strategic and innovative services is somewhat influenced by the level of automation, size and type of product. In contrast, within the southern group a greater variability of behaviour is observed and the demand for services is less influenced by structural variables than by 'performance'; establishments are engaged in more advanced production and have more diversified and extended output markets (see also I.Ter. 1987). Finally, the fact that only a small part of the variation is explained by the variables considered in the analysis, as well as the great variance observed in the southern sample, suggests that other factors should also be considered. Among these one can mention: individual corporate strategies, especially in the case of large corporations with varying organisational structures; the position branch plants occupy in the corporate division of labour; individual entrepreneurial and managerial capacities in the case of small firms (see also Giannola 1987b); the regional context, for example, being located in an urban, densely industrialised area or in a more rural, isolated setting. Many of these factors are not easy to measure.

The modes of procurement

Having assessed the role of ownership and other production and market characteristics, the second aim of the work was to identify differences in behaviour between southern and non-southern establishments concerning the modes of supply of services.

Four supply modes were retained: (a) in-house (internal to the establishment); (b) from the parent organization, whether headquarters or affiliates (external to the establishment but internal to the firm or group structure); (c) from an external, free-standing, specialised supplier (whether a consultant, a company or an institution); (d) from the client firm. To investigate this aspect, the average percentage of services secured in each different modality over the total number of services activated was considered.

Table 11.9 Distribution of services used in southern and non-southern establishments by type of supplier (% of total services used)

Service areas	Southern plants					Non-southern plants					No. establ.	
	I-H	PF	EXT	CUST	Total	I-H	PF	EXT	CUST	Total	S	N-S
MNGMT	86.0	10.3	3.8	0.0	100.0	56.2	42.5	1.3	0.0	100.0	(46)	(54)
FIN	54.7	6.2	39.1	0.0	100.0	28.8	39.4	31.5	0.3	100.0	(46)	(54)
ACC&L	46.4	8.0	45.7	0.0	100.0	52.3	22.7	25.0	0.0	100.0	(46)	(54)
SPECS	65.0	10.7	24.3	0.0	100.0	40.9	35.4	23.7	0.0	100.0	(25)	(44)
TLC	79.6	9.9	8.6	1.9	100.0	69.1	24.8	6.1	0.0	100.0	(27)	(48)
EDP	70.4	14.0	15.6	0.0	100.0	60.8	35.2	4.0	0.0	100.0	(36)	(53)
NTS	32.4	7.6	60.0	0.0	100.0	44.9	32.6	22.5	0.0	100.0	(35)	(46)
R & D	80.2	8.3	6.3	5.2	100.0	48.6	47.7	3.7	0.0	100.0	(29)	(48)
DES	73.6	3.9	9.3	13.3	100.0	53.5	37.8	4.3	4.3	100.0	(44)	(52)
MAINT	35.2	0.7	64.1	0.0	100.0	34.9	1.9	63.3	0.0	100.0	(46)	(54)
PROD	97.1	1.9	0.4	0.7	100.0	89.9	8.6	1.3	0.3	100.0	(46)	(54)
MRKTG	68.4	15.5	16.0	0.0	100.0	29.1	63.3	7.5	0.0	100.0	(43)	(53)
All services	69.3	7.5	22.1	1.1	100.0	52.2	34.5	13.1	0.3	100.0	(46)	(54)

Note: I-H = In-house; PF = Parent firm; EXT = External supplier; CUST = Customer

Source: Author's survey of 100 electromechanical establishments located in the Mezzogiorno, 1984

Figures presented in Table 11.9 point out two relevant patterns. First, both southern and non-southern establishments provide in-house the absolute majority of the services they use (69 per cent and 52 per cent, respectively), although the former show a significantly higher aggregate propensity to internalise. Second, and as expected, non-southern plants depend on the parent organisation for a substantial part of their services (35 per cent), whereas southern establishments rely to a greater extent on external suppliers (22 per cent on average against 13 per cent in non-southern establishments).

The first pattern can be explained by the fact that a number of the listed services are traditionally provided in-house. But it is also likely to be reinforced by the absence in the Mezzogiorno of a local external supply, which forces establishments either to internalise or to secure services long distance, as will become clearer further on. Moreover, owing to size, branch plants have greater opportunities to internalise certain services than their local counterparts.

As to the second aspect, the high recourse to the parent firm observed for non-southern plants contributes to explaining why, despite the higher aggregate demand for services, the branch plants sample records an average share of managerial, technical and clerical employment quite similar to that of local establishments (25 per cent compared to 23 per cent). Further, and more importantly, the recourse to the parent organisation occurs especially in the more strategic and/or innovative areas: marketing (63 per cent of all services activated in this area), R & D (48 per cent), management (43 per cent), finance (39 per cent), design (38 per cent), whereas only in the area of production (90 per cent), telecommunications (69 per cent) and electronic data processing (61 per cent) are services provided internally to a significant extent. The highest average shares of services purchased from external suppliers are instead found in maintenance (63 per cent), in financial services (32 per cent), in accounting and legal services (25 per cent), in special secretarial services (24 per cent), and in new technology services (23 per cent). These services are either traditionally carried out by independent suppliers or too specialised to be internalised, even by large firms.

Southern plants, which do not have a large parent firm structure to rely on, must secure services either in-house or through external suppliers. The latter mode is most frequently adopted in the same traditional or specialised areas mentioned in the case of branch plants. However, the aggregate propensity to use external suppliers is higher in southern plants than in their non-southern counterparts, for both types of service. This supports the hypothesis that despite the lower aggregate demand of local plants, those which do activate services cannot always afford to internalise them.[12]

It is also worth noting that the few cases where the services are secured from client firms are confined almost exclusively to southern plants (generally subcontractors) and are limited to the areas of design and product development.

Further information emerged from the analysis of contingency tables for individual services. First of all, little differentiation of supply modes occurs within those areas where non-southern plants are more dependent on the parent firm (marketing, R & D, design, electronic data processing). This means that the strategic choice between internalising or securing services from the parent organisation concerns entire functional areas rather than specific services. This functional division of labour between branch plant and parent organisation was also confirmed in the course of the interviews. An exception to this pattern, however, is found in the management area, where there is a straight partition between routine management activities (internalised) and strategic planning activities (secured from the parent firm).

In contrast, contingency tables show that in some areas where the reliance on external suppliers is higher (new technology, finance, legal and fiscal services, special secretarial skills, maintenance), it is a number of specific, consistently externalised services, which influence the overall area values: software services, leasing, factoring and auditing, legal and fiscal services, translation and interpreter services, maintenance of office equipment. These services are traditionally supplied by freestanding organisations; but it should be noted that many branch plants substitute parent firm support for external suppliers.

The analysis of the procurement modes supports the initial hypotheses. The scarce decision-making autonomy of branch plants and their dependence on the parent firm, especially in the most strategic or innovative service areas, is confirmed. Also confirmed is the limited propensity of branch plants to establish external service transactions: the firm's economies of scale allow individual establishments to replace external supply with parent firm support. It is important to stress, however, that relevant differences occur among different ownership groups within the non-southern sample. As mentioned in Chapter 6, the strategic choice regarding the development of a service at the plant or at headquarters' level depends also on corporate structures and strategies. In this case, the behaviour of state-owned corporations proves significantly different from that of private national and foreign corporations, since the former have also decentralised a number of strategic functions to the Mezzogiorno.

In contrast, although they record a lower, less diversified and less innovative aggregate demand for services than their exogenous counterparts, local establishments show a greater propensity to enter into service transactions with external suppliers.

The location of suppliers

Significant differences between southern and non-southern establishments emerged also with regard to the geography of service transactions.

Considering the totality of services supplied from outside the establishment (see Table 11.10), branch plants secure on average as much as 69 per cent of the services they do not provide internally from outside the Mezzogiorno, against only 11 per cent from local plants. The only service areas where branch plants rely to a significant extent on regional suppliers are maintenance (89 per cent of all services not provided in-

Table 11.10 Mean percentage of services secured ex-house, by location of suppliers

Service areas	Mezzogiorno S	Mezzogiorno N-S	Ex-Mezzogiorno S	Ex-Mezzogiorno N-S	Total S	Total N-S	K-W[1] test	No. establ. S	No. establ. N-S
MAINT	97.8	88.9	2.2	11.1	100.0	100.0		(46)	(51)
ACC&L	96.1	51.5	3.9	48.5	100.0	100.0	*	(45)	(51)
SPECS	76.9	51.3	23.1	48.7	100.0	100.0		(13)	(39)
EDP	92.3	34.9	7.7	65.1	100.0	100.0	o	(13)	(35)
NTS	83.3	30.3	16.7	69.7	100.0	100.0	*	(30)	(33)
PROD	100.0	28.4	0.0	71.6	100.0	100.0	+	(5)	(22)
FIN	88.1	19.9	11.9	80.2	100.0	100.0	*	(35)	(54)
DES	72.5	17.7	27.5	82.3	100.0	100.0	*	(20)	(33)
R & D	62.5	16.9	37.5	83.1	100.0	100.0	+	(8)	(34)
MRKTG	69.5	11.8	30.5	88.2	100.0	100.0	*	(28)	(48)
TLC	94.4	10.7	5.6	89.3	100.0	100.0	*	(9)	(28)
MNGMT	70.9	8.7	29.1	91.3	100.0	100.0	*	(11)	(43)
ALL SVCS	88.5	30.6	11.5	69.4	100.0	100.0	*	(46)	(54)

[1] Kruskal-Wallis test significance level:
* = .001; o = .01; + = .05

Source: Author's survey of 100 electro-mechanical establishments located in the Mezzogiorno, 1984

house), legal and fiscal services (52 per cent), and special secretarial services (51 per cent). The above aggregate results are obviously biased by the large dependence of branch plants on services supplied by their parent structures, which are all located outside the Mezzogiorno (Rome, Milan, and Turin but also abroad in the case of some foreign firms). However, when services obtained by external suppliers alone are considered, the average share of services obtained by branch plants outside the Mezzogiorno remains high (36 per cent). Again, services most significantly found in the Mezzogiorno concern the maintenance area (maintenance of office equipment), special secretarial (translation and intepreter services) and legal and fiscal services. For the other externally secured services, branch plants turn to extra-regional suppliers, generally 'through' the parent firm.

Local establishments in contrast purchase almost the totality of the services they do not provide internally in the Mezzogiorno (89 per cent). As shown in Table 11.10, the service areas where the recourse to non-regional suppliers appears most significant are R & D (37 per cent), marketing (31 per cent), design (28 per cent), special secretarial services (23 per cent) and new technology consulting (17 per cent). Evidently, for some of the most advanced services within these areas, southern plants do not find an adequate local supply and have to turn to extra-regional suppliers.

The thesis that branch plants have a low propensity to activate local linkages, especially in services, is thus confirmed. The non-southern subsample shows a limited propensity to activate linkages external to the firm in general. And even for those that are actually externalised, these branch plants favour extra-regional suppliers and limit their linkages with the local economy to the most traditional and less innovative services.

It is also interesting to mention that the development of telecommunications may actually have reinforced intra-corporate service linkages and branch plant dependence. In five out of the 54 non-southern establishments interviewed, the introduction of 'on-line' communication systems with headquarters had resulted in a further concentration of services at the headquarters level, with a shift of functions previously performed at plant level (such as accounting, inventories control, payroll, etc.) to the parent firm.

Conclusions

The empirical evidence provided for the Mezzogiorno illustrates how the industrial and corporate structure is a major determinant of the demand for and the development of producer services.

In the first place, the analysis shows that corporate structure and ownership significantly influence the level and diversification of service demand. Branch plants show an average propensity to use services which is significantly higher than that of small local plants, especially in the most strategic and innovative service areas. This behaviour is partly explained by the larger size of operations and hence the more extended technical division of labour of exogenous establishments. But size being equal, the fact of belonging to a large, multilocational corporate structure – as, by definition, branch plants – proves determinant.

Second, the analysis also confirms the important role of corporate structure in explaining the form of service procurement and the spatial structure of transactions. Branch plants express a more diversified and advanced service demand. They tend to use procurement channels that are internal to the corporate structure: a very large portion of their services is secured from or through the parent firm. The spatial structure of service linkages is thus polarised towards external centres of decision-making and 'bypasses' the regional economy: in the Mezzogiorno, about 50 per cent of services used by branch plants is procured totally outside the region.

Local small firms, in contrast, although their average demand is still low, little diversified and more traditional in character, show a much greater average propensity to secure their services from local external suppliers. None the less, in the case of more advanced services, many of these firms must turn to extra-regional suppliers to compensate for the lack of an adequate local supply. This is certainly an additional cost and a deterrent to their modernisation process, which strongly affects their potential competitiveness.

Thus, the quantitative constraint (the limited development of manufacturing) is reinforced by a qualitative constraint (the characteristics of the industrial market). The Mezzogiorno's productive structure does not express a sufficient service demand to stimulate a market response. The low aggregate regional demand is due to branch plants' 'deviated' demand and local firms' insufficient organisational development. This low demand is unable to sustain the development of a local supply of services. A classic 'vicious' circle unfolds, whereby the limited overall level of regional demand does not stimulate the development of a local service supply; the absence of external services, in turn, depresses demand, especially from small firms; the scarce use of services further limits industrial growth.

More generally, the above findings support the theory which explains unequal regional development as a function of the spatial division of labour carried out by large multilocational corporations, whether at the international or intra-national level. They also highlight the obstacles to growth encountered by indigenous capital in those peripheral regions characterised by the lack of significant nuclei of local large firms and/or integrated industrial systems.

Notes

1. The empirical work presented in this chapter is drawn from the doctoral dissertation prepared by the author at the University of California, Berkeley in 1986. Only the most important results are reported here.
2. With the term 'dualism' a set of interrelated characteristics is intended here: the substantial weight of exogenous operations in terms of employment: the significant differences in size and productive specialisation; the limited integration that exists between local and exogenous production.
3. Three broad regions have been retained: the northwest, which is the historical industrial core of Italy; northeastern-central Italy, which is characterised by a small-sized, specialised and fairly integrated industrial structure (the 'Third Italy'); and the Mezzogiorno, which includes the six administrative regions below Rome (Abruzzi, Molise, Campania, Puglia, Basilicata and Calabria), plus Sicily and Sardinia.
4. Although it must also be stressed that this sub-sector hosts many kinds of 'black' and other unrecorded forms of labour (family work). Census data are thus likely to underestimate actual employment.
5. Tertiarisation quotients for business services in these provinces are 1.82; 1.62; and 1.16, respectively. It is worth noting how Milan appears more specialised in advanced services such as marketing, advertising, organisational consulting and information technology services; Rome has more banking and finance services, as well as public R & D; Turin records instead more private R & D and advertising.
6. 1.83, 1.63, and 1.30, respectively. The latter result is more directly imputable (than in the case of external services) to the dualistic structure of the Mezzogiorno manufacturing structure, characterised by a strong presence of branch plants and by a very fragmented and organisationally poor local

industry. Most large firms' headquarters are in fact located in the above metropolitan areas.

7. Data on the sampling population come from the IASM–CESAN data bank of Naples, which covers virtually all manufacturing establishments with ten or more employees operating in the Mezzogiorno and provides information not only on size, product and location of operating units but also on capital ownership. With regard to ownership, two stratifying classes were retained: establishment fully owned or controlled by non-southern capital (including foreign corporations, private domestic corportions of north-central Italy and state corporations), and establishment of southern entrepreneurs. Also for size two classes were considered: small (20–99 employees) and medium-large (100 or more employees). It is important to mention that although a 'proportional' stratifying procedure was followed with regard to all classes, for the small-southern cell of the stratification matrix a 'disproportionate' procedure was chosen, since small establishments represented the over-whelming majority of the southern population and a statistically workable number of observations had also to be gathered in the other cells. Therefore, the small-southern stratum has been slightly penalised and represents a smaller proportion of the corresponding population than the other strata. This means that the analysis is partially biased in favour of larger establishments.

8. In the electrical equipment industry southern plants mainly manufacture switchboard equipment and control panels for custom industrial appli-cations, as well as some electro-mechanical telephone equipment, whereas non-southern establishments mostly operate in the mass fabrication of wires, wiring equipment and household appliances. In the machinery industry, local plants (especially in Campania) have a historical specialisa-tion in the manufacture of equipment for the canning industry, and to a lesser extent in light handling and conveying machinery, whereas exo-genous ventures are mostly engaged in the manufacture of heavy construc-tion, pumping and drilling equipment. As to transportation equipment, non-southern establishments as expected dominate the automobile, mass transport and aircraft industries, whereas local firms have a traditional specialisation (especially in Puglia) in the customised adaptation or trans-formation of commercial vehicles' bodies (trucks, trailers, etc.) and also operate in the repair and maintenance of mass transit vehicles (trains). A number of southern plants have also developed for the production of components and parts. In the electronics industry, finally, the few southern establishments are mostly confined to the production or assembly of elementary components for the telecommunication industry, whereas non-southern plants manufacture complete systems, whether computing equip-ment, industrial automation or telecommunications.

9. The automation level indicator was constructed, on an ordinal scale ranging from 0 to 4, combining several parameters. In a nutshell: 0 indicates total absence of automation; 1 indicates the presence of elements of automation, mostly at the level of conveying equipment and in some elementary phases of the transformation process ('rigid' automation); 2 indicates a low level of automation, with elements of flexibility (numerically controlled machinery); 3 indicates a medium level of automation with elements of integration (computerised numerical control and automation of complex phases); 4 indicates a high level of automation and integration (several integrated computer-controlled machines, and/or robots and/or wholly automated lines

of production).

10. The statistical significance of the observed differences in means was tested with the Kruskal–Wallis statistic. This is a non-parametric or 'distribution-free' analogue of analysis of variance statistics, useful to test the statistical significance of differences in means in the case of small samples, which do not fit the traditional assumptions of a normally distributed population. It is a conservative test, based on ranking procedures and highly sensitive to the number of observations. Briefly, the test is based on the comparison of the sums of ranks in each category.

11. About a quarter of the southern subsample has not yet introduced any R & D, telecommunications or special secretarial service; a tenth has not yet introduced any form of electronic data processing.

12. Further information emerged from the analysis of contingency tables for individual services. First of all, little differentiation of supply modes occurs within all those areas where non-southern plants are more dependent on the parent firm (marketing, R & D, design, electronic data processing). This means that the strategic choice between internalising or securing services from the parent organisation concerns 'whole' functional areas rather than specific services. This functional division of labour between branch plant and parent organisation was also confirmed in the course of the interviews. An exception to this pattern, however, is found in the management area, where there is a straight partition between routine management activities (internalised) and strategic planning activities (secured from the parent firm). In contrast, contingency tables show that in the areas where there is higher recourse to external suppliers (new technology, finance, legal and fiscal services, special secretarial, maintenance), it is a number of specific services, consistently externalised, which influence the overall area values (software services, leasing, factoring and auditing, legal and fiscal services, translation and interpreter services, maintenance of office equipment). Most of these are services traditionally supplied from free-standing organisations, but even in these services many branch plants replace parent firm support for external suppliers.

References

Amin, A. (1982) 'La ristrutturazione alla Fiat e il decentramento produttivo nel Mezzogiorno', *Archivio di Studi Urbani e Regionali*, **13/14**.

Cercola, R. (1984) *L'intervento esterno nello sviluppo industriale del Mezzogiorno*, Naples, Guida.

Del Monte, A. (1984) 'Gli effetti della politica regionale sullo sviluppo industriale del Mezzogiorno', *Mezzogiorno d'Europa*, **4**.

— (1987) 'Politica di industrializzazione, intervento pubblico e questione meridionale', *Nord e Sud*, **1**.

— and Giannola A. (1978) *Il Mezzogiorno nell' economia italiana*, Bologna, Il Mulino.

— (1984) 'Imprenditoria locale e sviluppo del terziario nel Mezzogiorno d'Italia: una nuova politica per il Sud?', *Rivista di Politica Economica*, **10**.

Dunford, M. (1986) 'Integration and Unequal Development: the Case of Southern Italy, 1951–73' in A.J. Scott and M. Storper (eds), *Work, Production, Territory*, London, Allen & Unwin.

Giannola, A. (1982) 'Industrializzazione, dualismo e dipendenza economica del Mezzogiorno', *Economia Italiana*, **11**.

— (1986) 'Industria manifatturiera e imprenditori del Mezzogiorno', Naples, Guida.
— (1987a) 'Problemi e prospettive dello sviluppo economico nel Mezzogiorno d'Italia' in Ente Einaudi (ed.), *Oltre la crisi*, Bologna, Il Mulino.
— (1987b) 'Politica industriale attiva e sviluppo dell' impresa locale nel Mezzogiorno', *Nord e Sud*, **1**.
Graziani, A. (1977) 'Il Mezzogiorno nell' economia italiana', *Inchiesta*, **29**.
— and Pugliese, E., (eds) (1979) 'Investimenti e disoccupazione nel Mezzogiorno', Bologna, Il Mulino.
I.Ter.-Eni (1987) *I servizi alla produzione per le imprese manifatturiere. Un' indagine in tre aree del Mezzogiorno*, Naples, I.Ter.
Martinelli, F. (1984) 'Servizi alla produzione e sviluppo economico regionale: il caso del Mezzogiorno d'Italia', *Rassegna Economica*, **1**.
— (1985) 'Public Policy and Industrial Development in Southern Italy: Anatomy of a Dependent Industry', *International Journal of Urban and Regional Research*, **9**.
Martinelli, F. (1986) Producer Services in a Dependent Economy: Their Role and Potential for Regional Economic Development, Ph.D. Dissertation, Department of City and Regional Planning, University of California, Berkeley.
Martinelli, F. (1989) 'Struttura industriale e servizi alla produzione nel Mezzogiorno', *Politica Economica*, **5**, 1, pp. 129–87.
Svimez (1987) *Rapporto 1986 sulla' economia del Mezzogiorno*, Rome, Svimez.
Vinci, S. (1984) 'Il quadro macroeconomico per lo sviluppo del Mezzogiorno', *Mezzogiorno d'Europa*, **4**.

12 Transnational business service firms and developing countries

Thierry Noyelle

F23 O19
L89

Introduction[1]

Since the 1950s, world-wide employment and output in business services have expanded at rates markedly higher than employment and output in the world economy as a whole, with growth accelerating further during the 1980s. The reasons for such development are many and complex. To a large extent, however, it is the outcome of a fundamental transformation in the mode of production of industrial economies, associated with the increasing substitution of service inputs for material inputs in the process of production. A discussion of this transformation is well beyond the scope of this particular chapter.[2] Note however that while the growth of business services was at first overwhelmingly concentrated in advanced economies, that no longer is the case. There is considerable evidence that business services are also growing rapidly in developing countries.[3]

This chapter is about the role of transnational business service firms in the expansion of the world market for business services and the implications of their expansion for host developing countries. The chapter is organised in three main sections following this introduction. The next section provides a brief description of the world market for business services. It is followed by a discussion of the importance of transnational business service firms in world markets and the nature of their competitive advantage. The impact of transnational business service firms on developing countries is then discussed. This last major section is followed by a short conclusion.

The world market for business services

Business services cover a wide range of activities with several characteristics in common. First, they are services that are purchased primarily by other producers (that is by *firms*, not *individuals*) for the purpose of being consumed in further rounds of production. In practice, of course, a number of business services are used by both producers and consumers. For example, accountants fill out income tax returns for both corporations and individuals; law professionals assist both individuals and businesses and so on. Since no country is really equipped to distinguish statistically between the output of business service firms that is consumed by producers and that which is purchased by final consumers, most available government statistics lump both together. Second, business services mostly deliver expertise, necessitating a major input from skilled or highly skilled professional, technical and managerial personnel. Third, business services comprise a mix of activities, some of which are restricted to licensed or accredited professionals (usually, accounting, auditing, law and so on) and others that are open to all (usually computer software, advertising, management consulting, etc). Finally, business services can be delivered either by firms, ranging from the very large to the very small, or by self-employed professionals. Self-employed professionals continue to provide for a sizeable share of the business in areas such as management consulting or software, even in international markets.

This chapter draws on examples borrowed from five business services, namely advertising, accounting and audit, management consulting, legal services and computer software and services. Together, these five sectors represent a major share of the business services. This selection has the added benefit of covering both licensed and non-licensed professions.

Available measures of employment and output in professional business services leave much to be desired, rendering their analysis somewhat difficult. Most advanced countries have fair employment coverage of their professional business service sector for the 1980s, but many are lacking reliable employment data for the 1970s. Domestic output data are usually weaker than the equivalent employment data. As for international trade data, they are, for all purposes, non-existent. Finally, some developing countries have relatively good data on business service employment for recent years; many, of course, are less fortunate.

It is with these observations in mind that the reader should look at Tables 12.1 through 12.3. Table 12.1 compares employment growth in the business services and real estate sectors to total employment growth in seven advanced countries (Japan, Belgium, France, the Federal Republic of Germany, the Netherlands, Sweden and the United States) for the period 1979–86. The table also shows the 1986 employment share of business services in the same seven countries. Between 1979 and 1986, rates of employment increases in business services and real estate in the seven countries were 24 per cent or more everywhere (54 per cent in the United States and 50 per cent in Japan), compared to rates of total employment growth ranging from −4 per cent to +13 per cent. In terms of 1986 employment shares, business services and real estate as a per cent of all employment ranged from 3.3 per cent in the Federal Republic of Germany (the lowest) to 7.6 per cent in the United States (the highest). In the case of the United States, I have estimated elsewhere, using slightly different data than those used in Table 12.1 that employment in business services (excluding real estate services) as a share of total private-sector employment grew from 4.2 to 8.1 per cent between 1970 and 1986 – a truly remarkable increase.[4]

Table 12.1 Employment in business services and real estate[a], seven OECD countries, 1979–1986

Country	Employment in business services 1986 (thousands)	Employment in business services as share of total public and private sector employment 1986 (per cent)	Employment growth in business services 1979–1986 (per cent)	Employment growth all sectors 1979–1986 (per cent)
Japan	2,420	n.a.	50.2	n.a.
Belgium	122	4.0	29.8	−4.1
France	859	4.8	25.4	−0.1
Fed. Rep. of Germany	762	3.3	26.0	0.4
Netherlands	347	7.6	37.8	10.1
Sweden	217	5.1	24.0	2.1
United States	8,338	7.6	53.8	13.1

[a] Industry classification is based on Eurostat NACE System

Source: United States Department of Labor, Bureau of Labor Statistics, unpublished data

Table 12.2 World-wide and United States, estimates of revenues in five business services, 1983–1987 (billion dollars)

	1987		1983	
	World-wide	United States	World-wide	United States
Accounting/auditing	50–60	26.5	n.a.	17.0
Management consulting	80–90	45.0	n.a.	28.0
Software/data processing	100–120	60.0	n.a.	35.0
Legal services	n.a.	75.0	n.a.	48.0
Advertising (billing)	215	110.0	134.0	76.0

Source: Author's estimates based on *U.S. Industrial Outlook*, 1988 and 1989; McCann-Erikson's estimates of advertising billings (see Table 12.3); and figures published in *Datamation*, July issues

Table 12.2 shows 1983 and 1987 output estimates for the United States and the world market for the five sectors selected for special focus in this chapter. These measures have been estimated by the author using United States' government and industry associations' data. For 1987, the world markets for accounting and audit, management consulting, computer software and services and advertising (measured in billings) were

Table 12.3 Advertising spending, 1982–9

	United States		Rest of the world	
	Billion dollars	Annual per cent change	Billion dollars	Annual per cent change
1982	66.6	10.2	58.3	0.0
1983	75.8	13.9	58.2	0.0
1984	87.8	15.8	58.6	0.7
1985	94.8	7.9	63.3	8.1
1986	102.1	7.7	79.8	26.1
1987	109.7	7.4	102.9	29.0
1988	118.1	7.7	121.4	18.0
1989[a]	126.2	6.9	133.5	10.0

[a] Estimated

Source: McCann-Erikson

estimated, respectively, at $50–60 billion, $80–90 billion, $100–120 billion, and $215 billion. It is impossible to develop a reasonable estimate for the size of the world market in legal services, although the American market alone was estimated at $75 billion in 1987.

Several observations stand out when looking at Table 12.2. The first observation is the enormous size of the American market which, in most cases, accounts for half or more of the world market in percentage share. This observation could be somewhat misleading, unless one also takes note of the fact that, since the mid-1980s, the market for business services has often grown faster outside than within the United States. See Table 12.3, for example, for evidence of such development in the case of advertising. A second important observation is the fact that recent growth has not been evenly distributed among business service sectors. Whereas advertising billings increased by 45 per cent in the United States between 1983 and 1987, computer software and data processing increased by over 70 per cent during the same period. This is one of the reasons why large business service firms in some of the relatively slower-growing sectors, such as audit or advertising, have sought to diversify into faster-growing ones – public relations and direct marketing and management consulting and computer software services (more on this below).

A third interesting observation, based on Table 12.2, is that, with the exception of accounting/auditing, each of the five sectors featured in Table 12.2 had United States' output in 1987 larger than the output of the American domestic steel industry (approximately $43 billion for American domestic producers). This is remarkable evidence of the extent of economic transformation during the 1980s.

What does the future portend for these sectors? No one knows for sure, but one management consultant in one of the world's largest accounting firms recently ventured the following forecast: '. . . As for the years ahead, management consulting and computer software services will continue to grow at a torrid pace – 25 to 30 per cent annually during good years; 15 per cent during slow years. Furthermore rates of expansion will continue to be higher outside than within the United States'.[5]

The importance of large business service firms in the world market

Market concentration

The internationalisation of professional business service firms is a phenomenon that goes back to the 1910s and 1920s, although one that has gained speed and magnitude during the 1980s. The reasons are twofold.

With the increasing globalisation of business, business service firms have come under growing pressure to follow their transnational clients, wherever the latter have chosen to go and do business. In this respect, the internationalisation of business service firms has been *demand-driven*, in so far as they have had few choices; either to follow or lose large clients. However, as the market for their services has widened to include a growing number of medium- and small-sized business customers, business service firms also have felt under increasing pressure to expand their presence in many geographical markets, partly in order to generate the scale economies needed to bring down the cost of their services and, in turn, make them attractive to a wider base of customers. In that respect, the multinational expansion of business service firms has also been *supply-driven*, in the sense that firms have sought to reach out to a wider, typically mostly domestic, rather than multinational, client base.

The internationalisation of business services has, of course, helped in the formation of large transnational business service firms. Table 12.4 shows a distribution of the top 20 business service firms in 1988 in each of the five industries selected for study by country of origin. The table underscores the importance of American and British business service firms at the top of their leagues across the five sectors (65 and 18 of the top 100 respectively), with an additional, but more recent, strong showing of French and Japanese firms. Table 12.5, which shows percentage share of total world-wide industry revenue by top firms in the five sectors, suggests a wide pattern of market concentration, ranging from a highly concentrated accounting industry – with the top six accounting firms netting nearly 40 per cent of the industry's world-wide revenues – to a highly atomistic structure in the case of legal services.

It should be noted that concentration in accounting has increased markedly in the late 1980s. The group of firms that, for nearly two decades, constituted the so-called 'Big 8' has by now become the 'Big 6', following the merger of Ernst & Whinney with Arthur Young in March

Table 12.4 Top 20 business service firms in five sectors by country of origin, 1988

	US	UK	France	Japan	Other	Total
Accounting	10	8	—	—	2	20
Advertising	12	3	4	4	—	20[a]
Software/computer services	13	—	1	5	1	20
Management consulting	18	2	—	—	—	20
Legal services	12	5	—	—	3	20
	65	18	5	9	6	100

[a] row entries add to more than 20 because 2 of the top 20 advertising firms have multiple nationality (one U.S.-France; the other U.S.-France-Japan)

Note: Firms are ranked by revenues except for law firms that are ranked by a composite factor including number of foreign offices and number of partners.

Source: Directory of the World's Largest Service Companies, Series I, Moody's Investor Services and UNCTC, New York: December, 1990; and *Datamation,* July 1989

Table 12.5 Per cent share of world revenues for top firms in the five industries, 1987

Sector	number of top firms	Per cent share of industry's world-wide revenues
Accounting	8	40
Advertising	10	27
Software/data processing	30	18
Management consulting	20	8
Legal services		Atomistic

Source: Table 2 in *Directory of the World's Largest Service Companies, Series I* Moody's Investors Service, New York (1990); *Datamation,* July 1989

1989, and that of Deloitte, Haskins & Sells with Touche Ross in October 1989.[6] One reason for these mergers is the pressure on firms, with heretofore uneven geographical networks, to try to complement each other's geographical strength in order to satisfy global clients. The experiment of KPMG – itself the product of the 1987 merger of then-number two Peat Marwick and number five Klynveld Main Goerdler – suggests that, by filling up what were once voids in its geographical network of branches, the firm was able to gain major new global accounts after its formation.[7]

Still, one must be careful not to draw too hasty a set of conclusions based on some of these data. For one thing, the market share percentages shown in Table 12.5 are rough averages for world markets. In reality, market share concentration is often much less outside the American market than within it. Second, the lists of largest firms are at times somewhat misleading in that they suggest more market concentration than there really is. This is the case, for example, in management consulting, although not unique to that sector. Areas of specialisation in the field are numerous and many of the top 20 management consulting firms specialise in businesses that are quite distinct.

Third, according to the data shown above, it is only in audit that concentration is very high. But, audit is also the smallest and, for that matter, probably the slowest-growing market segment in the business services. Computer software and services, management consulting and legal services are growing much faster than audit and show much lower market concentration – insignificant concentration in the case of legal services. In other words, the market concentration trends in audit are not necessarily representative of what is happening in other fields. Fourth, one must be careful in emphasising that concentration does not necessarily imply a lack of competition. Even in audit, the field has remained, thus far, fiercely competitive, and audit fees have dropped consistently in most countries throughout the 1980s.[8] This is so in part because some firms have been able to use information technology better to drive prices down and because others have used audits as 'loss-leaders' intended to attract clients to other, more lucrative services: for example tax services and management consulting services.[9] Of course, whether or not audit fees will continue to drop in the years ahead remains to be seen.

In advertising, the other sector with relatively high concentration, competition also remains intense, and for that matter has intensified further in recent years, despite the process of mergers and acquisitions that has been underway throughout the 1980s. This process has led to the creation of so-called mega advertising groups, in which more than one world-wide agency network may be managed under the same corporate umbrella. But, this process of merger has been rife with instability. As once-high-flying Saatchi and Saatchi and WPP Plc have learned the hard way in recent months, bigger does not necessarily mean better.[10] More broadly, as in the case of accounting, despite market concentration intense competition has forced many advertising firms to drop the once-standard advertising agency fee – 15 per cent of billings – for a lower one. By the industry's own estimate, nearly 45 per cent of all fees charged by agencies in the United States are now below the traditional 15 per cent fee.[11]

In general, the fact remains that many of the markets for business services are both growing too fast and changing too rapidly to allow for stability. Continuing reshuffling of positions among the top players is to be expected in the decade ahead. And, there remains ample room for new firms, including those from developing countries, to emerge as major players in business service markets in the years ahead.

Modes of delivery of business services

In theory at least, transnational business service firms can deliver their services through three principal modes: they can deliver services through 'pure' cross-border trade (as defined below); they can entice customers to come and purchase services where the firm is located; or they can move some of the firm's factors of production to where customers are located. In businesses in which the need for traditional investment in machinery, structures or financial capital is often limited, the movement of factors of production implies primarily the movement of personnel and the movement of technology (mainly in the form of training embedded in the firm's personnel – see below).

In business services, 'pure' cross-border trade means the provision of a service via a business letter, a business report, a telephone conversation, computer-to-computer transfers of electronic information via telecommunications or similar means. In practice, however, business services are extremely rarely transacted in this fashion; if and when they are, it is almost always in conjunction with one of the other two modes of delivery, not as substitution for those other two modes. International trade in business services, in many instances, necessitates either the cross-border movement of consumers or that of the factors of production. Moreover, for a number of the business services, the movement of consumers is not even an option, further narrowing the possibilities of trade to those made possible by a movement of the factors of production.

These observations have major implications for the nature of the presence of transnational business service firms in foreign markets and of their impact on the economy of host countries, especially developing countries. These issues are explored in greater detail in the next major section of this chapter. In the remainder of this section, an attempt is made to explain why international trade in business services typically occurs in the ways suggested above – that is through foreign direct investment rather than 'pure' cross-border trade. I shall also explore the nature of competitive advantage of transnational business service firms in world markets. Before doing so, however, some aggregate empirical evidence supporting my earlier assertion on the nature of trade in business services will be presented.

In 1985, the Office of Technology Assessment of the United States Congress produced a major study of American trade in services. As part of its study, the OTA attempted to re-estimate the value of direct exports by American service firms and to compare these direct exports to the revenues derived from the sales of their affiliates.[12] To the best of my knowledge, this remains the only country-specific study of its kind.[13]

Table 12.6 Ratio of United States' exports to total foreign revenues, 1983

Travel	1.00
Franchising	1.00
Licensing	1.00
Education	0.98
Legal	0.95
Health	0.61
Transportation	0.61
Construction	0.61
Information	0.50
Telecommunications	0.50
Motion pictures	0.50
Miscellaneous	0.47
Management/consulting	0.45
Software	0.40
Engineering	0.25
Insurance	0.22
Data processing	0.17
Investment banking/brokerage	0.16
Advertising	0.15
Leasing	0.14
Accounting	0.08
Retailing	0.00
Total	0.42
Banking	n.a.

Source: United States Congress, Office of Technology Assessment, *Trade in Services: Exports and Foreign Revenues* (Washington, D.C., U.S. Government Printing Office, 1986)

Table 12.6 shows the 1983 ratios of American exports to total foreign revenues (that is exports plus sales of foreign affiliates) of American firms in 22 service sectors covered by the OTA study. A factor of 1 means that all foreign revenues originate through cross-border trade; a factor of 0 that all foreign revenues originate from the sales of foreign affiliates. The table suggests that, with the exception of legal services, American business service firms serve foreign markets primarily through foreign affiliates. Why do these patterns exist and why are business service firms not generating more revenues through pure cross-border trade? The answers lie in a combination of technological, economic and regulatory factors.

First, much of the process of production in business services remains embedded in the direct relationship between clients and producers. This is true even though information technology was once presumed to eliminate this geographical constraint. For example, systems analysts and programing managers who produce customised software must spend many hours on their clients' premises, identifying and developing the systems that the clients are demanding. In turn, programers must work under the supervision of the programing manager (wherever he or she may need to be located), and often, in the case of customised software, they must work directly on the computer equipment of the client. The same holds true for systems integrators, whose primary service is systems analysis and systems engineering. It is also true of producers of packaged software. Most packaged software demands technical assistance which is usually provided in the form of a 'hot line' staffed with locally based technicians (at the minimum they must speak the language of their customers). Most packaged software – at least for mainframe and minicomputers – necessitates a staff of locally-based trainers to assist customers when the new software is first installed. Finally, most packaged software necessitates some reprograming when it is introduced in a new market.[14] Similarly, in the accounting industry, audits necessitate that junior accountants and account managers spend many hours on the premises of their clients.

Second, from some of the examples given above, a corollary constraint emerges. Whereas in some cases business services can be rendered indifferently through the movement of customers or that of producers, in others there is no choice but for the producer to move where the customer is located. A systems analyst with an assignment to help automate a factory must be able to come and spend time in the factory to discover, understand and analyse, through structured interviews with engineers, supervisors and workers, the specific labour process that he/she is being asked to automate. In this example, the factory is simply not going to move where the producer is located.

Third, in a world in which attention to quality, service and local tastes and customs has become a formidable competitive weapon, business service producers simply are unable to compete as effectively as they need to unless they have people deployed where the market is. The importance of being able to adapt the product to local markets is best demonstrated by what has happened in the advertising industry where the early 1980s' dreams of 'global' advertising for 'global' firms – that is the same advertising message for all countries – have largely fizzled. As advertising firms have had to rediscover, a considerable amount of adaptation of advertising campaigns to local tastes is required to compete successfully and only locally based operations can deliver on that count.

Fourth, 'pure' cross-border trade or trade through movement of consumers is, at times, not possible, simply for regulatory reasons: individual countries forbid such modes of service delivery in order to protect their right to control, through licensing, who can and who cannot perform a particular service. Typically, countries forbid foreign-based auditors from serving local accounts unless they have gained relevant local qualifications and, often, also, gained residency. The same typically holds true for other licensed professions, such as law, real estate brokerage, tax advice, architecture, engineering and so on.

It is true that it is extremely difficult for countries to control or restrict business services that are rendered either through 'pure' cross-border trade or through the movement of consumers. After all, millions of business letters criss-cross the world every day, some of which contain business advice from business service firms from one country to clients located in another country. Similarly, a travelling business person may be able to purchase some business advice from a firm in the country in which he/she is currently travelling, even though in both cases the advising firm may not be allowed to advise on the particular business problem. However, as I have suggested earlier, many business services are difficult to render without the movement of factors of production. This is particularly true of many of the licensed professions such as law, accounting, tax and so on. In general, most foreign practising licensed professionals will be reluctant to deliver their services in another country without proper qualifications because of the high penalty and other costs inherent in risking being caught doing it. Further, clients will be loathe to get advice from professionals whose qualifications are not recognised under relevant local licensing requirements.

The competitive advantages of transnational business service firms

Principal factors behind the development of large transnational business services include the search for greater scale economies, the search for greater economies of scope, the search for exclusive access to privileged information, and, in the process, the desire to raise costs of entry for potential competitors. The strategy used to reach these goals involves, in part, the creation of special linkages, both geographical and institutional, that encourage clients to use an ever-expanding diversity of business services from the same supplier, while making it costly for them to switch over to competitors or to multiply the number of their suppliers. Here too, however, one must be careful not to overemphasise the importance of these developments.

In the early 1980s, ambitious claims were often made to the effect that the largest business service firms would develop into 'one-stop' service firms, where clients could fulfil their many and varied needs under one roof. A decade later, it is useful to assess what has really happened. The reality, I believe, indicates that while a number of the largest firms have indeed done quite well at diversifying their business, not all have, and most have failed at their attempts to 'cross-sell' and develop 'one-stop shopping'. In the next paragraphs both sides of the argument are reviewed.

Perhaps more than any other factor today, the cost of the new information technologies explains the need for scale economies. New information technologies are playing an increasingly strategic role in allowing for greater integration of information flows through the firm and, equally importantly, for changes in the nature of the service delivered to clients. Significantly, the cost of the new information technology often lies as much in the software or, more importantly, in the training of personnel, than in the hardware. For example, estimates of training costs in the 8–10 per cent range of total revenues are not uncommon among large accounting firms. This is clearly an area where large firms have often been able to gain an advantage over smaller competitors.

Another area where large firms have been able to build some advantage is in their geographical and institutional reach. I have noted the importance of geographical networks earlier on in the case of the accounting industry and the same can be said for advertising. However, while these networks may represent a particularly significant competitive edge when dealing with global clients and their global needs, these are far less important, in and of themselves, when dealing with medium- and small-sized business clients or even more so with individual consumers.

Institutionally, the 'Big 6' accounting firms have clearly been able to develop a special grip on the audit market of large companies. Publicly held corporations that are active on the world's two largest capital markets – New York and London – have little choice but to be audited by one of them if they are to expect the most favourable financial terms on those markets. This grip may be weakening, however, if only because extensive privatisation among publicly held corporations during the mid-1980s in the United States, and lately in Europe, is shrinking the list of firms that are forced to abide by some of the most complex statutory requirements.[15]

Large business service firms have also tried to expand their access to privileged information in order to increase the opportunity costs of a shift in supplier by clients: for example, advertisers have gradually become involved earlier in their clients' product-planning process, making them privy to more strategic information than in the past; accountants have similarly found new ways of expanding their knowledge of their clients. And yet, this has not prevented large clients from dropping long-standing business service suppliers when dissatisfied with the quality of the expertise provided by their supplier. Indeed, the 1980s have seen greater account turnover among both accounting and advertising firms than ever before.

As for economies of scope, it is true that large firms have been able to leverage their name and reputation to diversify and expand into new areas. For example, a number of the world's largest consulting firms are management consulting divisions of the largest accounting firms; in the same way, a large number of the world's largest public relations or direct marketing firms are owned, today, by advertising agencies.[16] Yet the advertising agencies' dream of 'one-stop marketing' has simply not taken hold, and the accountants' ambitions of cross-selling management consulting and systems integration services to each and everyone of their audit clients have had to be revised, mostly downward. As one observer of the advertising industry noted in a recent article:

Madison Avenue may know how well to sell soap and soft drinks – but it's still having trouble selling itself. That's becoming increasingly clear as the advertising industry attempts to hawk its most important, most expensive strategy in decades: the much publicized communications supermarket.[17]

The same article goes on to give examples of senior managers in the division of one of the world's largest advertising firms that were strongly urging their clients not to use the services of one of their sister divisions because of what they perceived as poor quality work. While, admittedly, this is a rather extreme example, it is indicative of the difficulties that cross-selling and one-stop shopping have met in business services.

Accounting firms, in essence, have met with many of the same difficulties. The partner in charge of the management consulting division of a 'Big Six' accounting firm estimated recently that cross-selling represented at most 15–20 per cent of the sales of his division. Like advertising firms, accountancies have found it difficult to get accountants and management consultants to work together and cross-refer clients to one another, partly because sharp differences in professional cultures have been a major source of tension and mistrust among them.[18] In addition, accounting firms have found it difficult to cross-sell services because of certain regulatory barriers. In computer systems integration for example, an area in which most of the large accounting firms have extended their expertise, developing a computer system for a client entails subcontracting relationships with providers of computerised equipment, sometimes even joint ventures to share the costs and the risks of a particular commercial project. But the United States Securities and Exchange Commission, however, bars accounting firms from sharing certain business interests with companies whose books they also audit, on the assumption that such ties may taint the auditor's independence.

This problem was reported as one of the major factors that derailed the merger negotiations between Arthur Andersen and Price Waterhouse. As one of the world's most successful system integrators, Arthur Andersen Consulting has extensive business dealings with IBM and other American suppliers of hardware and software for some of the projects that the firm develops for its clients; but Price Waterhouse also happens to be the auditor of a large number of computer equipment firms, including IBM. A merger of the two firms would have either forced Price Waterhouse to drop several audit accounts, including IBM, or prevented Arthur Andersen from undertaking future joint projects with IBM and other computer suppliers.[19]

Finally, however large they may be, business service firms, as corporate institutions, are potentially far more unstable than manufacturing firms because of where technology is embedded in the firm: mostly in people-based processes in comparison to machine-based processes in the case of manufacturing. As one senior executive in a major accounting firm recently put it: 'The trouble with a business service firm is that the inventory goes home every night. You can never be sure it will show up the next day.'

This is a problem that a number of the large business service firms have had to confront the hard way in recent years. For example, during the merger negotiations between Ernst & Whinney and Arthur Young,

Thorne Ernst & Whinney (Canada's largest accounting firm and a then-affiliate of Ernst & Whinney) announced that it would defect to KPMG rather than join the newly formed Ernst & Young.[20] In the merger of Deloitte, Haskins & Sells and Touche Ross, the new firm lost $615 million in annual billings as a result of the defection of five of Deloitte's affiliates, including its British and Australian affiliates.[21] In advertising, WPP Plc lost most of the key accounts (including the IBM account) of Lord Geller Federico Einstein – one of the major agencies that it had just acquired – in 1989 when senior executives of the agency decided to walk out and start a new firm.[22]

In sum, the capacity of transnational business service firms to expand their scope and strengthen their grip on the business service markets, especially on some of the newest and fastest-growing markets, has met with far more mixed results than was anticipated earlier in this decade.

The impact of transnational business service firms on host countries: a focus on developing countries

Very little information exists that describes or measures the impact of transnational business firms on host countries. A view commonly held by development economists is that the impact of transnational firms on host economies can be analysed in terms of five broad areas: employment creation, technology transfer, market development and interlinkages, balance of payments and business practices. In this section, the focus is on developing countries.

Employment creation

Because so much of the business of transnational business service firms in foreign markets is conducted through a local presence rather than through 'pure' cross-border trade or movement of consumers, a major impact of business service transnationals on host countries is employment generation.

In early 1989, the United States' Coalition of Service Industries (CSI) surveyed its own members and members of the Industry Sector Advisory Committee (ISAC) for the United States' government regarding the importance and nature of their presence in developing countries. This survey was prepared in relationship to the ongoing GATT negotiations on trade in services. While the survey was not limited to American business service firms but included other American service firms, and while survey results were published in a way that did not permit separating out the data for business services firms, the findings of the survey are nevertheless useful.[23]

Eighteen firms responded to the survey. Together, the 18 firms were found to operate in 91 countries. Summarising the data for 15 developing countries in which at least five companies had a presence, the CSI survey showed that, together, the 13 companies present in those countries employed 48,171 staff in those 15 countries – an average of nearly 250 staff per firm per country. Nearly 99 per cent (98.8 per cent) of their staff were nationals; among managers over 80 per cent (81.2 per cent) were nationals. I suspect, although I do not have the data to prove or disprove my point, that the ratio of expatriate managers varies from firm to firm depending in part on the home country of each business service transnational. Transnationals from countries such as Japan are likely to use a greater share of expatriate managers to manage their foreign operations than American firms do, with likely impact on labour relations issues, issues of technology transfer or issues of business practices. A higher ratio of expatriate to national managers may lead to greater resistance in responding to certain local labour market goals (for example, the employment of minority groups), may mean that local managers are more likely to be shunted out of strategic decisions and may also influence the extent to which the firm's business practices are adapted to local conditions. The problem is likely to be attenuated somewhat in business service firms that use local partnerships as their primary legal form, since local laws will typically require that these partnerships be controlled by national partners. Still, even in those firms, the world-wide board of partners that maps out the firm's overall strategy may not always reflect numerically the balance of the local partnerships.

Technology transfer

Technology transfer is another major impact of transnational business service firms on host countries. As I have noted in an earlier study:

In service industries, 'products' are mostly procedures which come into being in the course of a relationship between the firm and its client. 'Services' are largely 'relationships', and 'product knowledge' is in no small way behavioral knowledge on the part of both employees and customers. In a world characterized by increasing competition, firms must keep identifying new markets, innovating and introducing new products. In turn, this implies a never ending need for training in the handling of new products.[24]

If a multinational business service firm is to serve its client base in different countries with the same level of quality, consistency and personalised service, it must impart the same level of knowledge to all of its employees around the world. Arthur Andersen reports that, during 1987, it trained each and everyone of its employees for an average of 170 class-room hours. This is an extremely high number by almost any standard.[25] To the extent that there is uneven distribution of those training hours among employees, it is mostly in terms of a distinction between senior and junior personnel – with the latter receiving more than the former – not in terms of geography. To be sure, Arthur

Andersen probably ranks among the highest in terms of its training effort. Other business service firms may not rank quite as high, but many do deliver a significant amount of training.[26]

By virtue of the nature of the professional business service output, part of the content of the training effort must be adapted to the local market: tax laws vary from country to country, as do accounting principles, and so on. This insures, more or less, that it be done locally. But part of the training also involves the teaching of methods (for example audit sampling methods, systems analysis methods) that need not be done locally. Historically, large business service firms have tended to centralise this type of training, in part for reasons of scale economies and costs. It may be in the interest of developing countries to push transnational business service firms towards greater decentralisation of training not only to insure equal access to training opportunities but to enhance their contribution to the development of business service technology by firms. Still, there is some evidence that a number of large business service firms have begun decentralising their training facilities on a world-wide basis, typically by opening regional training centres.[27]

The training delivered by transnational business service firms has benefits which reach beyond the employees of the firms themselves. Many of the business service industries are characterised by relatively high employment turnover. High turnover means diffusion of training throughout the industry via the job-hoppers. Still, training can have implications for a developing country's balance of payments, since it may require sending students to a foreign location for a certain period, necessitating the use of foreign currency for tuition, room and board (more on issues related to balance of payments below).[28]

Interlinkages

Transnational business service firms also have an impact on the development of the local market for business services as well as on the broader economy, through backward and forward interlinkages. As far as backward interlinkages are concerned, business services traditionally use very few inputs other than labour. As a result, backward linkages are quite limited, with some exceptions, such as the case of advertising, which is a heavy consumer of media space and of technologies associated with the production of advertising copy, videos and so on. Also, in the 1980s, business services became intensive users of computer technology, resulting in demand for hardware and software.

Still, it is probably in terms of forward linkages that the greatest impact of business service firms is to be felt. As was indicated in the opening paragraph to this chapter, the rise of business services is directly linked to a fundamental transformation in the nature of inputs consumed by other firms in the process of production. For example, automobile manufacturers need more design and engineering inputs to develop a new car, more computerised hardware and software to run the factory floor, more market research services to identify their markets and so on. Each and everyone of those needs translates into demand for business service firms. In turn, many of these new inputs are needed to assist the performance of producers in the market-place. In the last analysis, business services are a necessity for the competitiveness of firms from developing countries in global markets; lack of access to such inputs by firms from developing countries puts such firms at a competitive disadvantage.

Balance of payments

Since most business service firms need very little capital, the primary impact of the sector on the balance of payments of developing countries is likely to come in either one of two ways: first, in the intra-firm transactions associated with the repatriation of profits, the sharing of costs (costs of training, development cost of new products and so on), and the sharing of fees when work assignments involve professionals in different countries; second, in the transactions associated with the purchase of business service inputs by final users, with a differing impact on a country's balance of payment depending on whether the user can purchase the service locally or must purchase it from abroad.

Business practices

Transnational business service firms operate world-wide with a particular set of business practices that are part of what makes each firm unique. In a recent study of 'Transnational Service Corporations and Transfer of Technology', the United Nations Centre on Transnational Corporations noted that some business practices may have a 'restrictive' nature in terms of interlinkages with local suppliers. In the case of professional business service firms, the same report suggests that a restrictive business practice may arise from the fact that firms may limit the clientele that their affiliate serves in one country to avoid a conflict of interest with other clients that another affiliate services in another country.[29] Whether or not such practice is 'restrictive' remains questionable, however, since it applies equally to all affiliates world-wide and is not a priori biased against any particular country. However, the situation might also arise whereby the head office of a professional business service firm would prevent one of its foreign subsidiaries or partnerships from exporting its services to another country already served by another affiliate of the firm. The truth is that little is known about potential restrictive business practices by transnational business service firms and their impact on host developing nations.

Conclusion

Despite evidence that the importance of business services in the world economy has grown steadily through many of the past 20 or 30 years, only in recent years have researchers and analysts attempted to develop a more elaborate understanding of these increasingly strategic sectors.

In this chapter I have tried to review what is known about the dynamic of the expansion of transnational business services firms in today's world economy and particularly about their impact on host developing countries. In so far as good access to quality business services has become as critical to the development of firms from developing countries as it has for those from developed economies, but to the extent that transnational business firms are likely to play a critical role in the development of business service sectors in developing countries, there are major public policy issues to be addressed by developing countries as they set out to promote the development of those sectors in their economies.

Because of the very nature of production in business services – specifically the fact that most business services must be produced where they are consumed, meaning locally – developing countries may not need fear that business services consumed locally will be produced from afar, losing them local employment opportunities and unduly draining their foreign exchange. There are, however, critical issues relating to technology transfer, the nature of competition or restrictive business practices which developing countries do need to pay attention to as they promote business services in their markets.

The Uruguay Round Negotiations on Trade in Services have provided an important forum for developing countries to begin thinking about these issues and articulating their interests in the negotiations with the developed countries (see also Lanvin, Chapter 13). Notwithstanding the fate of the Uruguay Round Negotiations (which have broken down at the time of this writing), the issue of how developing countries can best promote the development of competitive business service sectors in their economy, while promoting their economic development interests simultaneously, will need to stay high on their agenda in the years ahead.

Notes

1. This chapter is based on a longer paper 'Business Services and the Uruguay Round Negotiations on Trade in Services' published originally in UNCTAD, *Trade in Services: Sectoral Issues* (United Nations Publication, UNCTAD/ITP/ 26, 1989).
2. There now is a large body of literature on this topic. See, for example, J. Singelmann, *From Agriculture to Services: The Transformation of Industrial Employment*, 1979; R.K. Schelp, *Beyond Industrialization: The Ascendancy of the Global Service Economy*, 1981; T. Stanback, P. Bearse, T. Noyelle and R. Karasek, *Services/The New Economy*, 1981; The Softnomics Center, *A White Paper on the Softnomization of the Japanese Economy*, 1985; UNCTAD,

Services in the World Economy (United Nations Publication, UNCTAD/TDR/8/ Offprint, 1988).

3. UNCTAD, *Services in the World Economy*, 1988.

4. T. Noyelle, *Skill Needs and Skill Formation in Business Services: The Case of the Accounting, Management Consulting, and Computer Software Industries*, A Report to the US Department of Education, July 1989.

5. November 1988. Based on the author's research.

6. During the summer and fall of 1989, discussions were also held between Arthur Andersen and Price Waterhouse regarding a possible merger of the two firms. If such a merger had materialised, it would have reduced the number of very large accountancies further down. Discussions were abandoned in early October 1989, however.

7. 'Peat's Experience Shows Why Accountants are Rushing to Merge: Main Hurdman Link Causes Turmoil but Brings in New Multinational Clients', *Wall Street Journal*, 17 July 1989, p.A1.

8. V.B. Bavishi, *International Accounting and Auditing Trends* (Princeton, NJ, CIFAR, 1989), Chapter 11.

9. More on this below. See also T. Noyelle, *Skill Needs and Skill Formation in Business Services*, 1989.

10. Having built a highly diversified network of activities during the 1980s, mostly through mergers and acquisitions, Saatchi and Saatchi began running into serious operating difficulties in 1988. In the spring of 1989, the company put its management consulting division up for sale. In October 1989, the Saatchi brothers were forced to hire a new Chief Financial Officer by their Board of Directors. The firm has now sold most of its management consulting business and cut sharply its operating costs. The firm is currently trying to recapitalise. WPP Plc, assembled in the late 1980s in a like fashion as Saatchi and Saatchi, but even faster, has run into remarkably similar problems as those faced by the Saatchi brothers.

11. C. Rigg and A. Breznick, 'Crumbling Empire: A Midlife Crisis Jolts the New York Ad Industry', *Crane's New York Business*, Special Report, 8 May 1989, pp. 31 ff.

12. Office of Technology Assessment, Congress of the United States, *Trade in Services: Exports and Foreign Revenues* (US Government Printing Office, Washington, DC, 1986).

13. Since the original publication of the OTA study, the Bureau of Economic Analysis (BEA) of the US Department of Commerce has altered its statistical gathering apparatus to improve its statistics of United States trade in services. BEA now publishes new estimates of service trade, consistent with OTA's revised estimates, beginning with 1987 data.

14. In some cases, it may necessitate almost complete rewriting, as was discovered by Lotus, the producer of 1–2–3, when it introduced its best-selling worksheet software in Japan.

15. *Forbes* magazine estimates that nearly one-third of the top 400 privately held companies in 1989 in the United States were firms taken private in the late 1980s (mostly from among the Fortune 500), with 39 large publicly-held United States' firms alone taken private in 1988. 'The 400 Largest Private Companies in America', *Forbes*, 11 December 1989.

16. See 'Market Research' in *The Directory of the World's Largest Service Companies, Series I* (Moody's Investor Service and UNCTC, New York, 190), pp. 367–94.

17. 'Ad Firms Falter on One-Stop Shopping. Coordination Among Units Hard

to Foster', *Wall Street Journal*, 1 December 1988, p. B1.

18. See T. Noyelle, *Skills Needs and Skill Formation in Business Services*, 1989.
19. 'Slow Progress in Andersen-Waterhouse Talks', *New York Times*, 5 December 1989, pp. D1 and D6.
20. Ibid.
21. 'Deloitte Touche Merger Done', *New York Times*, 5 December 1989, p. D7.
22. C. Rigg and A. Breznick, 'Crumbling Empire', 1989, p. 33.
23. Coalition of Service Industries, *Company Operations in Developing Countries* (Washington, DC, April 1989).
24. O. Bertrand and T. Noyelle, *Corporate Strategy and Human Resources: Technological Changes in Banks and Insurance Companies in Five OECD Countries* (Paris: OECD, 1988), p. 85.
25. Arthur Andersen & Co., *Annual Report*, 1987.
26. Also, T. Noyelle, *Skills Needs and Skill Formation in Business Services*, 1989.
27. For an example of regional training facilities, see Coalition of Service Industries, *Company Operations in Developing Countries*, 1989.
28. For a more extensive discussion of the issue of technology transfer by business service firms to developing countries, see T. Noyelle, 'Skills and Know-how in the Services: Issues for Yugoslavia', Eisenhower Center Working Paper #90–02, July 1990 and 'Computer Software and Computer Service in India, Singapore, The Philippines, Hong Kong, and the Republic of Korea', Eisenhower Center Working Paper #90–03, October 1990.
29. United Nations Centre on Transnational Corporations, *Transnational Service Corporations and Developing Countries: Impact and Policy Issues*, UNCTC Current Studies, Series A, No. 10 (New York, UN Publications, September 1989).

13 Services and new industrial strategies: what is at stake for developing countries?

*Bruno Lanvin** F13 L80

ō19 ō14

Since, at the GATT Ministerial Meeting of November 1982, the United States officially proposed to include services in a New Round of Multilateral Negotiations, many dramatic changes have affected international relations, including developments in Eastern Europe, and, more recently, in the Persian Gulf. The governments involved in the Uruguay Round, which was eventually launched at Punta del Este in September 1986, agreed that 31 December 1990 would be the deadline for completion of the negotiations.

In the course of seven years (from November 1982 to December 1990), much progress has been made, not only in the negotiations themselves, but also in the analytical approach economists and decision-makers are taking to services. With a number of key issues, not directly concerned with services, unresolved by this deadline the negotiations nearly collapsed but it has been agreed that the search for a solution should continue into 1991. Progressively, analysts, negotiators, policy-makers and private business have come to agree on a number of important points, including the following:

(1) traditional (orthodox) trade theory is in need of substantial refreshing. Comparative advantages are dynamic (they can be built through policies and competitive strategies, and are less strictly dependent on natural factor endowments);
(2) the functioning of the multilateral trading system needs to be revised. In particular, the mandate and scope of GATT and other international institutions dealing with trade issues need to be re-examined. This could be done, *inter alia*, in the context of setting up the long-awaited World Trade Organisation envisaged in the Havana Charter of 1947;
(3) trade in services is increasing rapidly, posing new challenges to macro-economic policies. The concept of 'globalisation' of the world economy is of particular relevance for understanding such challenges.

* Special Assistant to the Deputy-Secretary General of the United Nations Conference on Trade and Development (UNCTAD), Geneva. The views expressed here should be considered as the author's own. They do not necessarily reflect the positions of UNCTAD.

It is from this latter perspective that the present chapter attempts to explore the relationship between services on the one hand and industrial policies on the other. This will be done with a particular emphasis on the concerns of developing countries. The main conclusion presented here is that, in the 'global trade' of the 1990s, developing countries will have to avoid two pitfalls, namely: (1) gearing their development strategies to 'service policies' insufficiently linked to (and based on) more traditional industrial policies; and (2) designing their development strategies and industrial policies without taking note of the dramatic changes which have already started to affect international economic relations through services-led globalisation.

The first section of the chapter assesses different aspects of the growing importance of services in domestic economies and international transactions. In the second section, the stakes of developing countries will be studied in detail, and the potential of 'adapted' industrial policies will be outlined.

Myths and realities of the 'post-industrial' society

Much has been said (especially in the North-American-based literature of the 1980s) about the growing importance of service activities and the 'hollowing out' of industrial economies. Reality, however, is probably slightly more complex: important and significant as it may be, the growth of the tertiary sector in the output and employment of developed market economies does not mean that the post-industrial society will be a non-industrial society.

The growth of services in industrialised economies: an assessment

Over the last 25 years or so, all groups of economies have known a remarkable shift in the sectoral distribution of their gross domestic product: the share of agriculture has continued to decrease, while that of services increased markedly. In low-income countries, the growth of industrial output generally outpaced that of services. In most other countries, however, the growth of service activities caused a relative decrease of the share of industry and manufacturing in total production (see Figure 13.1). As far as employment is concerned, a similar pattern occurred which was more striking in the case of advanced countries (see Figure 13.2), thus giving credibility to concepts such as 'hollowing out', whereby industrial economies were seen as progressively giving up on manufacturing and replacing productive activities with low-productivity service jobs. One alternative interpretation of these data is the following: services are a heterogeneous set of activities, some with a high productivity (or high-productivity effects), some with low productivity; it seems that many of the service activities which generate strong competitiveness and productivity effects for the rest of the national economy are not significant providers of employment.

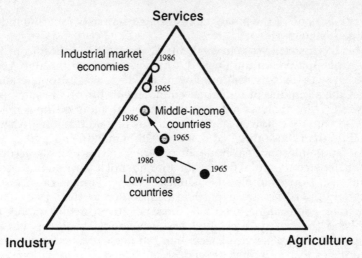

Figure 13.1 Sectoral shifts in GDP (1965–1986)

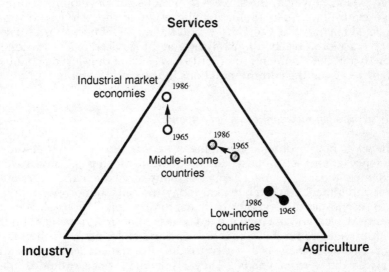

Figure 13.2 Sectoral shifts in the labour force (1965–1986)

Such a statement has important policy consequences. It also underlines a fundamental misunderstanding about services. In many
advanced economies, where unemployment was seen and felt as a
priority issue, governments have been tempted to rely on the tertiary
sector to create jobs, hence feeding the 'hollowing out' vision, and
further obscuring the necessity for strong policies in favour of 'strategic

services' as one of the means of restoring a seriously faltering industrial competitiveness.

This has been the case in the United States, for instance: from 1980 to 1985, unemployment diminished. This was achieved through a spectacular growth in services' employment which was strong enough to offset the shrinking of industrial employment during the same period. However, few analysts noted at the time that many of the service jobs created were of a 'lower quality' (in terms of qualifications, wages and stability) than those that had disappeared in manufacturing.

As far as international trade is concerned, services now account for about 20 percent of total flows. For a number of advanced industrialised countries, (for example the United States, France or the United Kingdom), services are a positive contributor to their trade balance, which, on goods alone, would be more negative. A consequence of this has been that many developed and developing countries have been tempted to design 'service-based' trade strategies, whereby comparative advantages lost in industry could be re-created in internationally tradable services.

The so-called 'services revolution' had triggered such high expectations that disappointments were bound to be commensurate. To a large extent, however, the success stories of some developing countries have contributed to perpetuating the myth of the 'service panacea', expected to cure all of the Third World's ailments. It may thus be useful to take a more objective look at the role of services in the process of growth and development, in order to assess what developing countries can expect from the current mutations in the world economy.

The 'services phenomenon' needs to be nuanced

Whenever new economic phenomena appear, there is a well-known tendency among economists to 'shoot from the hip' at any existing 'orthodox' theory. The peculiarities of many service activities have often been underlined: you can buy a car today and sell it tomorrow; but there is no second-hand market for haircuts, for example; if you sell your car tomorrow, you will not own it the day after tomorrow, whereas you can sell a piece of computer software today and still own it for the rest of your life, etc. Analysts have concluded from such peculiarities that 'services differ from goods'. They argue that, since orthodox trade theory was formulated as a way of explaining commodity trade flows, we need a new theory to explain services flows. A more conservative verdict would be that orthodox trade theory (that is the Hecksher–Ohlin–Samuelson formulation of Ricardo's law of comparative advantages) needs to be re-examined in the light of growing service transactions.

The rapid expansion of services has even led to more spectacular statements in the sociological field, where, not so long ago, some were still forecasting a global service-based full-employment economy. In such a golden-age type of society, developing countries were expected to rapidly de-link their comparative advantages from natural factor endowments and become true competitors in international service markets. Since then, many opposing views have been heard, which cautioned policy-makers against abrupt switches to 'all-services' economic strategies.

It is all the more important to dispel the mythical aspects of the services phenomenon that beyond the indisputable lacuna of currently available theories and data, there is indeed a truly revolutionary phenomenon. Among the many preconceived ideas which distort our present vision of services, some are more damaging than others. As to the influence of the growth of services on industrial policies, three common mistakes deserve special attention. They respectively stem from: (1) excessive trust in available data and statistics; (2) oversight of the cyclical component of the services phenomenon; and (3) underestimation of the importance of dynamic links between the tertiary and secondary sectors.

STATISTICS CAN BE MISLEADING

It is a well-known 'fact of life' that neither in national accounts nor in international statistics, existing categories and aggregates are adequate to describe service activities and transactions. The main reason for this rather sad state of affairs is that most of the currently existing statistical frameworks were built long before services began to assume the importance they have today. Many of these frameworks were actually created before some major service activities even came into being, at least as internationally tradable items. The most blatant example of this situation is probably in the countries of Central and Eastern Europe, where, until recently, the measure of national output was the so-called NMP (Net Material Product), which, by definition, excluded any 'immaterial' activity. In most countries, as well as in the IMF Balance-of-Payments Manual, services are often seen as a residual activity and are therefore dealt with at a much higher degree of aggregation than other sectors.

Service activities remain difficult to track statistically because they are more 'mobile' than most other economic activities. This means that, contrary to many other activities, they can be shifted rather easily from one 'host sector' to another; this phenomenon is often described in the services literature as 'internationalisation/externalisation'. It will be better understood through a concrete example: if Mr X, an accountant by training, is employed by General Motors, his production (that is in GDP terms, his salary) will be accounted for under 'automobile industry', that is within the industrial sector; if, for economic, fiscal, legal or other reasons, GM decides not to employ a full-time accountant any more, Mr X may be encouraged to set up his own accounting firm, of which GM will become a customer. Actually, Mr X's job may remain exactly the same (working out GM's accounts); the difference for GM is that they will have substituted a contractual relationship for an employment

relationship, thus gaining in flexibility (fixed costs are diminished); the
other major difference is that Mr X's earnings will now be taken out of
the automobile production sector and considered as part of the tertiary
sector output. In periods when large companies try to become leaner,
such externalisation phenomena can become quite significant. Even if
they are partly offset (statistically speaking) by internalisation phenomena (for example large manufacturing companies buying out smaller
'strategic' providers of software, design or engineering services), they
remain a potentially important cause of statistical over-estimation of the
importance of services in national economies.

IS THE SERVICES PHENOMENON OF A CYCLICAL OR STRUCTURAL NATURE?

The above-mentioned phenomenon will tend to develop in a certain
type of economic and legal context, namely that of increased competition in the manufacturing sector, with greater flexibility to adjust
variable costs through contractual relationship than through salary adjustments. Other macro-economic elements can also have a significant
impact on the relative growth of services output and employment: for
example, high interest rates will tend to penalise physical investment
and thus push entrepreneurs away from activities which make a rather
intensive use of fixed assets (machinery, plants); similarly, in times of
relative instability, the availability of quick and high returns on financial
markets may increase the opportunity costs of inventories and thus spur
the development of many services to the industrial sector in areas such
as consultancy or 'just-in-time' delivery services. It is also worth recall-
ing that some cyclical 'dysfunctions' of the market will tend to increase
demand for certain services, either to cope with undesired situations
(lawyers, psychiatrists), or to re-vitalise faltering demand (advertising,
marketing).

All of these causalities can be considered as 'cyclical': they tend to
contribute to the growth of the service sector in a particular type of
situation (uncertainty, fierce competition and high interest rates) and
should weaken significantly when that situation changes. Thus, the
current size of production and employment in services should not be
considered as the result of a non-reversible trend. The structural components of the service revolution are undeniable, but they are partly
buried under a set of more immediate, visible and cyclical syndromes.

SERVICES ARE NOT 'THE FUTURE OF INDUSTRY'

Another excessive assessment of current trends has led some analysts to
consider the inter-sectoral dynamics of modern economies as an illustration of the 'stages of development' theories (à la Rostow). According
to such views, the more advanced economies are progressively 'subcontracting' their industrial production, thus giving a chance to developing countries to upgrade from 'primary' economies (dominated by agriculture and raw materials production) to 'secondary' ones (that is

relying mainly on industrial production). This simplistic vision neglects two important realities.

First, services and industry are not easily separable: the higher the degree of development of an economy, the tighter the relationship between services production and demand from manufacturing industry. Competitive industries need competitive services and vice versa. Both require efficient and reliable infrastrctures, in particular information networks.

Second, de-localisation does not necessarily mean transfer of value added. It is true that modern services (in particular information-intensive services) have opened new possibilities for manufacturing abroad. It is also a fact, however, that host countries with limited or no access to the underlying management and information networks of 'global companies' remain in a relatively weak bargaining position when it comes to distributing profits, transferring technologies or improving their own competitive edge.

What is at stake for the developing countries?

The economic importance of the service phenomenon goes far beyond the increase of the tertiary sector in output and employment. The service phenomenon is of a truly dynamic nature and affects the 'how to produce' even more than the 'what to produce'. Such changes have been greatly facilitated (and sometimes induced) by rapid technological advances in micro-electronics and information systems. This undeniable 'industrial base' of the service revolution gives a renewed importance to industrial policies. At the same time, however, it does alter the intrinsic meaning and nature of such policies.

As far as developing countries are concerned, industrial policies are all the more needed since the current services-led mutations bear the distinct possibility of a fragmented world economy, within which most developing economies could very well be further marginalised.

The renewed importance of industrial policies

The reshuffling of roles in the emerging world economy will stress the prominent and strategic importance of services. Among the many forces at play, three will be particularly relevant in this context: de-materialisation, globalisation and de-regulation.

DE-MATERIALISATION

The steady decrease in the relative importance of materials in total costs of production is well illustrated by the case of the automobile industry. But any other 'mature' consumption product would provide evidence of the same trends; the competitiveness of manufacturers now lies more in design, management, marketing and financial services than in the product itself. Strategic alliances (for example Mitsubishi–Mercedes Benz,

General Motors and Saab, Volvo and Renault) and acquisitions (for example Jaguar by Ford and, to some extent, Rover by Honda, Lotus by General Motors, SEAT by Volkswagen) should be expected to multiply in the next few years. Automobiles are a perfect example of a good around which many services (upstream and downstream services) are being amalgamated. It is the way in which the final combination goods/services is organised which now conditions the profitability and competitiveness of the industry.

De-materialisation becomes even more spectacular as one goes up the ladder of technologies. For example, it has been noted that the total cost of all materials needed to produce the more advanced microcomponents (for example DRAMs) did not exceed 2 to 3 percent of their final production cost. (E. Larson, *et al.* 1986). It is also worth keeping in mind, for example, that fifty kilos of optical fibre carry over the same distance as many telephone messages as one ton of copper and that producing these 50 kilos of optical fibre requires fifty per cent less energy than producing a ton of copper wire.

Altogether, since 1900, the quantity of raw materials needed to produce one unit of output has decreased by an annual average rate of 1.25 per cent, and this phenomenon is definitely accelerating. Japan is a case in point: for the same amount of national production, the necessary quantity of raw materials has diminished by 60 per cent between 1973 and 1984. This was done at the price of tremendous changes in production techniques, which are now more advanced in Japan than anywhere else in the world in a certain number of industries. In this regard, Michael Porter (1990) is certainly entitled to quote Japan's need to 'dematerialise' as a possible explanation for the current competitiveness of its economy.

At the same time, an increasing number of large manufacturing companies have tended to compete with each other on services rather than on products. One example of this phenomenon can be found in the computer industry. Twenty-five years ago, the turnover of the industry was roughly distributed in the following proportions: 80 per cent for hardware, 20 per cent for software. Now, the proportion has been reversed, and software is clearly leading hardware in many segments of the market (especially in the fastest growing ones such as workstations and personal computers). The phenomenon is further exacerbated by the fact that, within the software industry itself, the 'services' component (that is maintenance, updating, trouble shooting) has been steadily increasing over the last decade or so. Some companies (like Tata Consultancy Services of India) have been thriving on international markets for this type of services (Lanvin, 1990).

GLOBALISATION

The trend towards an ever-increasing importance of services in the final value of output is particularly clear in all activities involving information-intensive services. Large multinational companies have rapidly identified possibilities to reach global markets and to organise production on a world-wide basis through the development and intensive use of international telecommunications and data services networks (ITDSNs). Coupled with the intensification of financial alliances (mergers and acquisitions, cross participations, etc.), the interweaving of the resulting global networks has again taken competition to new grounds. By deliberately increasing the proportion of information in their final product, global companies like American Express have been able to establish quasi-monopolies on a number of world-wide markets, thus reaping considerable economies of scale as well as economies of scope. In an increasing number of sectors (air transport, banking, tourism *inter alia*), networks are clearly emerging as a major source of competitiveness (Lanvin 1986).

Such networks are emerging as the common underlying structure of so-called 'global enterprises'. For any given product (good or service) the tendency of production and distribution to globalise will generally grow with the information-intensity of the product. This means that information-intensive services such as advertising, consultancy, engineering, design, software maintenance, etc.) are almost global by nature. In the area of banking and financial services, the industry will tend to offer an increasing number of 'pure' information services, likely to generate global economies of scale (*Time Magazine* 1986).

One can then speak of 'geo-finance' (Goldfinger 1986). In such global operations, markets tend to outgrow their traditional definitions and overlap each other. This is clearly the case for financial services and insurance services. American Express markets both types of services, and other competitors are expected to weave strategic alliances to the same effect; the recent deal between Aetna Insurance (American) and Vickers-Da Costa (British) can be seen in this context. Another example of overlap is that of the computer industry and the telecommunications sector. The progressive dismantling of national monopolies in both areas is feeding aggressive strategies by key players: IBM, for instance, has attempted (with limited success so far) to expand into telecommunications services, while AT&T was striving (with similarly limited success) to produce and market its own computer equipment on a global basis. Japanese and European companies should not be expected to remain on the sidelines for long.

DE-REGULATION

In the 1980s, the apparent complexity and unexpected duration of the economic crisis have considerably diminished the credibility of macroeconomic policies and measures. This phenomenon contributed to putting the 'invisible hand' back in fashion in several industrial economies. One of the consequences of this situation was an increasing and widely spread tendency to 'de-regulate' large sectors of national economies. The first 'real time' experiment of this type was that of the deregulation of air transport in the United States, starting in 1978.

One of the particularities of de-regulation, however, is that it tends to permeate national borders. Those industries which had emerged as winners in the national game of de-regulation were logically led to exert pressures (through their respective governments) in order to ensure a 'globally de-regulated' international environment. For a number of analysts, the proposal made by the United States in 1982 to include services in a New Round of Multilateral Trade Negotiations was an immediate result of the de-regulation of several domestic service markets, including those for transport (air, road, rail), telecommunications and banking.

As early as in the mid-1980s, however, it became clear that de-regulation had not brought all the benefits it promised (*Business Week* 1986). Moreover, the stock market crash of October 1987 led to a partial re-regulation of some activities and a very wide reassessment of the rationale for further domestic and international de-regulation.

In many sectors, one of the results of de-regulation had been the strengthening of dominant actors, especially those which had benefited from a headstart in terms of 'networking', as competition rapidly led to the emergence of 'hub-and-spoke' types of organisations. In air transport as well as in road, rail and maritime transport, a few 'hubs' (or 'nodes' in networking terminology) can be found at the starting and ending point of 'main lines' (trunk lines), whereas all other points in the network can be reached through secondary lines (feeders). The main beneficiaries of such architectures are the operators (who can adapt their fleet to the volume of activity) and the hubs (who concentrate the major part of the traffic). Secondary points, on the other hand, become more dependent on decisions made by (or with) the hubs: they constitute the 'periphery' of the network. This type of architecture is not exclusive to transport activities. It can be found in telecommunications, in financial services and even in some manufacturing industries, as exemplified by the famous Dresser-France case: in a globally de-regulated service economy, the dependence of peripheries on network-hubs (decision centres) is significantly increased. In such a context, potential peripheries can only avoid marginalisation by adopting resolute and well-designed policies (see Figure 13.3). In such a context, industrial policies (if appropriately adapted and fine-tuned) remain an important element of the limited panoply available to developing countries.

New peripheries in the making

For developing countries, the so-called service revolution is indeed a controversial issue. On the one hand, the emergence of new international markets for services is undoubtedly good news to the ears of many poor countries caught in the vicious circle of debt and commodity dependence. But on the other hand, many of the characteristics of these new markets could very well lead to strengthened centre–periphery hierarchies, thus further marginalising developing countries.

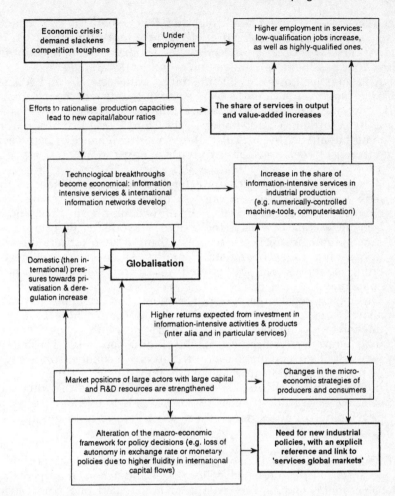

Figure 13.3 Mutations in the world economy and renewed importance of industrial policies: a causal diagram

MORE PARADOXES ABOUT THE SERVICE REVOLUTION

At first sight, a globalising world economy, making an ever more intense use of such a perfectly mobile factor as information is precisely the kind of prospect developing countries have been anxiously awaiting for decades. Indeed, one can easily see the advantage which such countries could draw from a world economy in which competitiveness relies more and more on 'grey matter': in such a context, comparative advantages become more a matter of policies and strategies than one of natural factor endowments.

The success stories of Singapore or Bahrain (financial services), India (software), Brazil (engineering), or South Korea (construction) confirm that this vision was not academic, and that, when the opportunity arises, developing countries are perfectly able to identify and latch on (Lanvin 1990). Services can indeed provide some developing countries with better possibilities of integration in international trade.

Such examples, however, remain limited, both sectorally and geographically. Moreover, a careful look at some of the current organisational and economic trends in most service industries, provides reasons to think that a further marginalisation of the Third World may result from on-going mutations. In particular, the increasing reliance of many service markets on 'networks' has two types of implications:

1. It leaves out in the cold any actor who is not a member of the networks; in many cases, once such networks have reached the critical mass necessary to offset their functioning costs, they tend to become 'exclusive'. This is the case of networks resulting from so-called 'strategic alliances', whereby firms weave intricate links of 'competition cum cooperation'. In most cases, suppliers from developing countries will be offered much competition and little cooperation.
2. The increasing degree of sophistication of information networks allows large organisations to attract and combine the best production factors on a world-wide basis. However, this does not mean that whoever contributes to the production and distribution network of such an organisation will receive a commensurate share of power and profit in that organisation. Actually, an increasing number of networks are now of a 'multi-layered' type, allowing only selective access to strategic resources. A selective by-passing of developing countries remains a distinct possibility in this type of set-up.

This should remind all analysts and champions of globalisation that, in the absence of coordinated political will and action, the upcoming 'global economy' might very well be a fragmented one. The Global Village would then have its centre, its suburbs and its slums.

TOWARDS A NEW INTERNATIONAL DIVISION OF LABOUR?

The above-mentioned tendencies allow for the sketching out of possible shifts in the present international division of labour (see Figure 13.4). Three groups of countries have been considered in this simplified diagram, namely the industrialised countries (OECD), the Newly Industrialising Countries (NICs) and the 'poor countries' (most other developing countries, with capital-scarce and technology-scarce economies).

As industrialised economies move from mature goods such as automobiles towards innovation-intensive services with a high proportion of R & D and analysis, they will vacate room to NICs in manufactures. The poorer countries will then be able to identify and use new opportunities

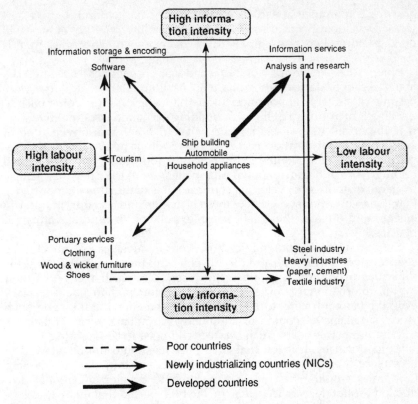

Figure 13.4 Possible shifts in the international division of labour

to move away from pure commodity dependence and export more semi-finished products. In other words, the first group will specialise in information- and capital-intensive productions, whereas the other two groups will keep a strong interest in labour-intensive activities. It is important to note, in this framework, that one of the areas in which competition is likely to be fiercer than anywhere else is that of labour-intensive information services (LIIS); these include a large share of the software market (encoding and trouble-shooting), for example.

Conclusion: whither service strategies for developing countries?

In the emerging global information economy, no country, however powerful, will be in a position to develop an economic strategy (even less a trade strategy) without considering two elements: (1) the strategies and aims of other actors (both public and private); and (2) the growing importance of services, particularly information-intensive services. Developing countries more than any other type of country will need to formulate and pursue their development strategies in this context.

When the keywords of international economics become de-materialisation, de-regulation and globalisation, inter-sectoral dynamics become of strategic importance. Industrial policies, thus, come back to the limelight as potential tools for building up national competitiveness. It is important to realise, however, that in a network-driven type of competition, globalisation is not automatically synonymous with integration. Since a fragmented global economy (one dominated by regional trading blocs and transnational oligopolies) would further marginalise the large majority of developing countries, it is of the utmost importance that these countries should take these elements into account, in order to design and follow the best possible policies, including industrial policies.

One needs to be pragmatic, however. In most cases, developing countries are not in a position to develop rapidly enough the domestic capacities necessary to produce those services which will boost their overall international competitiveness. More often than not, they lack even the basic infrastructures necessary to generate and transport such services (reliable telecommunication networks in particular). Thus, for a certain number of years, such services will need to be imported.

In many circles, it is felt that such imports should not be allowed to take place on a pure free-trade basis because if they did, developing economies would never be in a position to develop a national production of strategic services. It is thus to be expected that many developing countries will tend to offer access to their national markets for services in exchange for some degree of access to the underlying technologies and networks. There is quite a lot of room for compromises and cooperation in this area which should be reflected in the end results of the Uruguay Round of Multilateral Trade Negotiations.

References

Business Week (1986) 'Is deregulation working?', 22 December.
Fortune (1986) 'The market share fight over auto loans', 27 October.
Goldfinger, C. (1986) *La géofinance*, Paris, Le Seuil/Odyssée.
Lanvin, B. (1986) 'Réseaux et compétitivité', *Bulletin de l'IDATE*, **25**, Montpellier.
— (1990) 'Le Tiers-Monde regorge de matière grise et il a l'intention de s'en servir', *Le Temps Stratégique*, **35**, Geneva.
Larson, E., Ross, M., Williams, R. (1986) 'Beyond the era of materials', *Scientific American*, **254**, 6.
Porter, M. (1990) *The Competitive Advantage of Nations*, New York, Free Press.
Time Magazine (1986) 'Stock trading goes global', 27 October.

Index

accountancy, 79, 120
  case studies of, 137–44, 181–3,
    188, 189–90
'act', services as, 60–61
adverse selection problem, 49
advertising, 4–5, 50, 66
  case studies of, 180, 183, 186,
    188–9, 190
agent behaviour models, 5–6, 7
agglomeration economies, 10, 75,
    100, 108–9
Alcantara, D. d', 49
appropriation of knowledge, 32–3
Aronson, J. D., 76, 79
Arrow, K., 33, 35, 37
automobile industry, 203–4

Bacon, R., 135
Bailly, A. S., 145, 148
balance of payments, 193
banking system, 8
  case study of, 51–5, 56, 131
Baran, B., 79
Barcet, André, 60, 61, 109
Baudrillard, Jean, 49
Baumol, J., 41
Bearse, P. J., 24
behaviour models, 5–6
Belgium, 99, 178–9
Bell, Daniel, 1, 15, 16, 114, 136
Bertin, G., 38
Beyers, W. B., 106, 137, 145
Bhalla, A. S., 18
Blackaby, F., 136
Blumenfeld, H., 105
Bonamy, J., 5, 63, 120, 121
Bourdieu, Pierre, 49
branch plants, 71, 79, 81, 82–3, 86
  Mezzogiorno case study of, 152,
    157–73

Braverman, H., 15, 22
Britton, J. N. H., 82
Browning, H. C., 136
Business Administration System, 1
business services, 21

Canada, 55, 103
car industry, 203–4
Castells, M., 16, 17
Cavanagh, J., 141
central place theory, 99, 103, 105,
    109
centralisation *see* concentration
Chandler, A., 2, 10, 22
Chikhaoui, Y., 118
Christaller, W., 109
Clairmonte, F., 141
Clark, C., 1, 15
classification and definition of
    services, 17–21, 60, 61, 72
Claval, P., 101
Coase, R., 42, 77
Coffey, J. W., 111
Cohen, R. B., 74, 75
collective goods/services, 20, 42, 52
collusive behaviour, 49–50
competition
  and complementarity, 66–7
  forms of, 23, 24
computers
  hardware for, 120, 132, 204
  software for, 120, 185–6, 204
concentration of services
  case studies of, 131, 133, 136–7,
    139–41
  reasons for, 10, 70–75, 80–81,
    97–100, 108–9, 115–16
confidence, crises of, 50
consumer services, 18, 20
consumption